Children and Computers Together
in the Early Childhood Classroom

Children and Computers Together in the Early Childhood Classroom

Master Teacher
University of Delaware Laboratory Preschool
University of Delaware
Newark, Delaware

DELMAR PUBLISHERS INC.®

124083

NOTICE TO THE READER

Delmar Staff
  Associate Editor: Jay Whitney
  Project Editor: Christopher Chien
  Design Coordinator: Susan Mathews
  Production Coordinator: Linda Helfrich

For information, address Delmar Publishers, Inc.
2 Computer Drive West, Box 15-015
Albany, New York 12212

Printed in the United States of America
Published simultaneously in Canada by Nelson Canada
A division of International Thomson Limited

10 9 8 7 6 5 4 3 2 1

Library of Congress Cataloging-in-Publication Data

Davidson, Jane Ilene, 1948-
   Children and computers together in the early childhood classroom /
Jane Ilene Davidson.
      p.   cm.
   Bibliography: p.
   Includes index.
   ISBN 0-8273-3341-2 (pbk.).   ISBN 0-8273-3342-0 (Instructor's
guide)
   1. Education, Preschool—Data processing.   2. Early childhood
education—Data processing.   3. Children and computers.   I. Title.
LB1140.53.C64D38   1989
372'.21'0285—dc19
                                          88-25750
                                            CIP

Contents

Preface   xi

Acknowledgments   xiii

1

Why Use Computers with Young Children?

Some Say That Computer Use Has Many Values   2
    INPUT FOR TEACHERS: What Does It Mean?   2
    INPUT FOR TEACHERS: What Is Software?   4
Some Feel That Computer Use Has Many Potential Problems   8
Computer as Chameleon   12
Guiding Principles for Computer Use Must Be Based
   on a Developmental Awareness of Young Children   17
Summary   19

2

How to Begin: Setting Up the Computer in Your Classroom

What Is a Computer?   22
    INPUT FOR TEACHERS: Input/CPU/Output   29
Connecting the Parts   29
Purchasing a Computer System   29
    INPUT FOR TEACHERS: Identifying Cables   29
Getting Acquainted with the Computer   32
How Many Computers Are Needed, and Where Should
   They Be?   33

Putting Computers in the Classroom   35
Introducing the Computer to Children   38
Summary   41

3

In Search of the "Ideal Software"

Searching for the Elusive "Ideal" Software   43
Characteristics To Consider in Reviewing Software   44
Putting Together a Software Collection   50
Hands-On Approach Is Essential for Software Evaluation   51
    INPUT FOR TEACHERS: Software Guides   53
Summary   54

4

How Can Children Use the Computer If They Can't Find the Keys? Methods for Developing Computer Skills

Are We Hurrying Children to Expect Them to Learn
   These Skills at So Young an Age?   56
Providing Support for Children Who Are Developing
   Computer Skills   59
    INPUT FOR TEACHERS: Sample Dialogues   60
    INPUT FOR TEACHERS: A Note of Caution   61
Should Children Be Helped To Develop These Skills
   Before Using the Computer?   61
Why Spend So Much Time on Computer Skills?   61
Summary   62

5

Activities To Help Develop Skills for Computer Use

Turning the Computer On and Off   66
    INPUT FOR TEACHERS: Asking Questions   67
    INPUT FOR TEACHERS: Goals for Activities   69
    ACTIVITIES TO BUILD SKILLS IN TURNING THE COMPUTER ON AND OFF   70
Selecting Software and Loading Disks
   into the Disk Drive   74
    **ACTIVITIES TO SUPPORT DEVELOPMENT OF SKILLS FOR
    SELECTING AND LOADING SOFTWARE**   77
Learning To Locate Necessary Keys on the Keyboard   78

ACTIVITIES TO DEVELOP KEYBOARDING SKILLS   82
Learning To Use a Single Keystroke   90
Summary   90

6

More Activities for Developing the Skills Needed for Using the Computer

Selecting from a Menu   93
    INPUT FOR TEACHERS: Designing Activities for
        Specific Pieces of Software   96
    ACTIVITIES TO BUILD MENU-READING SKILLS   98
Following and Beginning To Design Multistepped Procedures   107
    INPUT FOR TEACHERS: Single-Serving Recipes   108
    ACTIVITIES TO DEVELOP SKILLS IN FOLLOWING AND
        GENERATING PROCEDURES   109
Following Picture Directions   117
    ACTIVITIES TO DEVELOP PICTURE-READING SKILLS   119
Summary   123

7

What Can Children Learn About Computers?

Should Children Learn About Computers?   125
Must Children Know About Computers in Order To
  Use Them?   126
Using the Computer Teaches Children About the Computer   128
When Should Children Learn About Computers?   130
    INPUT FOR TEACHERS: Defining "Formal" Teaching   132
What Can Children Learn About Computers?   132
Summary   134

8

Helping Children To Learn About Computers

Computers Are Made Up of Parts That Work Together   137
    INPUT FOR TEACHERS: Computer Terms Children Can Learn   139
    ACTIVITIES TO TEACH ABOUT COMPUTER PARTS   141
Computers Need People To Give Them Commands   150
    ACTIVITIES TO TEACH ABOUT COMMANDS   152
A Computer Can Remember a Whole Series of Commands   162

ACTIVITIES TO TEACH ABOUT PROGRAMMING   164

Summary   173

9

Computers in Our World: Building Concepts About What They Do and What We Must Do

Computers Can Do Many Things   176

    INPUT FOR TEACHERS: Planning Good Field Trips   180

    INPUT FOR TEACHERS: Dramatic Play   183

    ACTIVITIES TO TEACH ABOUT COMPUTER USES   184

Computers Have Both Strengths and Weaknesses   190

    INPUT FOR TEACHERS: Emergent Literacy   191

    ACTIVITIES FOR TEACHING ABOUT THE COMPUTER'S
    STRENGTHS AND WEAKNESSES   194

Computers Take Input, Process It, and Produce Output   196

    ACTIVITIES TO TEACH ABOUT INPUT/CPU/OUTPUT   198

Computer Hardware and Software Are Made By People and Controlled By People   205

Summary   206

10

"This Software's Almost Perfect But . . .": Activities To Support the Use of Specific Software and Hardware

Determining, Then Developing the Skills Needed for Independent Use of Specific Pieces of Software and Hardware   208

    INPUT FOR TEACHERS: Two-Step Commands   211

    ACTIVITIES TO TEACH TURTLE-ROBOT SKILLS   212

    ACTIVITIES TO TEACH GRAPHING SKILLS FOR BUMBLE GAMES   222

    ACTIVITIES TO SUPPORT THE USE OF AUXILIARY DRAWING DEVICES   229

Providing Ways To Circumvent Skills That Are Too Difficult for the Children   231

Software-Generated Activities To Facilitate Developmental Goals   234

    DEVELOPMENTAL ACTIVITIES GENERATED BY SOFTWARE   235

Summary   237

11

Integrating the Computer into the Early Childhood Curriculum

Using Computers To Support a Unit   240
    INPUT FOR TEACHERS: "Teaching" Skills to Children   240
    ACTIVITIES TO SUPPORT LEARNING ABOUT BOTH
       COMPUTERS AND DINOSAURS   244
Using Computers To Help Develop Skills   248
Using Computers To Support Development of the
    Whole Child   249
Conclusion   255

Appendix I: List of Software   257

Appendix II: List of Activities   265

Bibliography   268

Index   271

Preface

Five years ago, my colleague Cindy Paris got excited about integrating computers into her classroom. I listened to her excitement but could not join in. My only experience with computers had been as a graduate student, tussling with a computer system that (a) rarely seemed to do what I wanted, and (b) continually balked at my many errors and lack of technical skill. The experience was less then joyful. I left with the data analyzed and a vow to avoid the computer in the future.

Besides being scared of computers myself, I was concerned that the computer might decrease social interaction, discourage language, provide closed-ended, computer-structured activities that would not allow children to explore, and demand large quantities of my time, forcing me to neglect other important teacher roles. I could not see what it would add to my classroom. However, after watching the children in Cindy's class and in CAPP (Computers As Partners Project) summer camp use the computer, I was converted. The children gathered around the computer sharing ideas, making suggestions, solving problems, exploring and discovering what they could make the machine do. The children quickly learned to use the computer independently and often taught their peers and teachers new ways to use software.

As I began to use the computer in my own classroom, I discovered how simple it was to use and how many possibilities it offered to children. I have grown to see the computer as an excellent addition to the preschool and kindergarten classrooms. However, I have not become a fanatic, like some of the early converts to computer use. Computers are not magical. They do not teach academic skills earlier or better, nor should they. They are one of many media that can make an early childhood classroom a rich learning environment that encourages the development of each individual child.

I wanted to share my excitement and knowledge of computers with other teachers. This book is for the teachers who are afraid of the computer, for those who want to use computers in their classrooms but do not know how to start, and for those who are already using computers but want to expand their use and knowledge of computers.

For the beginning computer user, this book is full of easy-to- follow practical information about computers. There are clear directions for setting up computers in the classroom (Chapter 2); guidelines for selecting software that best fits a particular class (Chapter 3); suggestions for ways to support computer use in the classroom (Chapters 4–10); methods for using the computer to support the rest of the curriculum (Chapter 11); and illustration and discussion of countless teaching strategies throughout the book.

The "Input for Teacher" boxes in each chapter highlight teaching techniques and resources. A glossary has been incorporated into the body of the text, which defines words as they are used, to assure that the reader clearly understands what is being said.

The book is also highlighted by the more than 70 off-computer activities to support computer use. The activities are imaginative, simple to follow, and provide many suggestions for adaptation and expansion to fit each unique group of children.

The best way to learn about children's computer use is to watch children using computers. Because I cannot enclose children in the book, I have done the next best thing. I have filled the book with photographs and numerous anecdotes of children's interactions with computers.

If the computer was merely a machine to teach about and to learn to use, separate from the rest of the learning and curriculum in the early childhood classroom, I would question the value of its use. But the computer is not merely a separate entity that children can learn about and can learn to use, divorced from the rest of the curriculum. The computer can be used to support wide range of learning and development in the early childhood curriculum.

Acknowledgments

This book flows out of the hard work and ideas of many people. I may be the one who wrote the ideas down for others to read, but without those who developed and sustained CAPP, the Computers as Partners Project at the University of Delaware, I would have had nothing to write about. In 1983, Cindy Paris, Sandy Morris, Dene Klinzing, and Alice Eyman obtained a grant from the Office of Computer Based Instruction at the University of Delaware to supply computer equipment for a summer computer camp for 4- and 5-year-olds. The aim of the grant was to evaluate whether computers could be integrated successfully into a developmental preschool curriculum. The project continued growing to include the development of college courses on using computers with young children, a variety of research projects, the expansion of the camp to include children 4 to 8 years old and the integration of computers into the 4- and 5-year-old classrooms at the University of Delaware Preschool. Leon Campbell, the provost of the University of Delaware, was extremely supportive of CAPP. His support was instrumental in its growth.

Thanks to all those mentioned, as well as Nancy Edwards, Daniel Shade, JoAnn Springsteen, and Debbie Brady, who continue to expand and develop techniques for using computers with young children. The practicum students from the course, "Computers in Early Childhood," played an integral part in the development of activities and methods for using computers with young children. Their contributions are greatly appreciated.

Another large group of people who must also be recognized for making a major contribution to this book are the children in CAPP and the preschool who showed us how to make computers best fit their needs. Many exciting ideas came from children's suggestions and their discoveries on the computer. If you really want to learn the best way to teach and guide young children, the children themselves are the ideal teachers.

This book, like most books, has grown and changed during the writing and rewriting process. Many people were instrumental in the revision process. My reviewers offered pertinent suggestions on the first draft, which helped to clarify what needed to be added, expanded, or clarified in the final version:

Faith Coddington, Education Specialist, Head Start Program,
    Montgomery County, Maryland

Sue Haugland, Director, Center for Child Studies,
    Southeastern Missouri State University

Marlene Bumgarner Eltgroth, Coordinator Early Childhood
    Education, Gavilan College

Joan P. Isenberg, George Mason University

Mary Ellen Abell, John A. Logan College

Betty Larson and Candace Spence, San Antonio College

Jay Whitney, my editor at Delmar, always shared the excitement with me as the book grew and took shape. Jim Hadlock, senior programmer/analyst at the University of Delaware, provided invaluable technical assistance, both as I was learning about computers and as I was writing about them. Daniel Shade kindly offered to use the rough draft of my book in the Computers and Young Children course, offering me valuable insight into the impact of the book on students.

I wish to acknowledge and offer miles of thanks to two colleagues who have supported and assisted me while writing this book. Marion Hyson read and commented on each chapter. She offered praise, suggestions, corrections, and questions that helped me to clarify and improve what I was trying to say. Alice Eyman, the director at the University of Delaware Laboratory Preschool, supported my work in the Lab School as a teacher and supervisor and enabled me to take on the additional work of writing.

Last, but most important, I must thank my family. My husband, Jeff, taught me how to use the word processor; willingly listened, or at least pretended to listen, to the many times I read parts to him; took on extra household and family chores when I had deadlines; and got excited with me over new thoughts, and completed chapters. My children, Lily and Michael, were tolerant of my preoccupation, and overly busy schedule. They kindly offered many suggestions, although many, like Michael's insistence that I should finish the book with "THE END," were appreciated more for their intent, than for their content.

1

Why Use Computers with Young Children?

Should computers be used in early childhood education? This issue has been hotly debated since the introduction of computers into classrooms. As with any new educational innovation, there are those who say that this is the new wonder machine that will revolutionize education, as well as those who predict dire results if the demon machine is let into the classroom. The following two quotes show the differences between those who view the computer as a "messiah" and those who see it as a "monster" (Mathews, 1980).

> The computer, if it is allowed to infiltrate the very heart of education . . . will destroy education . . . we will be transformed into a culture of psychopaths (Sardello, 1984, p. 631).

> It is in the elementary grades, perhaps even among preschoolers, that microcomputers may ultimately challenge and radically alter traditional instruction modes (Martin, 1981, p. 41).

Until recently, there has been little research on computer use with young children. A number of articles have reviewed the existing research and theoretical statements and set suggested research agendas for the future (Barnes & Hill, 1983; Clements, 1985b; Goodwin, Goodwin, & Garel, 1986). As Goodwin et al. point out, there are numerous "pronouncements and speculations" about the value of, or problem with, using computers with young children. Although I certainly do not want to denigrate research, the value of most materials used in the preschool has NOT been verified through research. For example, *The Block Book* (Hirsch, 1984), one of the best books on block use, cites no research. It discusses the many uses and virtues of unit blocks, describes children using blocks, and, based on observations and child development knowledge, suggests that children can benefit from such use.

No one would advocate disposing of unit blocks until we have proof of their value. In the same sense,

Computers can be a captivating social activity. (Photo courtesy of Robert Cohen)

the lack of research proving the value of computers should not cause them to be banned from the classroom. Classroom use should continue as long as teachers see evidence that computers add to the learning environment of the classroom. If subsequent research shows that computers (or, for that matter, blocks, sand play, or other materials used in the classroom) are harmful to children, these materials should certainly be removed.

At this point, it is wise to take a cautious stand. Teachers should observe how computers are used. Are there problems? Can their use be modified to alleviate these problems?

This chapter presents the values and possible concerns of using computers with young children, followed by a discussion of the roles and characteristics of the computer itself. Some of the claims for the computer's potential, both good and bad, may be unsubstantiated. But it is important for teachers who are considering the classroom use of computers to be knowledgeable about this debate and aware of which positions have been verified and which are still hypothetical.

SOME SAY THAT COMPUTER USE HAS MANY VALUES

According to advocates, computers in the classroom have many potential values.

Computer Use Increases Social Interaction and Cooperation

Early critics suggested that computers would decrease social interaction among children, but the research has not shown the predicted negative effect on social interaction. In fact, many studies indicate that the computer encourages social interaction (Borgh & Dickson, 1986; Lipinski, Nida, Shade, & Watson et al., 1986; Swigger & Swigger, 1984). Other studies have shown that computers encourage social interaction of 4-year-olds (Muller & Perlmutter, 1985) and older children (Hawkins,

---

Sheingold, Gearhart, & Berger, 1982) involved in problem-solving situations. Social interaction is not limited to problem-solving situations. Wright and Samaras (1986) describe many instances of children working jointly on the computer creating a make-believe reality. If given appropriate *software,* children often work together on computers.

Meaning?   SOFTWARE

Software is a set of instructions used to direct a computer to perform some activity. The software children use is usually stored on a disk. The type of software loaded into the computer determines what the computer will do.

Many other studies have shown that computers do not affect the social interactions in the classroom either positively or negatively. Children's social interactions on the computer are similar to those seen elsewhere in the classroom (Hoover & Austin, 1986; Lipinski et al., 1986; Shade, Nida, Lipinski, & Watson, 1986). While using computers, children often work together to discover how to make the computer do what they intend. Observational studies reported

Cooperative computer ventures are common.

Children are often constructively involved in solitary activities such as drawing.

that the computer is often a group activity with two or more children clustered around a single *monitor* (Campbell & Schwartz, 1986; Church & Wright; 1986; Shade et al., 1986). In one study in which children were initially encouraged to use the computers singly, the children's need to use them together was so strong that the researchers adjusted their rules (Swigger & Swigger, 1984). Peer teaching is often evident as children share their discoveries or past experiences with each other (Paris & Morris, 1984; Shade et al., 1986).

Meaning? MONITOR

A **monitor** is the visual display for the computer, usually a picture tube like that used on a television.

It is true that children do sometimes play alone at the computer, but it is also not uncommon to see a child sitting alone looking at a book, engrossed in a puzzle, drawing intently, or constructing a block building. Many activities can be done either independently or socially.

Computer Use Bolsters the Child's Self-concept

If the right *programs* are selected, each child can be in control of the computer. The child becomes someone who is independent and powerful (Burg, 1984; Ziajka, 1983). According to Wright and Samaras (1986), "The child's self-concept as a craftsman becomes more positive as he or she masters the machine" (p. 77). Being successful at, and in control of, an adult kind of activity, such as computer use, can lead to increased feelings of self-confidence and self-worth (Beaty & Tucker, 1987). There has been a great deal of research to show that young children can use the computer independently (Shade et al., 1986; Paris & Morris, 1985; Borg & Dickson, 1986). Weiner and Elkind (1972) suggest that at the preschool age, children "begin to recognize the difference between past and present skills" (p. 258). They see new behavior as compared to old behaviors and are therefore able to recognize their own achievements, "achievements that can have a lasting influence on an individual's sense of personal competence" (p. 259). Although there has been no experimentally designed research assessing a child's self-concept before and after computer use, many of the observational studies do demonstrate the child's pleasure with independent use (Hyson & Morris, 1985; Shade et al., 1986; Wright & Samaras, 1986).

Meaning? PROGRAM

Program has two different but related meanings: (1) A program is a series of commands or instructions to the computer. Some programs are short; others require a whole disk to store all of the commands. (2) The word *program* is often used to refer to a piece of software.

Computers Increase Thinking, Reasoning, and Problem-Solving Skills

Papert (1980) states that the use of computers allows users to develop intimate contact with their own thinking. Many have claimed that using the computer, especially being involved with the computer language, **Logo,**[1] does increase children's

---

INPUT FOR TEACHERS:
WHAT IS SOFTWARE?

In discussing how children use computers, this book mentions many different pieces of software. At times, the software is described in the text; at other times, it is not. If readers are unacquainted with a named piece of software, they should refer to the software appendix at the end of the book.

---

thinking skills. Research to date has been contradictory in regard to **Logo's** effectiveness with young children. Pea (1983), in a study of younger elementary school children using **Logo,** found that the children did not gain in either specific or generalizable knowledge. Papert (1986) refutes Pea's work, claiming both that the way in which **Logo** was used was unclear and that the posttest did not accurately test whether the children's cognitive skills had increased because it tested the wrong attributes. Clements and Gullo (1984) found that 6-year-olds using **Logo** had increased skills in the following areas: fluency, originality, general divergent thinking, reflectiveness, metacognition, and the ability to give accurate directions. Studies of older children using **Logo** have been more uniformly positive.

Although **Logo** may not increase children's problem-solving skills, this does not preclude computers from facilitating thinking skills. In observing children using computers, it is clear that they are engaged in productive thinking. For example, 4-year-olds enjoy typing random series of letters on **Bank Street Writer** (a *word processing* program).[2] Initially, They type lines of gibberish, as children do when first exploring a typewriter. When the last line on the monitor is filled, the text moves up, making space for new text. To the children, it looks like the typing has vanished. They are amazed with this new prop-

---

[1]**Logo** is a programming language developed by Seymour Papert. The commands needed to create graphic designs and to write programs for recreating pieces of the design can be simplified to a single character making it easier for children to use.

[2]The use of **Bank Street Writer** described here was observed in the four-year-old lab school class in 1987.

erty of the program and type faster to see if they can make it happen again. Some children may then discover that the *left arrow* [←] erases what has been typed. When the erasing has emptied the screen, the text written earlier moves down, filling the screen again. Children exclaim over each new discovery, bringing other children to watch and comment.

Meaning? WORD PROCESSING

Word processing involves using the computer to record and print words in a manner similar to a typewriter. Word processing programs allow the writer to enter, edit, store, and print text.

These children are involved in problem solving, though perhaps at a different level than children using **Logo**. They are exploring the reactions of the computer to their actions. They then repeat actions to see if they can reproduce the previous results. Children also put together actions in new ways to speed the desired result. One child was eager to have the text move up and found that typing only a few characters then pressing the **[*Return*] *key*** would make the cursor reach the bottom of the page faster, and in consequence make the page move up more quickly. Numerous such examples of children exploring and manipulating the actions of the computer can be found when watching children interact with open-ended software.

Meaning? RETURN

The **[Return]** key on the computer is used in many programs to tell the computer that you have finished your entry or made a choice. On the IBM and some other computers, the **[Enter]** key fulfills these functions.

Meaning? KEY

A **key** is a button on the computer keyboard, with symbols, letters, numbers, or words, which you push to give the computer instructions.

Computers Help Children Construct and Revise Concepts

According to Piaget (Forman & Kuschner, 1983; Kamii & DeVries, 1978), children learn by constructing their own knowledge. They learn physical knowledge about objects by manipulating objects. Piaget also discusses another form of knowledge: logico-mathematical knowledge. Despite its name, this knowledge is not limited to mathematical knowledge. Children construct logico-mathematical knowledge by putting past experiences, knowledge, and concepts into relationships. A child builds a concept of gravity, although in a rudimentary form, by dropping many objects and seeing the results. The child concludes that objects fall when dropped. In the same way, children using **Bank Street Writer** are creating concepts about the functioning of the computer. When they get to the bottom of the screen, some of the letters will disappear. The child who tried pressing the **[Return] key** to get the text to move up faster may have been taking a concept developed while using the typewriter and seeing whether it would apply to the computer as well.

According to the National Association for the Education of Young Children (NAEYC) criteria for developmentally appropriate practice, ''Learning is a complex process that results from the interaction of children's own thinking and their experiences in the external world'' (NAEYC [Bredekamp, Ed.], 1986, p. 47). Children learn while playing with sand, water, blocks, paint, and dolls. While playing, they are constructing new concepts and revising old ones. The computer is another material that stimulates children to construct and revise concepts. As with other materials, the child's conclusions are not always correct, but it is this process of learning to understand the world that is important, not the particular information that is learned. "Knowledge is not something that is given to children as though they were empty vessels to be filled. Children acquire knowledge about the physical and social worlds in which they live through playful interactions with objects and people" (NAEYC [Bredekamp, Ed.], 1986, p. 48).

The Computer Is a Medium That Can Stimulate Children's Play

"Play is the child's medium for learning," proclaims the title of Sponseller's book (1974). The importance of play in the development of young children is widely acknowledged (NAEYC [Bredekamp, Ed.], 1986; Fein, 1986; Sponseller, 1982). Wright and Samaras (1986) cite many examples of children using the computer to become involved in imaginative play. When I first introduced **Kidwriter** (a program that allows children to select a scene and characters to create a picture, then write a story to go with the picture), the children used the option for moving the characters to a preferred spot as a means for "animating" their pretend stories. If a figure is moved on top of another figure the stationary figure seems to disappear. A favorite activity was to have the spaceship "catch" the other characters by slowly covering them. Children also use the **Explore-a-Story** software for dramatic play. And children animate the figures in **What Makes a Dinosaur Sore** to create a variety of dinosaur adventures. Children will use *graphics* programs for make-believe as well.

This creation of fantasy around materials is common in all areas of the preschool. The film, *Dramatic Play—An Integrative Process for Learning* (1973), shows children's pretend play not only with blocks

This building toy has become a rocket zooming through outer space.

Meaning?   GRAPHICS

Graphics are drawings or other nontext designs (i.e., designs not made with characters normally found on a typewriter) created on the computer. Graphics programs are programs that enable the computer to make such drawings.

and in housekeeping where one would expect it, but also with playdough and finger painting. Pretend play can also be seen at the sand table, the water table, and even while doing puzzles. While putting together a puzzle, the child (a) may take on a special character and be doing a puzzle in the game or (b) may give life to the puzzle pieces, using them as the actors in dramatic play. The computer provides another medium for imaginative play.

Barnes and Hill (1983) are concerned that the play offered on the computer is two-dimensional and does not allow for the use of all senses. This is true, and one would certainly not recommend computers as the only outlet for dramatic play. But it is an acceptable addition to the many possibilities already available in an early childhood classroom.

Early Use of Computers Teaches Computer Skill and Develops a Positive Attitude toward Computers— Both of Which Are Needed for Later Computer Use

Studies have shown that children can develop the skills needed to use the computer (Paris, 1985). Shade et al. (1986) and Wright and Samaras (1986) all describe children as using computers independently of teachers. To do this, the children must have mastered basic computer skills. But as critics have asked, just because children can learn the skills needed to use the computer, does it mean they should (Cuffaro, 1984)? It is pointed out that older children seem to learn to use the computer without having had early experience. This type of argument—that we should use computers with young children so that they will be ready for later life—is all too reminiscent of the people who urge more formal and rigorous education of young children to prepare them for school. This desire to prepare children for later experiences at younger and younger ages is robbing them of their childhood (Elkind, 1981). Barnes and Hill (1984) suggest that using computers too early may be asking children to work on a developmental plane that is too high and thus may be creating the kind of "hurried child" that Elkind decries. Perhaps this positive benefit should not be stated as a *reason* to use computers with young children, but instead as a *by-product* of using them.

Favaro warns against beginning computer use at too young an age, especially if the tasks are too difficult and frustrating. Early inappropriate computer use "is likely to cause enduring negative perceptions of the computer experience and keep some children permanently turned off to computers" (Favaro, 1983, p. 158). This threat is certainly worth attending to. Inappropriate use of computers could have a negative impact on how children view computers, as would inappropriate use of any material. The descriptive studies have shown that appropriate use of computers creates enjoyment and positive

Early computer use by both boys and girls may prevent later labeling of the computer as a "male activity."

feelings in children indicative of a positive feeling about computers (Hyson & Morris, 1985; Shade et al., 1986; Wright & Samaras, 1986).

Early Computer Use Inhibits Sex-Role Stereotypes

The research on computers in the later grades has shown that boys tend to use computers much more than girls (Clements, 1987). Although most of the research with preschoolers has not shown this sex-role stereotyping to occur, a few studies have found slight differences by gender. Swigger, Campbell, and Swigger (1983) found that boys tend to experiment more with the software, while girls follow the rules. These differences have not been found in other studies (Sherman, Divine, & Johnson, 1985). Lipinski et al. (1986) found that boys used the computer more often than girls did in the larger of their two study groups. Boys appeared to be more aggressive in their attempts to gain turns at the computer and therefore used it more. This seems to indicate a need either for more computers, to decrease the wait for turns, or for additional teacher help to ensure that more aggressive children do not exclude other children from using the computer.

Despite a smattering of research to the contrary (Beeson & Williams, 1985; Klinzing & Hall, 1985), the majority of research shows no difference between boys and girls in the amount or type of computer use (Hess & McGarvey, 1987); Hoover & Austin, 1986; Lipinski et al., 1986; Muller & Perlmutter, 1985; Shade et al., 1986; Sprigle & Schaefer, 1984; Swigger et al., 1983). Watson, Nida, and Shade (1986) feel that early use by both genders may decrease the stereotyping at the later age because these children will already have defined computer use as an activity for both boys and girls.

SOME FEEL THAT COMPUTER USE HAS MANY POTENTIAL PROBLEMS

On the other side of the debate over the computer's value are the "gloom and doom" worriers who see dire effects of using computers with young children.

Children Need To Be Physically Active; Using the Computer Is a Passive Activity

Many critics condemn computer use because it is a passive sedentary activity. In many computer programs, children do nothing but respond to what the computer puts on the screen. Even in programs that allow children to make more choices, children still exhibit almost no physical activity. It is true that computers tend to generate more sedentary activity, but then so do puzzles, books, or crayons—all common preschool/kindergarten activities. If computer use was either mandatory or the only part of the curriculum, this would be a legitimate concern. As part of a total curriculum, where the computer area is one of many choices and activity is encouraged in many areas, this need not be a concern.

Although computers do tend to be a more sedentary activity for adults, the children who use computers at the University of Delaware Preschool

Kindergarteners dancing to Astro-Grover's song. (Photo courtesy of Nancy Edwards)

do not seem passive. Children are jumping up to observe each other's work, looking around the back of the computer for characters that they have removed from the screen, moving their bodies with the actions of the characters on the screen, and in some cases even dancing to the music on the program.[3]

Computer Use Decreases Opportunities for Language Use and for Exposure to Appropriate Linguistic Models

Barnes and Hill (1983) suggest that children who are working on computers are often isolated and thus deprived of opportunities to use language and to hear good language models in meaningful situations. This argument would be of grave concern if children really did use computers in isolation. But computer use tends to be a social activity (Borgh & Dickson, 1986; Lipinski et al., 1986), thus providing a forum for language use rather than a place at

---

[3]One year the five-year-old class found the music on **Astro-Grover** exciting. Whenever the music played they would dance around imitating Grover's jerky space dance in time to the music.

Children discuss, describe, and debate as they use the computer.

which it is lacking. Like other materials in the room, computers can be used alone or with peers. The language generated would depend on the way the material is used on a particular day. Teachers can also increase the language potential of the computer. They can stop to talk with computer users, providing vocabulary, encouraging conversation, and providing language models in the same way they facilitate language in other areas of the classroom.

Computers Are a Symbolic Medium: Preoperational Children Are Still Working at a Concrete, Not a Symbolic, Level

One common objection to using computers with young children is that such use requires skills beyond the developmental level of preoperational children (Barnes & Hill, 1983). Sheingold (1986) points out that there has been a change in thinking about children's symbolic development. Children do use a wide variety of symbols, though not perhaps in as sophisticated a way as when they are older. Lan-

guage, blocks, dance, art, and dramatic play are all symbolic activities. In the block area, children use stacked pieces of wood to symbolize buildings, jails, caves, or roads. In dramatic play, the child uses objects to represent props and people to represent characters. In many cases, single gestures or objects symbolize whole activities. "The symbolic nature per se does not make it (the computer) incompatible with or inappropriate for use by young children" (Sheingold, 1986, p. 27). She goes on to stress that the true issue is not whether children can use a computer, which is a symbolic medium, but "how the child engages with a particular symbol system via the microcomputer" (p. 27).

Cuffaro (1984) and Barnes and Hill (1983) both feel that the computer is too abstract a medium for young children, who need experiences with real things. Early childhood educators stress that "learning activities and materials should be concrete, real, and relevant to the lives of young children" (NAEYC [Bredekamp, Ed.], 1986). It is true that the computer creates symbols, and that computer use involves the indirect manipulation of these symbols, but the computer itself is certainly a real object. It is obviously more complex than a block, but it is no less real. Children can act on the computer, by pressing keys, moving the ***joystick,*** turning on and off the power switches and then watching how it reacts to their actions. The complexity of the machine makes it harder for children to understand the reason for the reaction, but it makes it no more difficult to observe. For example, when you press the right-arrow key when using **Magic Crayon,** the ***cursor*** on the screen moves to the right.

Meaning? JOYSTICK

A **joystick** is a device that can be attached to a computer. It is a box with an upright stick attached. Moving the stick will move the cursor on the screen.

Meaning? CURSOR

A **cursor** is a blinking light or box on the screen that shows where the image or letters will appear. The cursor may also highlight the current selection on a menu.

Cooking is a recommended part of early childhood programs (Hendrick, 1985). One of the values of cooking is that children can discover how heat changes ingredients. When the cookies are put into the oven, they are soft, pliable, and moist. When they come out, the cookies are hard, dry, and rigid. The children can observe the cause-and-effect relationship. Putting the cookies into the hot oven changes the way the cookies feel, look, and taste.

In the same way, children can observe that pressing the right arrow key changes the position of the cursor and leaves a line. The children cannot understand how either the oven or the computer accomplished the transformation, yet the result is equally apparent in both cases. The computer can be seen as another concrete material with characteristics that can be explored. It is also important to remember that the computer is not intended to replace other experiences, but only to add another medium that a child can choose to explore.

Another layer of this argument is that children learn by doing, by interacting with real things in the environment. Computer use may limit the amount of time children have for such interactions. If this were true, it would be a strong argument against computer use. Research has shown that computer use does not change the types of activities in other areas of the classroom (Hoover & Austin, 1986; Lipinski et al., 1986). If computers are used as a required activity and seen as a "better way of learning," this might threaten the child's chances to interact with and learn from real objects in the environment. Unfortunately, some advocates of computer use do take this position (e.g., Lee, 1984), causing others to cite such misuse as a reason for avoiding computers. As

a replacement for parts of the curriculum, it might have the feared effect, but as an addition to the developmental curriculum, the computer does not prove a threat.

Early Childhood Educators Recommend Open-Ended, Child-Directed, Creative Activities; Opponents See Computers As No More Than Animated Workbooks

A majority of the software programs available for young children are no more than glorified workbooks. Nonetheless, the addition of color, animation, and immediate feedback makes these workbooks more inviting. Goodwin et al. (1986) list a variety of skills that may be encouraged by using computers as workbooks: development of visual skills, alphabet recognition, basic math skills, and spatial and relational concepts. Although there has been some research to verify the effectiveness of "workbook-type" *computer-assisted instruction (CAI)* in teaching content, one must ask if computers are the most effective medium for teaching these skills.

Meaning?
CAI =
COMPUTER-ASSISTED
INSTRUCTION

Computer-assisted instruction, or **CAI**, refers to computer programs designed to instruct users through drill and practice, simulations, or tutorials.

Cuffaro (1984) argues, quite justifiably, that spatial relations can be learned more effectively with three-dimensional objects than on a two-dimensional computer screen. Cuffaro (1984) and Barnes and Hill (1983) question the use of computerized workbooks when paper workbooks are generally frowned on as developmentally inappropriate

(NAEYC [Bredekamp, Ed.], 1986; Kamii, 1985). The computer may add flashing color and animation, but many programs are still uninteresting and unchallenging, stereotypical, and mindlessly repetitious (Cuffaro, 1984). Another concern is that administrators who place computers in early childhood classrooms may want proof that they are being used and may encourage utilization of various workbook-type programs that offer classroom management options.[4]

Much of the concern with such programs comes from the fear that they will be required of children. Good early childhood classrooms are already rich in letters and print. There are letters and words in books, on puzzles, on blocks, on matching games, on the typewriter, and so on. These materials can be used as desired by the children. Alphabet programs can be added to the classroom as yet another way of adding letters to the environment. As with other letter and word materials, they can be selected and used by those children who want to use them, as one of many choices provided in a good early childhood classroom.

It is important to realize that although the majority of software is drill and practice, there are also more open-ended pieces available—graphics programs that allow children to draw and create; word processing programs that can be used for free typing or creating words, depending on the skills and interests of the children; and other programs that allow children to move characters around the screen to animate their own stories. Teachers can select software for their classroom that provide the more open-ended, rather than drill-and-practice approach.

Computers Cannot Be Used Independently; They Take Teacher Time That Could Otherwise Be Spent in Other Areas

If children need a great deal of help with the computer, this takes away from the time teachers have to

[4]Some computer programs offer the option of keeping track of what parts of the program the child has used, and for how long.

interact with children involved in other activities. Cuffaro argues that "the one-to-one attention and extended preparation required serve to underline the gap that exists between the abilities of the young child and the skill needed for programming" (1984, p. 560). Some of the early research on computer use with young children involved trying to simplify **Logo** programming for their use. In many cases, this did involve a great deal of extra teacher time. There is still a lot of question about whether **Logo** is what young children should be doing on computers. Some programs have simplified **Logo** to the point that little teacher help is required. But to do more advanced **Logo** activities, additional teacher time is still required. There are, however, many programs for young children other than **Logo.** Many studies have shown that children can successfully use computers independently (Borgh & Dickson, 1986; Lipinski, 1986). Although more teacher time may be needed initially, follow-up time is similar to that in other areas of the classroom.

Computer Graphics Cannot Offer the Richness of More Appropriate Art Media

Many early childhood educators are aghast at the thought of "computer painting" (Cuffaro, 1984; Barnes & Hill, 1983). The critics decry the important characteristics of paint that are missing from "computer painting"—the fluid quality of the paint, the rich smell of paint, the tactile stimulation, and the ability to mix colors. It is true that the computer does not offer any of these properties, but crayons also lack messiness, fluidity, and the ability to mix colors. Each art medium is different, offering different potentials and limitations. Computer programs such as **Delta Draw** or **Magic Crayon** allow the children to create with straight lines and segments of line, something not within their skill level when using crayons, paint, or markers. Two frequent themes that occur in the computer drawings among my 4-year-olds at the University of Delaware Laboratory Preschool are stairs and cities. Many children just make designs, but those 4-year-olds in my classes who have chosen to use the computer for represen-

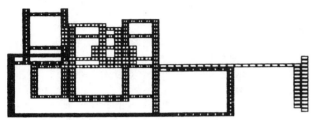

*A city made with **Magic Crayon**.*

tational drawings seem to find that it lends itself to themes not so easily explored in other ways.

Many argue that computer drawings are not even art, just some mechanized lines or designs. One could spend hours debating what qualifies a creation to be labeled "art." When photography first emerged, many claimed that it was not art, as it just recaptured life. Others argued that it was a different art medium that created pictures by capturing particular segments of reality. The fact that art museums collect photographs seems to substantiate the supporters of photography as an art form. In the same way, the computer is a new art medium with its own limitations and possibilities, a medium that can be used for creation and self-expression.

One would not ban crayons from the room because paint is available. In the same way, the addition of computer graphics should not detract from the other art media available in an early childhood classroom. The computer is merely another possible medium with which to create.

Summing Up: Computers Can Be Useful Additions to Preschool Classrooms If Used Wisely

The earlier "messiah" or "monster" definitions of computers are seen less often now. More people tend to take a middle ground regarding computer use. The more moderate view is the one adopted in this book. The computer is seen as a material with many potential benefits and many potential problems. If it is used wisely, with the principles of early

childhood development in mind, it can be a valuable addition to a developmental-based classroom. Although the computer has much to offer an early childhood classroom, its absence from the classroom will not be disastrous.

COMPUTER AS CHAMELEON

The computer has been called a "chameleon in the classroom" (Center for Children and Technology, 1983) because, like a chameleon, it can take on many different guises. It can provide a word processor, a drawing medium, a *simulation*, a drill-and-practice machine, an entity to program, or more. This chameleon quality of the computer, its ability to fulfill so many roles and take on so many different characteristics, may be responsible in part for the diametrically opposed views of the computer's value for young children. Because the computer has so many uses, each with its own unique characteristics, it is hard to evaluate "the computer" in a global sense. The values and faults depend on the use to which it is put. The opinions formed about the computer by early childhood educators depend on how they perceive the computer.

Meaning? SIMULATION

A **simulation** is something that represents an object or action in real life through a model. Many computer programs create simulations, or representations of real life. One example is a flight simulator, which allows the user to simulate the experience of flying an airplane.

It is as if two early childhood educators were debating the value of watercolor painting for young children. One of the discussants is remembering watching an artist gently squeeze out blobs of water-color onto a palette, carefully smoothing the bristles to a point, then meticulously dabbing a bit here, a bit there so that the colors remain separate. Occasionally, the artist adds a bit of water to blend two colors in a precisely measured way. Obviously, if this is "using watercolor," the process requires too much fine motor control and precision for young children. Watercolors by this definition are not developmentally appropriate for young children.

The second participant in the debate recalls 5-year-olds with a metal box containing eight small pans of hard watercolor. The children wet brushes and rub off the colors as needed. They watch the colors run and blend on the paper. They delight in changing the color of the water by rubbing the brush on the paints, then stirring the water with the colored brush. In observing this use of watercolors, it is apparent that watercolors are indeed appropriate for young children. Although the two educators have reached opposing views of the value of watercolors, each is right because they have defined "use of watercolors" in different ways.

In the same way, people's judgments of computer use for young children are based on their perceptions of what such use entails. For an early childhood educator who has used a computer in college to search for data or who began to master the many procedures of a word processing program, the thought of children using computers may be mind-boggling. Young children cannot handle the complexity and precision required by either of these uses (although children can use much simpler forms of word processing designed for their use). For the teacher who has observed children lined up in rows using drill-and-practice software for a half hour a day, computers also appear inappropriate for young children. But for teachers who have seen children working together to figure out how to fill in every part of the screen in a **Color Me** picture, or creating elaborate imaginative stories while moving the figures in **Bald-Headed Chicken**, it is equally obvious that computers are developmentally appropriate for young children. The computer is not a single entity, but a machine that can do a wide variety of things.

*This child has chosen to fill the whole screen on **Color Me** while classmates are busy with many other choices.*

Early childhood educators must strive to find ways to use it effectively.

Because the types of computer use selected are crucial in determining its usefulness in the classroom, it is essential to stop and look at its many different forms. The diverse uses for the computer become apparent in the many analogies that have been devised to describe it.

Taylor (1980) began this proliferation of analogies for the computer by describing three modes for using computing in education. He devised a framework to help organize the "somewhat chaotic range of activities" (p. 2) available for the computer. He describes the computer as a *tutor*, *tool*, and *tutee*. Clements (1985a) presents six possible metaphors for the computer—the computer as tutor, subject, tool, pencil, sand castle, and building block. Beaty and Tucker (1987) suggest seven metaphors—the computer as paintbrush, playmate, alphabet book, abacus, building block, crayon, and chatterbox.[5] A closer look at all of these analogies helps to clarify

---

[5]The following discussion focuses on metaphors for the computers that describe child use. Two of the metaphors represent teacher uses of the computer. When Clements calls the computer a tool, he describes how teachers can use it as a tool for teaching, rather than as a tool for child use. Beaty and Tucker's computer as chatterbox presents the computer as a means of encouraging children to talk with one another.

the multiple roles the computer can take, thus making it possible to pinpoint those roles that can be used in the early childhood classroom.

Meaning? THE COMPUTER AS A TUTOR, TOOL, TUTEE

The **computer as a tutor** refers to the computer as a "teaching machine."

The **computer as a tool** refers to the fact that the computer can be used as a tool for writing, drawing, recordkeeping as well as in many other ways.

The **computer as a tutee** refers to the computer's capacity for being instructed by the user. In this role, the user "teaches" the computer to do things, usually through a programming language, such as **Logo**.

Taylor's original three analogies for the computer—tutor, tool, and tutee—cover most of its uses. Let us look at these and see how the other metaphors fit within these larger categories.

The Computer as Tutor

When the computer is used as a **tutor**, it presents information to the user, sometimes in the form of games, sometimes in the form of drill and practice. The computer can evaluate the user's response, using this evaluation to determine the level of material to present next. "At its best the computer tutor keeps complete records on each student being tutored; it has at its disposal a wide range of subject detail it can present; and it has an extensive and flexible way to test and then lead the student through the material" (Taylor, 1980, p. 3). This type of computer use is often referred to as CAI (computer-assisted instruction).

The majority of the currently available early childhood software fit under this use. This software is designed to teach children letter recognition, numerals, opposites, spatial relations, or some other concept deemed important for young children to master. CAI software ranges from relatively straight drill and practice, in which the child is asked a question and then must respond, to more playful forms. For example, **Letter-Go-Round** asks children to do such things as find the matching letter and match uppercase to lowercase letters, but the program adds lively animation to make it seem less like drill. The letters go around on a giant Ferris wheel. Big Bird appears with a letter to match and dances when you stop the Ferris wheel at the matching letter.

Clements lists tutor as one of his metaphors for the computer, and three of Beaty and Tucker's analogies are forms of **computer as tutor**. They describe the **computer as an alphabet book**, with which children learn letters on the computer; the **computer as an abacus**, with which children learn math concepts; and the **computer as a set of building blocks**, with which children learn spatial relation concepts.

The Computer as a Tool

The computer can also be used as a **tool**, a means to reach some end. Unlike a ruler, a needle, or a hammer, the computer is a multiuse tool. It can be used in such diverse ways as word processing, calculating, making music, drawing, making masks, or creating simulated models. There are a number of available programs that allow children to use the computer as a tool. Kurland (1983) suggests that this is where software development should focus, for with strong tool programs, the computer can be used to support learning in all areas of the curriculum.

Beaty and Tucker suggest two analogies that belong in this category. **The computer as a crayon**, which describes graphics programs that produce straight lines and segments, and the **computer as a paintbrush**, which includes graphics programs that allow for curving lines.

The Computer as Tutee

In this mode of computer use, the child is the tutor, and the computer is the **tutee**, or recipient of the tutoring. In order to teach the computer, the child must learn how to "program, how to talk to the computer in a language it understands" (Taylor, 1980, p. 4). To teach or program the computer, the child needs to give the computer a series of **commands** that it can follow sequentially to obtain the intended result. **Logo** is a programming language most often recommended for young children. In **Logo**, children can "teach" the computer to make a shape or design by telling the computer the series of commands needed to make that shape. The children can then label this process. Once the process is labeled, the child may simply tell the computer the label in order to make the computer follow the sequence and repeat the process again.

Meaning? COMMAND

A **command** is a direction to the computer. Commands must be given in a way that the computer can understand.

One of the benefits claimed for peer tutoring is that in order to teach others, the tutor must learn the information being taught more thoroughly. The same is true when a computer, rather than a peer, is the tutee. "The human tutor of the computer will learn something both about how computers work, and how his or her own thinking works" (Taylor, 1980, p. 4).

Bamberger's **computer as a sand castle** (1983) analogy, which appears on Clements's list as well, is also a form of computer as tutee. It describes programming the computer as a way of developing a richer, deeper understanding of what you know. When programming the computer, "the most common sense aspects of the things that otherwise re-main hidden emerge, helping us to account for, and to build on, what we already know how to do so well but can't say" (Bamberger, 1983, p. 39).

The Computer as Thought-Provoker

Taylor suggests that his "**tutor, tool, tutee**" framework may need to be expanded or modified, to more clearly delineate the computer's potential uses. His analogies encompass many of its uses but do not communicate what is perhaps its most valuable use for young children—the **computer as a thought-provoker**. The computer allows children to experiment, creating and revising concepts as they interact with the computer. As discussed earlier, children learn by constructing concepts with which to comprehend their exploration of and interaction with the world. As children interact with the computer, they construct and revise concepts based on the reaction of the computer to their manipulation. In using the term **thought-provoker**, it is important to clarify that it is the child, not the computer, who constructs the thoughts. The computer is the medium that the child explores, and its actions are the basis for the child's construction of these new concepts.

I had considered calling the computer a "thought reflector," but the computer does not reflect preexisting thought. I had also considered calling it a "thought constructor," but this implies that the computer is constructing the thoughts, whereas the child actually does so. Interaction with the computer provokes new thoughts and encourages the child to put old and new ideas together in new ways. New concepts are developed as a response to interaction with the computer.

Beaty and Tucker's **computer as a playmate** falls into this category. They describe playful interaction with the environment as the child's mode for learning, and the computer is an excellent material for such interaction.

Clements's **computer as a building block** is another version of the **computer as thought-provoker**. The computer is compared to blocks. "As are the building blocks of the classroom, the computer is limited only by the imagination of the children. The same set of materials worked on by different hands and different minds can be anything from a spaceship to a home, to a weight for papers blowing in the wind. Not limited in scope or purpose, the materials can grow with the child, ever increasing in complexity and depth. They can be used alone, but are especially enjoyed when they are shared and used with others'' (Clements, 1985a, p. 5). He suggests that the computer has different meanings. All children perceive computer interaction in light of their own past experience, knowledge, and interests. So, for each child, the knowledge generated from this interaction is unique.

The Computer as Tutor, Tool, Tutee, and Thought-Provoker: Which Uses Belong in the Early Childhood Classroom?

The computer can be described as a tutor, tool, tutee, and thought-provoker. Which of these four uses are appropriate for the early childhood classroom? The **computer as a tutor** holds the fewest possibilities for young children. This use turns the computer into an animated workbook, teaching skills such as number, letter, and spatial relations in a rote, stereotypical way that is not recommended for young children (NAEYC [Bredekamp, Ed.], 1986, p. 49). Children learn best when the information is meaningful to the child ''in the context of the child's experience and development.''

On the other hand, some of the alphabet-letter drill-and-practice software could be made available as a way of adding other letters or numbers to the classroom environment, if there is no requirement or pressure to use them. When children get excited about writing they may fill a whole page up with the alphabet, friends' names, ''mom,'' ''dad,'' or other words or letters that are meaningful to them. Teachers certainly would not require a child to sit down and do such writing, but neither do they discourage it. The classroom has paper and pencils, and it provides a supportive atmosphere for those who want to write, as well as those who do not. In the same way, some software that allows exploration of letters, or other skills, might be available for those children who want to explore it, as long as (a) this is not the only or even the main kind of software available, and (b) it always remains a self-selecting, rather than a required activity.

The **computer as a tool** can easily be integrated into the early childhood classroom. There are a variety of tool programs that children can explore. Music programs allow children to explore the computer as a tool for composing and recording musical creation. Many graphics programs are simple enough for young children to use independently. As with other media, children first explore the computer's many properties before using it as a tool for creating a desired product.

Word processing programs also allow children to use the computer as a tool. As with graphic programs, children first explore the properties of the word processor. They type lines of random letters or of letters with special personal significance. Some of the more cognitively mature 4-year-olds, some 5-year-olds, and many 6-year-olds begin to use the word processor as a tool for recording words or sentences. Children often use the computer as a tool for quickly capturing a story they narrate, with the teacher doing the typing. One 4-year-old used a computer with a *voice synthesizer* as a ''reading machine.'' He laboriously typed out text from a book, then listened as the synthesizer read it back to him.

Meaning?   VOICE SYNTHESIZER

A **voice synthesizer** is a device that allows the computer to synthetically create the speech sounds of the human voice.

Kurland (1983) feels that the potential for the computer as a tool is great and will only be limited by the availability for software for this age group.

The **computer as a tutee** is often seen as the ultimate educational computer use. With older children, programming certainly does offer many excellent opportunities for problem solving and social interaction. But, because *computer languages* are so rigid, and require knowledge of and manipulation of numbers and directions, young children cannot yet easily program independently. Young children can create a series of commands, if the method is simple enough, but they cannot yet string together series of programs to achieve an end result. To use **Logo** with young children requires a great deal of teacher time. At this time, *programming languages* do not allow young children to be independent computer programmers.

Meaning? COMPUTER LANGUAGE OR PROGRAMMING LANGUAGE

A **computer language** is a set of instructions to the computer in a form that it can understand. BASIC and Logo are two computer languages. Each language requires the user to give instructions to the computer in different ways. This may also be referred to as **programming language**.

The **thought-provoker** use of the computer is **definitely** appropriate for this age child. If the teacher views the computer as a material the child can manipulate, explore, and experiment with in the process of creating new concepts, it becomes merely another of the opportunities for similar exploration and learning in the classroom.

The Computer as Subject

The four metaphors suggested—the computer as a **tutor, tool, tutee,** and **thought-provoker**—are able to describe most of the ways in which children

can use computers. But one of Clements's metaphors does not fit here—"the computer as subject." This refers to students studying about the computer. Clements suggests that not only can the children use the machine in many different ways, they can also learn about the computer, making it the "subject." The computer as subject is discussed in Chapters 7-9.

GUIDING PRINCIPLES FOR COMPUTER USE MUST BE BASED ON A DEVELOPMENTAL AWARENESS OF YOUNG CHILDREN

Clements points out that computers, like all new technology, bring advantages and disadvantages.

"Computer technology offers us a new way of thinking about learning and about thought itself. But we may have to give up some of the old comfortable notions and ways of teaching. In addition, we have to work so that children benefit and do not suffer. We need to make sure that we use these tools to extend and enrich the life of the thinking child and also that of the imagining and fantasizing child. But we also need to ensure that these are an addition to, rather than a replacement of, other experiences. We need to let the child see beyond the video arcade. To do this we require a set of directions or principles, to guide us" (Clements, 1985a, p. 6).

To ensure that computers are an asset to the early childhood program rather than a liability, it is important that their use be guided by an understanding of young children. The NAEYC provides these guidelines in its *Developmentally Appropriate Practice* (NAEYC [Bredekamp, Ed.], 1986) criteria. An appropriate learning environment for young children "is planned to be appropriate for the age span of the children within the group and is implemented with attention to different needs, interests and developmental levels of those individual children" (p. 3). The curriculum encourages the development of the whole child in an integrated approach, realizing that all areas are interdependent. Learning is viewed as an interactive process in which children learn

Computers offer opportunities for social interaction, cooperation, and peer teaching.

one of many opportunities for furthering the development of the total child.

As Papert (1986) notes, what children learn from the *microcomputer* depends on the culture of the classroom and the school. "How computer activities are presented may be as important as the software. In a classroom sensitive to the social organization of work, the microcomputer can provide an opportunity for children to work cooperatively in small semiautonomous teams (Borgh & Dickson [1986]; Kull [1986]; Wright & Samaras, [1986]). In a classroom sensitive to children's striving for autonomy and success teachers will guide without precluding discovery and encourage discovery without permitting children to flounder. One consensus . . . is that the classroom context will influence what children learn from or about the software just as it influences what children learn from other educational devices" (Campbell & Fein, 1986, p. 7).

through exploration and interaction with teachers and peers. Learning materials should be concrete and real. A variety of activities and materials should be provided so that each child can select personally meaningful activities. Activities should span a range of levels to provide challenge and success to each individual child.

To meet these guidelines, computers must be integrated into a developmental classroom without disrupting the existing environment. The computer should allow for interactive learning, which children can select or not select, depending on their individual needs and interests. The computer should be viewed as a material that can complement the development of the whole child, not just as a material to boost cognitive development. Socially, the computer can offer opportunities for interactions with classmates, cooperation, and peer teaching. Emotionally, computer use can provide the child with successful experiences adding to a feeling of self-worth. Physically, the computer can offer an opportunity to use a variety of fine-motor skills. Although the computer is one medium that can add to many aspects of development, it is not the only one. It should be merely

Meaning?   MICROCOMPUTER

A **microcomputer** is a small, self-contained computer system with its CPU (the central processing unit that both tells the other parts what to do and contains additional codes) implemented on a single integrated circuit, called a "microprocessor." A microcomputer is often called a micro.

In a developmentally appropriate early childhood classroom, the children play and work individually and in small informal groups. Large group lessons occupy at most only a small part of the day. These classrooms are filled with children who are independently involved in child-directed, open-ended activities. If the computer is to become an accepted part of the early childhood classroom, it must allow for this same type of independent, child-directed, open-ended use. If the classroom environment encourges experimentation, exploration, social interaction, conversation, and creativity, then the computer can offer these same things. On the other hand, if the classroom culture is restrictive, teacher-directed, right-answer-oriented, the computer is likely to mirror these qualities. The computer is a material whose values are dependent on the way people choose to use it.

In looking at a busy early childhood classroom, the observer sees some children cooking in the house area, others building with blocks, driving trucks, doing puzzles, playing in the water, using the computer, painting pictures, stringing beads, and looking at books. It would be impossible to pinpoint one of those activities and claim that it is more important than the others. Each activity adds to the richness of the classroom environment. Each provides developmentally appropriate activities for the children in that class. The computer is only one of many activities; it does not have a higher value or a unique status. The fact that this entire book discusses computer use is not meant to imply that it is better or more important than other classroom materials. The aim is to help teachers better understand the computer, enabling teachers to treat computers like the blocks, puzzles, dolls, or other materials with which they are more familiar.

SUMMARY

The debate over the appropriateness of computers for early childhood classrooms has been heated. Descriptions of the computer range from "monster" to "messiah." Many of the fears have been proven unfounded. When used in developmentally appropriate ways, the computer does not cause isolation, decrease opportunities for social and language development, encourage gender segregation, decrease child-teacher interactions, or change the atmosphere and activities of the classroom. Although the computer cannot solve all ills, as some advocates seem to proclaim, it can be used by the children independently, it can encourage social interaction, it can stimulate imaginative play, and it can provide a forum for problem solving and thought construction. Chapter 11 examines these areas in greater detail.

The computer is like a chameleon with many different uses. It can be seen as a tutor, tool, tutee, or thought-provoker. The most appropriate uses for the early childhood classroom are as a tool and a thought-provoker. The culture of the classroom will affect what is learned from the computer. The teachers should integrate the computer into the classroom as an additional child-directed, individualized activity.

2

How to Begin: Setting Up the Computer in Your Classroom

Teachers who have never used a computer are easily overwhelmed by the idea of adding one to their classroom. There is much that must be learned. The machinery appears so complex, with seemingly endless *cables*, keys, and parts to learn about. The computer's cost also tends to daunt novice learners—what if they push the wrong key and something breaks? The computer terms thrown around by computer "jocks," salespeople, and manuals are bewildering. As with any new technology, fancy terms add a special mystique that separates those "in the know" from the uninitiated. Computer experts have generated a sufficient number of complex-sounding terms to impress, and scare, beginners. To those on the outside, the terms make everything seem difficult and hard to grasp.

Meaning? CABLE

Cables are the round or flat wires that connect the different components of the computer to each other.

However, once you have played with a computer, the numerous parts, keys, and wires become less baffling. It becomes apparent that you can easily use the computer without having to learn about each individual wire. Learning a few computer terms will take the mystique out of these words. It becomes clear that most terms merely describe simple things, and are easy to understand.

This chapter introduces the novice to enough computer terminology to cross the barrier from being fearfully in awe of the computer to actively exploring its potential. Ways to explore and become familiar with the computer are suggested. Once teachers are comfortable with the computer, they

Like other materials in the classroom, children can use computers independent of adult help.

must consider how to integrate computers into their classroom— where to put the computers, what kinds of electrical needs must be met, and other practical questions. Then teachers must decide how to introduce computers to the children. In other words, this chapter discusses what teachers should do to prepare themselves, their classroom, and their children for computer use. Additional information about the parts of the computer is in Chapter 8.

WHAT IS A COMPUTER?

A **computer** is a man-made machine that (1) takes in information, (2) processes the information according to the instruction(s) given by the user by changing it in some way, or by storing the information, (3) then shows the result of that processing (Clements, 1985a). What makes a computer unique is its ability to store information, and then to act on that information with amazing speed and accuracy. The computer is only limited by what people are able to program it to do. (**Program** is the computer term for "teaching" the computer to do something.) It would take a person a long time to multiply five 10-digit numbers. A computer can do this almost instantaneously. But computers cannot make decisions or weigh alternatives unless they are given the guidelines for such judgments by people.

In order to do its job of taking in information, processing and/or storing it, and then putting out the processed/stored information, the computer must have four parts:

- An **input device**
- A **CPU** or **central processing unit**, which processes the information
- A **storage component**
- An **output device.**[1]

[1]These terms are defined in full in the following section.

Input Devices

An **input device** is a mechanism used for entering information into the computer.

Keyboard. The most common computer input device is a **keyboard**. Each keyboard looks slightly different. Most **personal computers (PCs)** have keyboards that look like a typewriter with some extra keys. The number and type of extra keys vary according to the company that produces the keyboard, and often from model to model. Different kinds of computers have quite different keyboards. Many grocery stores have computerized cash registers with keyboards that have keys for entering the type of purchase and the quantity. Bank machines generally have 10 numeral keys and a few **function keys** to indicate what action you want the machine to undertake. McDonald's restaurants have computer keyboards with keys for each kind of food sold.

Meaning? PERSONAL COMPUTERS (PC) AND FUNCTION KEYS

A **personal computer,** or **PC**, is another name for a microcomputer, or a small, self-contained computer system. It is called a "personal computer" because it is designed for use by one person at a time.

Function keys are keys that tell the computer a specific set of commands. Different commands are assigned to the same function keys by different programs. These keys are often called "programmable function keys."

There are many other types of input devices besides the keyboard. I will discuss a few that seem most promising for use with young children. Some are used to move the cursor, a flashing line that

A bank money machine keyboard.

An Apple IIe keyboard sits under the monitor.

appears on the screen to indicate the user's current starting position. In many programs, the cursor highlights an item on a *menu*. When the user has moved the cursor to the desired choice, the user gives the computer a command to process this choice. On other programs, the cursor may indicate where the text will be entered. The cursor may take the form of a flashing box or line at the end of the text. On graphics programs, the cursor indicates where the "paintbrush" will begin painting.

A McDonald's keyboard.

Meaning? MENU

A **menu** is a list of choices or options in a program that appear on the screen in order for the user to make a selection.

The following devices may all be used to move the cursor.

Joysticks. Joysticks are familiar to many nonusers of computers already, as they are commonly used for moving objects in video games. Joysticks come in a variety of shapes and sizes, comprising a lever and two or more buttons attached to a small box. The child can move the cursor or other object on the screen by moving the stick (lever) left or right, up or down. The buttons are used either to enter a choice or to make the cursor leave a line trail. Both buttons may be on the box, or one may be on the head of the joystick. Joysticks vary considerably in their sensitivity to touch and their ease of manipulation. Before buying a particular joystick, it would be wise to have some children test it to see if they can

Children can use the joystick to control the cursor.

This boy is using the Koala Pad, a type of touch pad, to move the cursor. (Photo courtesy of Robert Cohen)

manipulate it easily. Many of the inexpensive models have too much tension for preschoolers to maneuver. Some children find joysticks with the button at the end of the stick hard to maneuver. They find it difficult both to move the joystick and to press, or not press, the button when needed. Some joysticks have dials underneath for adjusting the joystick. Children will often move these inadvertently when they pick up the joystick or hold it in their lap. Consider the placement of such dials before purchase. (There is more discussion of joysticks in Chapter 10.)

Touch Pad. A *touch pad* is an electronically sensitive pad that can be used with a *stylus* or other pointer (e.g., any bluntly pointed object or even a finger) to move the cursor on the screen. The child uses the pointer to indicate the cursor position on the pad. Two buttons are also located on the pad's outer frame.

Meaning? STYLUS

A **stylus** is a pointed, pencil-like object, used for drawing on a touch pad.

Children can use the mouse to draw on Color Me.

Mouse. The *mouse* is a small box enclosing a rubber ball that rolls along the surface when the mouse is moved. The user moves the cursor by moving the mouse's ball on a *mouse pad*. The mouse pad is a thin foam pad backed with rubber on which the mouse is moved. There are also from one to three buttons on the mouse, used for additional computer instructions.

Comments on input devices. In many programs, all *input* can be entered through these devices (though some programs require the child to use the keyboard initially to indicate the type of device that is being employed). In order to use the aforementioned devices, the computer must either have a *port* to attach them to or have the option to add an *interface card* that will run the device. The joystick, touch pad, and mouse can only be used with software designed to accept their input.

An Apple disk drive is to the right of this computer.

Meaning? INPUT, PORT, AND INTERFACE CARD

Input is information (e.g., commands) entered into the computer.

A **port** is an interconnection between the computer and an external device, such as a printer, joystick, or disk drive.

An **interface card** is a flat panel containing electronics and circuitry that can be inserted into the computer. Some computers use cards as intercommunication devices between the computer and external devices. Such cards have a port into which to plug the external device.

The preceding descriptions present these devices as moving the cursor. This makes their use sound rather limited. But in fact, this is not as limiting as it would appear. These devices can be used to select options from menus and to do a wide variety of things. For example, in **Color Me**, after the child uses the keyboard to select the type of input device that will be used, the rest of the program is controlled by the mouse, joystick, or touch pad. The child uses the chosen device to move the cursor, until it reaches the desired part of the menu displayed on the screen. The child then presses the button on the device to enter the choice. The device is used to draw, fill, erase, select line size, cut and paste, and control all parts of the program.

Speech Recognition. Computers have been designed that recognize and respond to human speech as the input device. This seems like an ideal type of input for preliterate children. Unfortunately, the technology is still far from perfected to the point where it can be used by children. To enable the computer to recognize words, users must speak clearly, pronouncing words accurately, and separating words distinctly—all three of which are difficult for many young children.

Disk Drive. An external *disk drive* is a box with an opening into which a *disk* can be inserted. Some disk drives are built into the box that houses the

CPU[2] or the monitor. The disk drive takes the stored information (i.e., the program) from the disk and copies it into the computer's short-term memory. For example, if a child is using **Facemaker**, the disk drive will copy the program from the disk, enabling the computer to display (on the screen) the menu of features for creating a face. The program enables the computer to understand the **Facemaker**-related commands that the child enters. In other words, the disk drive copies the programmed information from a disk into the computer's memory so that the user can use that program.

Meaning? DISK

Disks—often called **diskettes**—are thin, magnetized mylar circles enclosed in square plastic cases. Disks are used to store information—either programs or data entered by the user. The most common disks are 5.25-inch disks, which have flexible cases, and 3.5-inch disks, which have rigid cases.

Output Devices

The **output device** allows the user to see (or hear) the results of the processing that the computer has done with the input that has been entered.

Monitor. The most common output device is the **monitor**, which looks like a television set. The **output**, or information that has been processed by the computer, is displayed on the screen. For most children's programs, a color monitor is essential. It is important that the display on the monitor be clear and crisp, especially for programs in which children must decipher letters or numerals.

Printer. **Printers** allow the children to make copies of their work on paper (known as **hard copy**). Many child development sources proclaim that children are "process, not product oriented" (Hendrick, 1986). They would lead one to believe that a printer, which is designed solely to preserve the product, would be unnecessary. Yet children are fascinated by printers. If you watch children using a printer, most of them are excited by the process of printing, rather than with the product produced by the printer. Many children will watch intently as the print head races back and forth across the page leaving a trail of print behind it. These children may then take the copy of their work to show teachers, peers, or parents, as a proof of the wonderful process that has occurred. At this point, the print may be left unwanted on a table or shelf while the child proceeds to another activity. Children enjoy watching the working of the printer, and they are proud of their ability to control it.

Not all programs have options for printed output. It is important to consider what may be printed before investing in a printer. The **Print It** or **Finger Print** card can be added to the Apple II to enable the user to print most screen displays.[3]

Printers vary considerably in clarity and speed. A printer should print clearly enough to let children easily decipher numerals and letters that are printed. The printer's speed should also be considered. If only one computer is available, and the printer takes a long time to print, this decreases the amount of time children can use the computer and may make it impossible to print all the output before the children leave. A **print buffer** can free up the computer a bit. It can store the information to be printed until the printer can catch up, allowing the computer to do other things. Those familiar with adult use of computers may say speed is not important for children since their text output is short—thus requiring a relatively short printing time. But most of

---

[2]CPU is defined later in this chapter.

[3]**Print It** is produced by Texprint Inc. **Finger Print** is produced by 3rd Ware Computer Products.

Children are fascinated by the printer.

that are in color on the computer. Some children become intrigued by the different designs the printer uses to signify the different colors.

Speech Synthesizers and Digitizers. These devices enable the computer to produce comprehensible speech. Children are fascinated by the computer's ability to make sounds for the letters they enter. Those children who are beginning to read are tickled by the fact that they are able to read words more correctly than most synthesizers and digitizers because these devices slavishly follow the rules. If you enter a word that does not follow basic phonics rules of English, the computer will "misread" the word (i.e., "head" will be read as "heed"). The synthesizer synthetically creates speech sounds whereas a *digitizer* organizes previously recorded speech sounds to create the typed-in sounds.

Disk Drive. The disk drive was described earlier as an input device. It is also an output device. In some programs, such as **Bank Street Writer, Primary Editor, Magic Crayon,** and **Color Me**, the child can record what has been created on the disk to be retrieved later. This stored information on the disk is another way of presenting processed information.

Central Processing Unit or CPU

The *central processing unit*, or *CPU*, is the "brains" of the computer. This is the part of the computer that deciphers and carries out the instructions given to it by the program and the user. The CPU coordinates the actions of the rest of the computer. The CPU can only work on a small amount of information at a time. It relies on the computer's memory, retrieving and returning bits of information to the memory as needed.

Storage or Memory

It is the computer's ability to store information that makes it unique. Computers have two types of

what children print are graphics, which take considerably longer to print, especially if a color printer is used.

Color printers are exciting to watch. Children are intrigued by the way the printer uses the limited number of colors on the ribbon to produce a wide number of colors on the paper. They watch the printer print a line of red, then turn the line purple by printing over the same line with the blue part of the ribbon. Color printers have the disadvantage of being significantly slower because each line must be reprinted in each color. Black and white printers can be used to print black and white versions of graphics memory systems to create this ability—primary and secondary storage.

Primary Storage. *Primary storage* holds information and instructions in the memory inside the computer. The primary storage contains some information in its permanent memory, called **read-only memory**, or **ROM**. ROM contains instructions and information that are a permanent, unchangeable part of the computer. ROM may contain information that tells the computer how to interpret basic commands; for example, ROM understands the elementary loading instructions. What is contained in the ROM varies from computer to computer. **BASIC** (a programming language) is in the ROM of some personal computers. The ROM of some computers contains **sprites** (or programmed characters) that the user can call up to the screen. The information held in ROM remains in the computer when it is turned off. When the computer is turned on again, the information is still there.

Primary storage also houses more temporary information, or **RAM—random access memory**. RAM enables the computer to store information that either the user enters through the keyboard or the disk drive reads from the disk. This information is not permanently a part of the computer. When the computer is turned off, the information will disappear. While Bonnie makes a picture using a graphics program, the picture is contained in RAM. If Bonnie wants to continue the picture the next day, she must first record the picture onto a disk that's in the disk drive. The information stored on the disk is the output, containing instructions to the computer on how to recreate the picture. When the computer is turned off, the picture is "dumped" (erased) from the computer's memory, but it will have been stored onto the disk. The next day, when Bonnie turns on the computer, the picture will not appear. But when the "saving disk," or **data disk**, is loaded from the disk drive, the instructions for making the picture will be reloaded into the computer's RAM.

A computer's memory size is measured in terms of the number of **bytes** that the RAM can store. (One **byte** is required to store one character.) A computer with a 128**K** memory has the ability to store approximately 128,000 characters.

Meaning? DATA DISK, K

A **data disk** is a disk used to store pictures or text or other information that the user has created on the computer. On many children's programs, the data can be saved directly onto the program disk (the disk that stores the program). On other programs, the program disk must be removed, and a data disk is inserted in order to save what the user has created.

K is short for **kilobytes**, which represents the number 1,024 or 2 to the 10th power. K is often used to measure the size of the computer's memory. A typical typewritten page requires 2K of storage space.

Secondary Storage. The computer does not have room inside its RAM to store all the information that a user may ever need. To handle other storage, the computer uses **secondary storage**—other devices to hold extra information for the computer. Disks allow the user to store information that can be reentered into the computer's primary memory as needed. The disk drive reads the information from a disk into the primary memory, and it writes information from the primary memory onto the disk for later use. Some computer systems use cassette recorders and tapes instead of disks and disk drives. Tapes are considerably slower loading than disks. The disk drive can read information off any part of the disk (this is called "random access"), but a tape recorder must advance the tape to the correct spot ("sequential access") in order to get the information. The lengthy loading time makes tapes much less attractive for use with young children. Also, loading from tape may require several attempts while the user tries to get the tone and volume controls of the recorder properly adjusted.

Children are fascinated with following each wire to find what parts it connects.

CONNECTING THE PARTS

Looking behind a computer, a novice may be bewildered by the tangle of wires snaking here and there. The disk drive must be connected to the CPU and primary memory so that the information can be copied between the disk and the computer. The keyboard, or other input device, must also be connected to the CPU so that the entered information can be processed and then stored and/or acted on. The monitor, printer, and other output devices must also be connected to the CPU so that the processed information can be displayed. Each computer system has a slightly different method for connecting its different parts. Teachers do not need to be computer technicians, but a basic understanding of how the parts are connected is helpful. With this knowledge, teachers will have the needed information to deal with problems such as a suddenly blank screen. Is the monitor broken, or is the connection from the computer to the monitor faulty? Knowledge about how the computer parts work together is also important for helping children to gain a basic understanding about computers (this is discussed in more detail in Chapters 7-9).

PURCHASING A COMPUTER SYSTEM

What is the best computer system for young children? This question is not easy to answer. Purchasing a single computer or multiple computer systems is a large investment and should be given a great deal of thought.

What Do You Expect to Do with the Computer?

The first step should be to consider what you expect to do with the computer. Will it be exclusively for the children's use, or will it be used administratively as well? What kinds of software do you hope to use? Will you be using graphics programs, word processing programs, and/or other types of programs? What types of peripherals will you use? Discussion with other teachers who have used computers, and observation of classrooms in which children are using computers are often helpful in clarifying the options.

Will the Software You Want Run on This Computer?

Once you know the types of uses desired, the next step is to find software that allows this type of use. Note which machines can run the chosen software. (Software is the computer term for the program stored on disks, or other medium, which makes the computer perform the type of activity desired.) Each piece of software is designed to be used on a specific machine. Some software producers make more than one version of their program to run on more than one type of computer.

Often, "bargain computers" that are being discontinued by a company, or smaller *systems*, seem like a good deal until you begin looking for creative children's software, only to learn that there is little or none available for that machine. High-quality, open-ended software for young children is just beginning to emerge, and we hope that many new pieces will expand the choices. An outdated computer system will not be able to use the new materials that are being designed.

Meaning? SYSTEM

The word **system** is often used as shorthand for "computer system," which means all the components that make up the computer.

Who Can Offer You Advice?

After the staff has determined how the computer will be used, it would be wise to seek a consultant, preferably one who knows something about both children and computers. Discuss your needs and the systems you are considering. Visit other schools that use computers with young children to see how they are used. Ask the staff to assess the advantages and disadvantages of the school's computer(s). Talk to a variety of computer salespersons, asking each one similar questions, to assess the previous advice you have received.

How Much Memory Do You Need?

When selecting a computer system, one of the issues to consider is how much memory you'll need. Often, computer people assume that computers purchased for children's use need minimal memory capacity, as children do not (a) work on long complex documents, (b) need to manipulate data, or (c) do involved formatting—all adult tasks that require more memory. It is true that children do not need extended memory on their computers for these purposes, but animation and graphics also require substantial memory. It would be wise to consider the amount of memory required for the software that has been selected. Many systems can be expanded. A machine with a 64K memory can be upgraded to a

128K memory by adding a memory card. A system that is expandable will allow your computer to grow to accommodate new needs.

What Peripherals Will You Need?

Many children's programs employ a joystick, mouse, or touch pad. Look for a computer that can accommodate this type of peripheral. Some computers, while not packaged with these features, allow for their addition. If you know that you will want these peripherals, it may be wise to purchase them with the system, as the combined price may be less than the price of the parts individually. Some peripherals, like the printer, may require the separate purchase of a cable and an interface card to connect it to the computer. These can add greatly to the expense of your system if they are not included.

Printers are not compatible with all computers, software, or interface cards. It is important to determine compatibility before selecting a printer.

What Else Should You Ask?

Not all computers are able to produce graphics or pictures. Because pictures are necessary for preliterate children using the computer, it is essential to have graphics capacity in computers intended for children's use. Another important consideration is picture clarity. Children should be able to easily decipher the letters and graphics on the screen. Some computers come with two disk drives. This increases the available secondary memory. This is important for adult use, but not necessary on a system used solely by children. The availability of maintenance is a crucial consideration when purchasing a computer. It may be worthwhile to purchase from a local dealer—even if the initial expense is higher—if the dealer will quickly and reliably repair the machines. Having to send machines away to be repaired is costly, inconvenient, and time consuming,

making the computer unavailable to the children for a longer period of time (Clements, 1985a).[4]

Should Schools Consider Owning More than One Type of Computer?

Because each different system has different advantages and disadvantages, would it be wise to consider buying different systems if more than one computer is going to be purchased? This is an interesting question, with many pros and cons. School systems often buy all one type of computer, as this allows for good deals on purchase prices. Having a single type of system has other advantages:

- Children, parent volunteers, and teachers only need to learn one keyboard and loading procedure
- All software can be used on all machines
- Maintenance may be easier
- Technical assistance and classroom enrichment activities can be shared.

On the other hand, having more than one system allows schools to capitalize on the advantages of each system. Some systems have better graphics; others have higher capacity for animation; some excellent software is available on one computer but not on other models. Having more than one system allows the school to use each system for the activities it handles best. Because computer technology is developing rapidly, buying multiple systems is a way of hedging your bets. It is impossible to know which computer will have the most potential and run the most interesting software 5 years from now. Having more than one system makes it more likely that you will be able to take advantage of new developments.

---

[4]Douglas Clements has an excellent section on selecting *hardware* (the computer term for the components of the computer system) in his book *Computers in Early and Primary Education*, New Jersey: Prentice Hall (1985).

GETTING ACQUAINTED WITH THE COMPUTER

To successfully integrate any material into the classroom, the teacher must feel comfortable with that material. If a teacher is terrified of guinea pigs, a guinea pig is not an effective classroom pet. A teacher who is afraid of the pet does not communicate to children the curiosity, excitement, and affection for pets that their inclusion in the classroom is supposed to generate. A teacher who has never used Cuisenaire rods, read about them, or seen them used is not able to help children explore the full potential of the rods. In the same way, a teacher who is unacquainted with the computer is at a disadvantage in helping children to feel comfortable with one.

Unfamiliar Materials and Activities Can Change a Teacher's Teaching Behavior

The first year of the Computer As Partners Project (CAPP) summer computer camp,[5] the computers and software arrived only days before the children. Many of the teachers were still learning about the computers when camp started. The staff noticed that the normal teaching behavior of the experienced teachers changed for the worse when interacting with children and unfamiliar computers. When teachers were trying to learn the materials along with the children, they became more directive. They were often just as eager as the child to find out what would happen if . . ., and thus they were more likely to push keys themselves, or make intrusive suggestions to children who were busy pursuing their own ideas. Teachers were less likely to leave children to explore the machines independently, because the teachers were as intrigued with the exploration as the children.

This same phenomenon of changed teacher behavior in using unfamiliar computers is often noticed among student teachers and other practicum students in the University of Delaware Preschool.[6] Students not yet at ease with the computer tend to use less appropriate teaching methods than in other areas of the classroom. These students were more likely to ask questions that were neither true requests for knowledge nor an attempt to get the child to explore a novel idea. These teachers were also more likely to give unsolicited and unneeded help and to spend more time attending to the computer's reactions than to those of the child. Students who were more familiar with the computer were less likely to display separate "computer teaching" behaviors. They use the same teaching techniques for both on- and off-computer activities.

A similar change in teaching style in reaction to unfamiliar materials or activities is often seen in student teachers in other areas of the classroom besides computer use. Student teachers who are unsure about pretending display poorer teaching skills in the dramatic play area than in other areas of the room. Uncertainty tends to produce one of these behaviors:

- Less interaction with children
- More directive interaction with children
- Less responsiveness to the child's actions and interests due to more concern with their own actions
- Either much stricter discipline guidelines than necessary or an unwillingness to set any limits at all.

Teachers who were not completely familiar with the machines were more likely to panic when problems arose. Teachers who knew the machines were more likely to take problems in stride, even when they did not immediately know the solution. If you

[5]CAPP, at the University of Delaware, has run summer computer camps, for children 4 to 9 years of age, since 1983. CAPP also sponsors practicum-related early childhood computer courses for college students during the school year.

[6]Because student teachers start in the middle of the semester, they often do not have time to become familiar with all materials before beginning to work in the classroom.

basically feel comfortable with the computer you can calmly "troubleshoot," including the child in the quest for the problem's solution.

Teachers Should Be Involved in the Purchasing Process

Donohue, Borgh, and Dickson (1987), in a study of how preschools used their computers, discovered that computers were less likely to be used if teachers were uninvolved in the process of considering whether computers should be purchased and how they would be used. Borgh and Dickson (1986) noted that time to get to know computers and software was essential for creative use and integration into the classroom.

If teachers cannot be involved in the selection of *hardware*, they should at least be given a say in the selection of software. Teachers use materials more effectively that they feel support their style of teaching and the program in their classroom.

Meaning? HARDWARE

Hardware refers to the physical components of the computer system—printer, disk drive, monitor, peripherals, electronic circuitry, etc.

Ways To Get Acquainted

Time should be allocated for teachers to play with the computers and get to know them. Some schools have found that letting teachers take home the computer for a week or weekend allows for more leisurely exploration. Often, the ability to explore the computer individually or with the children in their own families allows teachers to use the computer, rather than to fear it.

Visiting classrooms in which computers are integrated into the curriculum is an excellent way for teachers to become at ease with computers and young children. Seeing children using computers along with blocks, paint, sand, and dress-up clothing reassures teachers that the computer will not have a negative effect on the classroom, and the teachers become more willing to investigate the computer with an open mind.

Getting to know the computer takes time. Teachers should not be expected to use computers in their classrooms the minute the machines are delivered. Time should be set aside for teachers to play with the machines. They should learn to set up the system. They should play with different pieces of software. In playing with the software, the teachers should think of what children would do. They should push the wrong keys to see what will happen. Are there keys that change what is on the screen? Can the original picture be retrieved? Teachers should explore the computer in the same way they explore a new art medium, manipulative toy, or other materials that will be used in the classroom.

HOW MANY COMPUTERS ARE NEEDED, AND WHERE SHOULD THEY BE?

If the computer is to be viewed as another child-directed activity in the classroom, it is essential that the computer be in the classroom. Preschool teachers would not consider having the dress-up area or blocks in a separate room where the whole class would go for a set period of time each day. This would reduce the child-directedness and spontaneity of the activity. Many elementary schools choose to have their computers in a computer lab rather than in the classroom. The lab advocates argue that

- Not having to move computers between classrooms decreases the wear and tear on the computers
- All children are able to work on the computers simultaneously
- The software is centrally available

- A teacher trained in computer use can supervise the area.

While this is all true, the disadvantages of a separate computer lab far outweigh the advantages for young children. A lab segregates the computer from the rest of the program. It makes computer use a required activity. When the class goes to the computer lab, everyone uses the computer. Each child is given a fixed amount of time to work regardless of individual interests and needs. The kind of spontaneous excitement about discoveries that occurs in a classroom is less likely to happen when children are each intent on their own computer work.

Even if the lab time is more flexible, allowing children to decide when to use the computer room, the lab still does not meet the needs of young children. When selecting a new activity, children look around the classroom for something that interests them. A choice that is housed in a different room does not provide a visual prompt and is often forgotten.[7] Having the computer in another room also eliminates the wonderful incidental learning and excitement that is generated among the children who wander by and watch the computer in use. Children often become intrigued with a new program, or a new way of using a program, which they observe when passing by. The **Bald-Headed Chicken** has a rather slow beginning. When it was first introduced, some children gave up before actually getting into the program. These same children later watched peers using the program and became so interested that they were then willing to wade through the slow beginning.

With more than one computer, arrange them so children can easily compare notes from machine to machine.

How Many Computers Are Optimal?

With unlimited resources, what would be the ideal number of computers per child? This is a hard question to answer. When the computer is first introduced, or a new piece of software is added, a classroom of 20 children could easily keep five or six computers busy. But this is true of any new material when it is first introduced to the classroom. Children are excited by any interesting new material, and most children want to have a chance to use it. When new puzzles are added to the classroom, they generate a sudden surge of interest in puzzles. When the dramatic play area is arranged in a new way, many children want to explore the new arrangement. The number of computers needed should be decided based on normal use, not on the unusually high use engendered by the novelty effect. The ideal number of computers varies from classroom to classroom, depending on such things as

- The other activity choices in the classroom
- The amount of time available for self-selected activities
- Available funding for computer purchasing
- The interests of individual classes and teachers.

[7]When computer use was first begun in the 4-year-old class at the University of Delaware Preschool, the children had to go next door to the empty 5-year-old classroom to use the computer. At the time, we had no microcomputers. The children used the university's mainframe computer (a large computer system accessed by many terminals). The children were excited about going to use the computer at first. During the first week, a number of children asked when it would be their time to go. But after the first week, the children no longer asked to go. Even children who seemed to enjoy the computer, and were eager to go when the teacher initiated the idea, did not think to ask for a turn.

Having more than one computer offers children the opportunity to compare notes between computers. For example, children may try to get their **Facemaker** faces or **Juggle's Rainbow** butterflies to match. Children using other programs may share new discoveries with friends using the same program on another computer.

Having two computers also reduces the time a child must wait to use the computer. A child who wanders by and gets excited by a classmate's block building may get inspired to begin building too. The same thing happens in the computer area. Children get excited and want to participate. The observers may sit down at the computer and work with the child whose work sparked the interest. But, going back to the block analogy, the entering child may want to build onto the first child's work, or may want to begin a new building from which the first child can be visited. In the same way, some children may want the opportunity to begin a new creation on the computer rather than joining the work in progress. If the class has only one computer, either the child must stand around and wait—a rather unproductive exercise—or the child may move on to other activities and forget about the interest in the computer. With more than one computer in the room, it is possible for a child to become inspired and immediately begin working on the computer.

Lipinski et al. (1986) suggest that there should be at least one computer for every 10 children. They found that one computer for 20 children tended to increase the aggressiveness around the machine. This increased aggressiveness tended to favor boys' use of the machine over girls. The girls in the class seemed less pushy in their attempts to get a turn at the computer, and thus the boys tended to monopolize computer time.

There may be a maximum as well as a minimum ideal number. Last year, I had three computers in my class of 18 4-year-olds. Because there were so many computers, children shared computers less often. The year before, and later in the year, when I only had two machines available, joint use of computers was much more prevalent. The ideal number of computers to make available also varies with the way the teacher chooses to use them.

Because having more than one computer encourages some interesting social and cognitive interchanges between users, I would encourage two computers per classroom if possible. If finances restrict the number of computers available to one per classroom, one way to accommodate this is to let each class have two computers for part of the year and no computer for part of the year, rather than having one computer in each classroom all year. Sharing computers in this way has disadvantages as well. Teachers cannot be as spontaneous in their use of computers because they must be used when they are available. Having computers come and go may also make it more difficult to build on earlier activities.

If a sharing arrangement is used, it would be wise to leave the computer(s) in each class for at least a month at a time, to enable children to get many consecutive opportunities to explore this medium. Rather than having the computer in one class for half a year, then the other class for half a year, a month-on, month-off arrangement may be more ideal. Teachers could build on previous computer time when the computer reappears in the classroom. Having the computer available only part of the time also may bring new interest with each reintroduction. Having long visits from the computer (shorter than a semester) allows each teacher to have the computer during different times of year when different uses might be expected, due to developing skills and changing curriculum. This would allow a more uniform integration of the computer across the year.

PUTTING COMPUTERS IN THE CLASSROOM

When deciding where in the room to locate the computer(s), a number of issues should be considered. It is impossible to have a room that has the ideal conditions for each type of activity. Teachers are always balancing the various demands of their classroom and making compromises. This is true of the computer area as well. The following guidelines are ideal recommendations. Teachers should keep them in mind but not expect to achieve them all.

Lighting

Monitor screens tend to reflect light and act as a mirror if they are not positioned wisely.[8] Avoid placing computers directly opposite windows or other light source. After selecting a location for the computer, try a variety of software. Sit so that you can view the screen from the same height as the child to assess the amount of glare.

Furniture

As in other areas of the classroom, it is important that the furniture be appropriate for the children's size. Most commercial computer tables are made for adults and are too tall for children's use. Using tables designed for young children ensures the appropriate height. Children should be able to sit at the computer table with their feet on the floor and the table slightly above their legs. The table should be large enough to hold the computer and the disk cover with its rebus guides, needed peripherals, and other support materials. The table should be large enough to easily accommodate at least two chairs. If the computer must be moved from room to room, casters can be added to a child-sized table.

Electrical

The computer must be located near a power source. It is possible that each part of the computer system—input device, output device, CPU, primary memory, and secondary memory—may each require a separate power source, meaning that each computer system may use up to five outlets. In fact, several parts of the system are usually housed together, sharing the same power source. The Apple II

[8]Hadlock and Morris (1984) was a resource for the following section.

system, for example, needs two separate power cords: one for the monitor, and the other for the keyboard, disk drive, CPU, and primary memory. Peripherals such as printers may require additional outlets.

Power strips (long narrow boxes that accommodate several plugs and can be plugged into one wall outlet) are an excellent way of providing for the multitude of plugs. Power strips with their own switches allow teachers to turn off the power to the computers when the machines are not in use. Some power strips also contain **surge suppressors**, which protect the equipment from sudden surges in power. Surge suppressors are important because they protect both the hardware and the software from surges in electrical power. Some surge suppressors also contain noise filters, which filter out electrical noise on the line. Power strips often come with extension cords to allow flexible placement of the computer regardless of the location of fixed outlets. It is important to run wires along walls or to attach them firmly to the ground with tape.

Environmental Considerations

Computers are sensitive to a number of environmental factors: heat, dust, liquids, magnetic fields, and static electricity. It is important to be aware of these when selecting a location for the computer.

Heat. Computers are sensitive to heat. They should not be used or stored near radiators or other heat sources. Software is also sensitive to heat. Disks should not be left in direct sunlight or on top of computer equipment that is being used.

Dust. Computers are sensitive to dust. Computers should not be placed near blackboards that are in use. If the best location is near a blackboard, be sure to wash it thoroughly to remove old chalk dust and put away chalk to prevent current use. Closing the disk drive when not in use helps to prevent airborne dust from entering. Plastic dust covers help keep the dust off at night or on the weekends when the computer is not being used.

Liquids.   Liquid can easily damage computers. Computers should not be positioned near sinks, cooking areas, or eating areas.

Magnetic fields.   Magnetic fields can damage computers. The magnetic field created by televisions, monitors, telephone bells, vacuums, and power tools should be avoided. Disks should not be stored on top of the monitor.

Static electricity.   Static electricity can also damage computers. If the computer is located on a carpeted floor, static electricity may be generated, requiring sprays, a humidifier, or special mats. (If you receive a shock when touching the computer, some preventive measures should be taken.)

The teacher is seated so she can see the children's faces and help with either computer.

Where Should the Computers Be Placed?

There is no ideal spot for the computer in the classroom. It can be added to the language area, placed near or in the art area (if such placement is possible without placing the computer too near liquids), located in the manipulative area, or have a spot all of its own. If you have more than one computer, it is important to put them near each other to encourage interaction between users. Placing the computers so that they are at right angles to each other allows children to observe the other computer with only a turn of the head. Placing at least two chairs at each machine tells children that this is a cooperative activity.

What Does the Teacher Do?

Although teacher assistance is certainly not needed at all times, it is wise to consider where the teacher can be when help is needed. Locating a chair at the point of the angle made by the two machines allows the teacher to view the children's faces easily and to see either monitor with a slight turn of the head.

When arranging the computer on the table, consider where the switches are located. If the switch is on the right, then locating the disk drive on the left makes the switch more accessible. Some computers, like the Apple II, hide the switch on the back of the machine. This out-of-the-way location is intended to prevent accidentally turning off the power. Unfortunately, it also makes it hard for little arms to reach the switch. If your computer has a switch on the back, place the machine far enough out from the wall or shelves behind it to allow children to see and reach the switch. If the machine is very deep, it may be necessary to place it near the side of the table with room for the child to walk around to where the switch is located. Be sure to consider the location of cords and cables to prevent accidents.

If you want children to be able to use the computer independently, signs and/or labels explaining how to turn on the computer can facilitate such use. Also helpful are numerical labels for each switch, indicating the sequence in which to turn on each part of the system. For example, on the Apple II computer, a "1" can be placed on the disk drive, indicating that the disk must be loaded first. A "2" can be placed on the monitor's power switch, and a "3" on the CPU's power switch. Because the switch for the CPU is located in the back where it cannot be easily seen, a label with a "3" and an arrow pointing to the back of the machine may be helpful. A chart

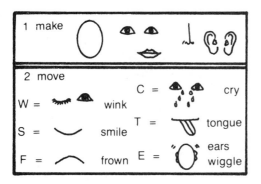

illustrating the steps can be used to supplement the labels if desired.

Displaying software so that children can easily select the program they want also facilitates independent use. CAPP finds pegboards an excellent way to display the software. A 5'' x 7'' index card is taped to the back of the *disk sleeve* so that it extends above the disk. A hole is punched in the top of the card for hanging the disk. The rest of the card can be used to provide a picture representation of what is on the disk. Because most children cannot read the names of the disk, a picture representation of the program helps the children to select the desired program.

The card can also be used to provide *rebus picture directions*, which might be needed for interpreting the menu, or successfully using other parts of the program. For example, **Facemaker** has four options. The child can make a face (menu option "1"), move the face ("2"), play a memory game about how the face moves ("3"), or ("4"), see a list of choices about sound and background color. Because the **Facemaker** menu describes these options with written words, nonreaders must either have teacher help, or memorize the choices. If a large "1" is on the card next to a blank face, the child can see that pressing "1" calls up the blank face to be filled in. A large "2" next to pictures (depicting the possible motions and the letters that command these motions) tells children that pressing "2" allows them to move the face. The movement pictures also illustrate which letters cause which motions.

Meaning? DISK SLEEVE, REBUS PICTURE DIRECTIONS

A **disk sleeve** is the paper pocket in which the disk is stored.

Rebus picture directions are directions with picture clues that nonreaders can interpret and follow.

INTRODUCING THE COMPUTER TO CHILDREN

There is no right way to introduce computers to children. The method used depends on the age of the children, their previous experience with computers, and the teaching style and philosophy of the teacher. Some teachers prefer to introduce computers with a unit on computers, tying in the use of computers with activities and discussion about the computer. Other teachers prefer to introduce the computers more briefly, as they would other new materials in the classroom. They provide the children with the information that is essential to use the

Pictures on the disk sleeves help children select software.

computer constructively and let the children learn the rest through experience. The younger the group of children, and the more limited their previous computer experience, the more important it becomes to use the latter method of introduction. Children need some experience with computers in order to understand abstract discussions of computers.

Many authors suggest introducing computers by constructing cardboard computer models, using posters of computers, or using other computer literacy materials. These materials have little meaning to children who have had no experience with computers. It is rather like encouraging young children to build a model of a sewing machine without ever having seen one. It is harder to conceptualize what a machine does from a model and discussion than from actual observation and use. However, models and discussion can be effective methods to encourage children to better understand what they have seen. They are good techniques for clarifying knowledge after computer use has begun. When deciding how to introduce computers, consider the past experiences of the children and use these as a gauge for when to begin talking about computers. This is discussed in more detail in Chapter 7.

What Must Children Know Before They Begin Using the Computer?

What essential information must be introduced before children can use the computer? There are five pieces of information to which children should be introduced before computer use.

1. A special procedure must be followed for loading and turning on the computer. Number labels and charts should be provided for prompting children to remember this sequence.
2. Disks must be handled in a special way, touching only the label. Improper handling damages the disk.
3. Different software makes the computer do different things. Each of the software holders displays one or more pictures indicating what the disk does.

4. Children need a basic understanding of how to move through the selected program. The rebus pictures can be introduced to show children how to remember when the teacher is not available.
5. Computers can be used by two or more children working together. Classmates can share knowledge with each other when someone is stuck.
6. Sand, water, and other messy substances should be kept away from the computer.

Each teacher must present the information in the way that best fits the individual class and personal teaching style. Some teachers prefer to have a group lesson showing the children how to load the computer. If desired, the entire class can be introduced to a piece of software and can then discuss what the teacher is doing to use the software. Other teachers prefer a more individualized way of introducing the computer. The computer may be mentioned to the large group as a new piece of equipment in the classroom, perhaps mentioning the need for dry, clean hands, and the proper way to hold a disk. Then the loading procedure and specific software can be introduced more informally to small groups of children during activity time.

The First Few Days of Use

No matter which way is selected, during the first few days, the teacher must plan to allow time for helping children get to know the computer. The teacher need not sit with children all day, but she or he must help each child or group of children through the process of

- Selecting software
- Loading and turning on the computer
- Getting acquainted with the user's actions for that piece of software.

The first few days the computer is in the classroom, the teacher may want to have a parent aide present (if it is a one-teacher classroom), and/or offer other activities that are of high interest to the class but require little teacher supervision. In many cases, the teacher need not spend as much time helping the last half of the class to use the computer. Many children learn from observing others use the machine. Classmates are also eager to share their new knowledge and skills with children who are just beginning.

It is wise to begin with a limited selection of software. Teachers must use their judgment of their own classes to decided on the appropriate number of choices to make available at the start. I recommend at least two kinds of software so that children know that (a) the computer can do more than one thing, and (b) the program they select determines what the computer can do. Depending on the difficulty of the programs and how much similarity exists between programs, up to five pieces may be available at the start. (Chapter 3 discusses the importance of considering software similarities in building an in-class software collection [p. 50].) It is important to remember that the children need not be introduced to all of a program's options at once. (Chapter 10 discusses how to introduce programs that can be used on a variety of levels.)

Continuing to Use the Computer

Periodic reinforcement of this information is necessary regardless of the introduction method used. Teachers can ask children to remind each other of the loading procedure when the computer is mentioned as an activity option. Teachers can praise appropriate behavior as a means of reinforcement (e.g., "I'm glad you are so careful to hold the disk on the label"). This encourages the child to continue to be aware of proper handling, and reminds nearby children as well. Teachers can ask questions to help children focus on the information (e.g., "What do you want to do on the computer today: make a face that can move, or draw your own picture? Which disk do you think will do that?"). If the child is unsure, encourage looking at the pictures on the disk holder.

Once each child has had an opportunity to play on the computer, the amount of teacher assistance needed will decrease. But, as in the use of any ma-

terial, some children need more time than others to develop the needed skills and understanding for independent use. When paper punches are first put out in my 4-year-old class, the children are unsure what to do with them. The teacher may have to demonstrate or assist children to place the paper in the correct slot, to push with a quick hard pressure, and to remove the paper gently without ripping. For some children, the demonstration is enough, for others the more direct assistance is needed, and for still others repeated help is needed before the technique is mastered. Some children continually seek help: some of these calls for help are truly warranted; at other times, the child uses help requests as a way to obtain some shared time with the teacher. This same range of assistance required is apparent also when children begin to use the computer.

If appropriate software is selected, children are quickly able to use the computer independently. At this point, teachers may supervise the computer in the same way they do with other classroom materials. They may

- Observe how the children use the material
- Stop to enjoy the child's work, and perhaps spend time sitting with the child as they work
- Ask open-ended questions when appropriate
- Provide help if the child has a problem.

Introducing Additional Software

To keep the computer a "fresh" and interesting area of the room, it is important to introduce new software periodically. How often new software is introduced depends on

- The children
- The other materials and activities available in the room
- Whether new ways to use the current software can be introduced

- The amount of appropriate software available for classroom use
- Many other factors.

New software can be introduced as often as every 2 weeks, or as infrequently as every month. How many pieces of software to introduce at one time depends on

- The children's level of computer skill
- The difficulty of the program(s) introduced
- The similarity of the new programs to each other and to the old programs
- The number of computers available.

If the new program is quite different from the old ones, it might be best just to introduce it alone. If more than one computer is available, you may want to provide either one new piece of software for each machine or multiple copies of the new software.

When new software is introduced, as when other new materials are introduced in the classroom, additional teacher time may be needed to help children explore its potentials. The amount of help required varies both by child and by how much the new software differs from previously used programs.

SUMMARY

Teachers do not have to be computer whizzes to use computers with young children. As with any material used in the classroom, teachers should become familiar with the new material, exploring its potential before introducing it to the children. To truly integrate the computer into the classroom, it is important that computers be in the classroom. The way the computer is introduced and where it is placed in the classroom varies by teacher and classroom, just as they do in the use of other materials.

3

In Search of the "Ideal Software"

Software is one or more computer programs, usually stored on disks, that make the computer do things. The incredible variety of available software is one of the factors that gives computers their chameleon-like nature. With one piece of software, the computer can be a sophisticated typing machine; with another, it can be an easel; with another, it can become an animated workbook page; and with another, it can become an electronic feltboard. These are only a few of the many kinds of programs that are available.

The value of computer use for young children depends on wise software selection. Carefully chosen software can make computer use an independent, child-controlled, interactive experience that encourages social cooperation. Poorly selected software can make the computer into a tedious electronic workbook, can encourage competition, can make the child feel frustrated and inadequate, can encourage sex stereotyping, and develop in children (and teachers) a dislike for computers. If the computer is to provide any of its potential benefits to children, it is important that teachers learn to select software wisely.

SEARCHING FOR THE ELUSIVE "IDEAL" SOFTWARE

The quantity and variety of software available, and the effort required to obtain copies for preview, make selection of software difficult. Software advertised for young children varies in type (graphics, word processing, tutorial, etc.), in quality, and in appropriateness for the advertised age range. Because it is difficult to wade through both the broad promises made by software producers and the mass of poor programs in order to find appropriate pieces,

Open-ended software allows children to interact with the computer.

43

teachers often ask for a list of "ideal software."[1] Such a list is difficult to supply because the criteria for determining "ideal software" depend on such things as the teacher's goals, the age of the children, the children's previous computer experiences, the amount of time children have access to the computer, and the teacher's teaching style. It is rather like asking "What is the ideal curriculum for a 4-year-old class?" There is no ideal curriculum. Teachers must design a program that fits both their personal teaching styles and the children's needs and interests, while taking into account sound developmental practices.

In selecting any type of material for the classroom, teachers must consider goals, the children's interests and skills, and the other materials available. If a teacher is going to select small manipulative building toys (like Duplo, Bristle Blocks, etc.), many characteristics must be considered. One characteristic to examine is the building toy's stability. Although a teacher can be encouraged to look at the blocks' stability, it is impossible to pinpoint the amount of stability that should be sought. For the inexperienced builder, instability can lead to frustration, but for the skilled builder, the challenge of making the structure balance may be an added benefit. Teachers must evaluate the stability and other characteristics in the light of their children's skills in order to find an appropriate match.

In the same way, it is possible to list characteristics that should be considered when evaluating software, but it is impossible to pinpoint the ideal dimensions of these characteristics, as these vary according to the experience of the children involved. When assessing whether a computer program can be used independently, the children's previous computer experience is an essential consideration because the characteristics that allow for independent use differ, depending on the ages of the children and their previous experiences with computers. For

those reasons, a guide for evaluating software should list general characteristics to be considered and evaluated with specific children, ages, and levels of experience in mind.

CHARACTERISTICS TO CONSIDER IN REVIEWING SOFTWARE

When selecting software, as with the selection of all classroom materials, it is important to keep in mind sound developmental principles. The software should enable children to use the computer for creative exploration and child-initiated activity without excessive teacher assistance. In reviewing software, there are a number of questions that teachers can ask. It is important to remember that although the best possible software should be sought, it is unlikely that any piece will be ideal in all areas. As with other classroom materials, teachers must decide which qualities are most important and look for pieces that reflect as many of these characteristics as possible.

Can Children Explore the Software without Adult Assistance?

Most writers agree that children should be able to use the software independently of adult assistance after a brief introduction (Haugland & Shade, 1988; Clements, 1985a; Beaty & Tucker, 1987). This is essential if the computer is going to be added without disrupting the normal functioning of the classroom. The ease or difficulty with which a piece of software can be used independently depends on a number of variables. The following questions may help to assess the ease or difficulty children may have in using a program independently.

Are the Instructions for the Program's Use Clear? Because most young children cannot yet read, it is important that the software include on-screen pictorial prompts, as well as (or instead of) written directions. If such prompts are not available,

[1]One of the most asked questions by teachers who attend the University of Delaware Computer Conference and visit the campus laboratory preschool to see computer use, or who observe CAPP (Computers as Partners Project) summer computer camp is "What software should we buy?"

Searching for a needed key.

would it be possible to make off-screen rebus sheets to clarify the steps for children? When the program requires children to make a choice, are the need for a choice and the options from which to select clearly presented on the screen? Is it clear how to exit the program?

Does the Program Require Reading? If so, it cannot be used independently by nonreaders without adaptation by the teacher. Chapter 10 discusses ways to adapt software to circumvent inappropriate sections.

How Many Specific Keys Must Be Located? The more keys that a child must locate, the harder the program is to use. Although increased exposure to the computer makes key location easier, programs that employ many specific keys for different functions may prove frustrating for beginning computer users who like to press letters randomly. Such children may unintentionally cause irreversible changes or even cause the product to vanish and not know how to retrieve it.

For example, children using **Magic Crayon** may accidentally press "R" for remember, temporarily removing their picture from the screen to replace it with directions for saving pictures. The child cannot return to the picture without pressing at least one

letter key and then **[Return]**. The child will probably need teacher assistance to discover how to retrieve the picture. The more keys that can unexpectedly produce results that are irreversible, the more likely a child will need a teacher's assistance. As children (or adults) become more familiar with computers, they become better able to understand and deal with keys that produce special commands.

Are the Specific Keys Needed for This Program Already Familiar to the Children? Do the special function keys play the same role as in familiar programs? If children have previously used programs that use the **[Return]**, spacebar, **[Esc]**, or arrow keys, any new programs that use these keys in the same way are easier to learn. In many programs for young children, the **[Return]** key lets the computer know that the user has made a choice, and the spacebar moves the cursor through the menu. If children have used other programs in which the **[Return]** key and spacebar function in this way, they may spontaneously use these keys the same way in new programs.

But in some programs, such as **Mask Parade**, the **[Return]** key and spacebar have the opposite functions. These programs can be confusing at first. This is not to say that such programs should not be used. However, they will be more difficult to use independently if children have used the other type of program. These programs should not be introduced until children have had enough experience with computers to understand that keys can have different functions in different programs.

How Many Separate Steps Are Necessary To Use the Program at the Most Basic Level? Using **Magic Crayon** involves only two steps—typing the user's name and moving the cursor to "draw." Other programs involve many steps. Even more important than counting the number of steps is to evaluate how difficult children may find the steps. For example, **Facemaker** involves many steps, but not all steps are equally difficult to learn.

1. To begin the program, the child must select a background color, decide whether sound should be audible, and then ask the computer for the face-building part of the program.
2. To begin building the face, the child must move the cursor to the feature the child wants to add (e.g., eyes), confirm the selection, move the cursor to the desired pair of eyes, and again confirm the selection made.
3. This selection process is then repeated with each feature.
4. Once the face has been constructed, the child must press "2" to ask for the part of the program that moves the face.

The children quickly learn the steps needed to build the face, as they are repeated over and over, but the steps to move from building to moving are much harder for the children to remember. It is not so much the number of steps that indicate difficulty, but how repetitive and logical they appear to the user.

What Previous Experiences Have the Children Had with Computers? In evaluating whether children can use a piece of software independently, it is important to consider the children's previous computer experiences. If children have used a variety of software already, they are likely to be able to use more difficult pieces independently. Children with little previous computer experience may find these same pieces too difficult for independent use.

Can the Child Control What Happens on the Computer?

As with other classroom materials, in order for the computer to be an interactive experience, it is important that the child be able to initiate and shape that interaction. Obviously, the software puts some constraints on the interaction. The child cannot make pictures on a program that is designed for word processing; nor can the child make curved lines on graphics software programmed to make linear designs. All materials place constraints on interac-

tions. Children can neither build towers with crayons nor balance blocks in ways that defy gravity. Children must always work within the limits of the chosen media, but the limits should be broad enough to allow room for exploration and experimentation. The following questions may help in determining whether children would be able to control a particular piece of software.

Can Children Escape to the Main Menu from Any Portion of the Program? In many tutorial programs, children cannot return to the main menu until they have completed the lesson. This takes the control away from the child. The child should be able to determine when and how to change what is being done with the computer (Haugland & Shade, 1988).

Can Children Initiate the Computer Activity and Determine the Sequence of Events, Rather Than Merely Responding to the Computer? Software should be selected such that "children are in control, acting on software to make events happen rather than reacting to questions and closed-ended problems" (Haugland & Shade, 1988).

If the computer is to be a thought-provoker, this characteristic is essential. To construct their own knowledge, children must be able to manipulate the materials in their environment. This exploration allows them to come to terms with and make sense of what they have discovered in light of their previous concepts and experiences.

Can Children Control the Pace of the Program? Can children repeat or skip sections if desired? Does the program have lengthy entrance displays (e.g., the boy running up the stairs on Spinnaker children's software) or long "reward displays" if the child is successful? Although such displays, when well done, are cute the first few times, they soon become tedious. Can the child skip these displays and get to a more active part of the program, or vary the length of the display as in **Dinosaurs**?

Are the Computer's Reactions to the User's Actions Predictable? In order for children to feel in control of software they must know what results their actions will have. For example, the child who has used **Stickybear ABC** a few times learns that to get the bear to cry, the letter "C" must be typed. If pressing it once brings a cake instead, then pressing "C" again will make the bear cry. The child can successfully control this software because the rules are clear. But in **Toy Box**, when the child pushes a key, the same shape always appears but the size, color, and location of the shape will vary randomly. The child cannot control this software. It is impossible to plan or use the shapes to create a desired design.

Are the Computer's Reactions to User Commands Easily Visible? In order to discover how to predict the computer's reaction, the child must first be able to discover these reactions. When children are using **Magic Crayon**, they can observe that when the up arrow is pressed, the cursor moves up, leaving a line. Visible reactions allow children to discover the relations between their own actions and the computer's reactions.

Does the Software Allow for Trial-and-Error Exploration?

Children learn through constructing their own knowledge. New information is integrated with old concepts. If exploration of new materials does not agree with previous concepts, the child will continue to explore until an acceptable solution is reached. It is important to be able to repeat and revise previous actions in the process of accommodating old concepts to new ideas. This characteristic is also essential in order for the computer to be used as a thought-provoker.

Although drill-and-practice software is not highly recommended, it can be used in conjunction with more open-ended software. If drill-and-practice software is used, it is important to consider how the program deals with errors that the child makes. A child's self-concept is not enhanced by hearing a buzzer that indicates an error has been made.

Is the Software Appropriate for Children This Age?

The appropriateness of software can be assessed in terms of a variety of characteristics.

Are the Pictures Understandable? Can the children understand the pictures? If the program is working on letter sounds, are pictures chosen that have only one possible label (e.g., a picture of a bunny could also be called a rabbit)? Do the pictures represent things familiar to most children this age?

Is the Print Used Based on Primary Print? Children who are just learning to recognize the alphabet have trouble understanding the more elaborate form of print often produced by typewriters: the "a" with the hood over it, the "t" with the curved tail and the "g" with the closed loop on its tail. If the software requires children to recognize letters, the letters should be made in primary print.

Is the Content of the Software Appropriate?

To determine whether the content of the software is appropriate, two questions must be asked.

Is the Software Free of Stereotypes and Materials That Conflict with the Moral Values of the Program? When selecting software, as in selecting any materials, it is important to avoid items that promote racial, ethnic, or gender-based stereotypes. Other values and goals of the school should also be considered. Many early childhood programs avoid guns and other violence-based items. Aggression and violence-based software should be avoided to accommodate this philosophy.

Is the Topic Appropriate? Is the material covered something children of this age are likely to find interesting and understandable? Is the material likely to coordinate with the content of the classroom curriculum?

Can the Software Hold the Children's Interest?

Will the software maintain the children's interest after initial use? Are the visual displays captivating? Does the program offer enough variety, either in what is presented, or in what the children are able to do with the material?

Is the Program Expandable?

Programs that can grow with the child can be used for a greater length of time. Haugland and Shade (1988) suggest that an important criterion for good software is that it should have a low entry level but be able to expand as the child explores. Ideally, the program can be used at a basic level by beginners. As the children use the software, they will develop skills to allow a more expanded use.

For example, in using **Color Me**, children can begin by just drawing. As they explore the software, the children will learn to change colors, adjust the width of the drawing line, explore the letter-making options, fill areas of their picture, and learn the other possible options. Each child will learn the options at a different rate and in a different order. This piece of software can be used at an extremely simple level, at a complex one, or at various levels in between. Programs that can be used on different levels are able to accommodate the different levels of children found in every classroom. Many programs offer a choice of skill levels as well.

Is the Software Well Made Technically?

It is important that the software be technically sound. If the picture is fuzzy, or the program runs slowly or erratically, both children and adults will find it difficult and frustrating to use. Following are some questions to ask in assessing the technical quality of software.

Is the Picture Quality Good? The picture should be crisp and well defined. Characters should be easily identified. Colors should be aesthetically pleasing and appropriate for the content. High-resolution software will have richer colors than the older low-resolution pieces. (It is important to remember that picture quality also depends on the quality of the monitor. When possible, preview the software on your own equipment before the final purchase.)

Is the Sound Quality Good? Does the sound add to the program? Can the sound be turned off if desired? Will the sound be distracting to children working in other areas of the classroom?

Does the Program Load Quickly? It is important that the program *load* quickly, so that children are able to begin their computer interaction without too long a delay. It is also important to consider the time required to move from one part of the program to another. Are there many instances in which the child needs to wait? The time required may depend on the speed of the computer system, as well as that of the software, so it is best to test software on your own machine if possible.

Meaning? LOADING A PROGRAM

Loading a program is the process of transferring information from the disk into the computer's memory.

Are Backup Copies Available? Does the software come with a *backup copy* or a means of making a backup? Can backups be obtained at a reasonable cost?

A GRL IZ TACEN A WOC AND SE FD A LT
DOG. SE TACS THE DOG HOM. THER WZ A
SNAC LAD OT ON THE TABL. THER WZ A TINE
VAZ ON THE TABL.
THE AND.

Children can use **Kidwriter** *just to make a picture or they can use it at a more advanced level like this kindergartner and compose an accompanying story.*

Meaning? BACKUP COPY

A **backup copy** is an extra copy of the program that can be used in case the original disk is damaged.

What Type of Peripherals Are Needed? How Much Memory Is Required? It is important to consider how much memory is needed to run a program. A program that requires 128K will not run on a machine that has only 64K. Does the program require special peripherals such as a joystick or a mouse? Many programs have the option of working with the keyboard or a peripheral. Sometimes, the quality of the program is affected by the device used. For example, **Explore-a-Story** can be used with either the keyboard, a mouse, or a joystick. Moving the cursor with the keyboard is more time-consuming than using the other two devices. This program can be used with the keyboard, although younger children may be impatient with the slow speed. It is important to realize that you must evaluate the program using the peripheral that will be used in the classroom, as the developmental appropriateness of the program may depend on the means available to run it.

Is the Software Easy to Load? If children are to use computers independently, it is important that they be able to load the program themselves. Some software require more elaborate steps for loading.

Does the Software Inactivate Unneeded Keys? It is important that unneeded function keys be made inactive so that children do not accidentally start an undesired function.

PUTTING TOGETHER A SOFTWARE COLLECTION

When evaluating software, it is important to think of building a collection of pieces that complement one another. The software should cover a range of types and levels in the same way that teachers select different types of manipulative building toys that complement one another. Some kinds of building toys seem to "expand," being used at one level by beginning builders and at other levels by more skilled hands. Other blocks are better only for the novice builder, yet others are better for just those with more building experience. Some blocks lend themselves to constructing vehicles, others encourage towers, and still others encourage a range of products. Teachers select an assortment of blocks that meet the needs of different skill levels and that encourage a variety of construction types.

Likewise, some software requires few skills at the entry level; some takes more skill to begin. Software can also enable the computer to be used in many ways—as a tool, tutor, tutee, or thought-provoker. When selecting software, teachers should select pieces that accommodate a range of levels and allow the children to explore the computer's various uses.

A Software Collection Should Provide Expandability

Although it would be ideal if each piece of software was infinitely expandable, moving from novice level to great complexity, this is not always possible. But by wisely selecting the software to be used and carefully sequencing its introduction, teachers can use a series of individual pieces to provide a similar progression.

For example, the **Explore-a-Story** series does not begin at an entry level. Children must move the cursor to select a page, then move it to the character they want to animate. These steps are relatively simple for children who have had experience selecting from a menu and moving a cursor with the arrow keys (or joystick or mouse, depending on the auxiliary being used). But the same steps are quite confusing to children who have never used a computer before. This program is easy for children to use independently after some initial exposure to other software. Therefore, this software would be incorporated later in a progression of software introduced into the classroom. Of course, there are always exceptions. Many children learn to use a piece of software without the prerequisite skills by watching and imitating a classmate's use.

A Software Collection Should Provide Variety

When selecting software, it is important to choose programs that allow children to explore the computer's many potential uses. The teacher must decide whether to emphasize one type of computer use or to balance the number of pieces for each type of use. A teacher who is particularly interested in stressing the computer's potential as a tool would select a larger quantity of tool software than a teacher who has another emphasis.

But even if the teacher decides to help children see the multiple dimensions of the computer and selects software with a variety of uses, it is still advisable to pick two or three programs with the same type of use. Early childhood classrooms provide materials with a wide variety of uses, such as building toys, art materials, and dramatic play props. Yet within each area, there are also many choices. The art area could include crayons, paints, paste, pencils, markers, and chalk. Each medium encourages different types of creation, expression, and exploration. In the same way, it is important to provide more than one graphics program. Graphics programs vary widely. Some allow only straight line drawing, others allow for curves or for filling in enclosed areas. By providing more than one piece of each type of software, the children are introduced to the richness and the seemingly limitless potentials of the computer.

A Software Collection Should Provide Balance

When selecting software, it is difficult to find pieces that are ideal in each of the characteristics evaluated. Some programs are superb for early independent use but rate less well in other areas. **Stickybear ABC** can be used independently by the novice computer user. It also allows the child to have some control over the software. The child controls the speed because the software continues each graphic until the child requests a new one.

The program allows for trial and error. If the child does not get the desired graphic, other keys can be pressed until the wanted picture appears. Yet this software is not expandable. It only allows for one type of interaction, which tends to lose children's interest more quickly than software with more possibilities.

Although the software does allow the children some degree of control (they can select the graphic by pushing the correct letter), the amount of control is relatively limited when compared to graphics programs in which children can make their own designs, or programs like **Explore-a-Story**, in which children can add and move their own characters and props to create a picture, story, or dramatic play environment.

Some teachers question the value or possible problems of using programs that have an easy entry level but that may not offer the open-ended, child-directed, computer-as-thought-provoker experience ultimately being sought (e.g., **Stickybear ABC** or **Juggle's Rainbow**). These teachers feel that such software encourages children to build narrow restrictive definitions of computer use that may be hard to alter. In the Lipinski et al. study (1986), the computers were introduced the first week in a demonstration mode, in which the screen display changed without anyone touching the keyboard. The second week, the keyboard activated the screen display. Many children were confused the second week. They expected the constantly changing screen display of the week before. Initial interaction has an effect on the way children perceive the computer, what they expect it to do, and the way they attempt to use it.

But other teachers suggest that some of this type of software is an effective introduction to the computer as long as it eventually leads children to software that does allow an open-ended, child-directed, thought-provoking experience. I take a middle ground about this type of software. If it is introduced with more open-ended pieces, such as **Magic Crayon**, the children will see a variety of uses for the computer and not have their perceptions limited by the more restrictive pieces. Whichever position you take, it is important to remember that children will build conceptions of the computer based on what they do with it.

If teachers see the computer as a machine that can be a thought-provoker, it is important that pieces like **Stickybear ABC**, which do not promote this use, be balanced with software that does. When compiling a collection of software to be used together in a classroom, teachers must not only weigh the merits of each individual piece of software but also consider the composite merits and weaknesses of the total software collection.

HANDS-ON APPROACH IS ESSENTIAL FOR SOFTWARE EVALUATION

In order to evaluate and select software, teachers must have access to software that can be sampled. Hands-on trial of the software is essential for a number of reasons. Many of the important characteristics for evaluation cannot be determined without ac-

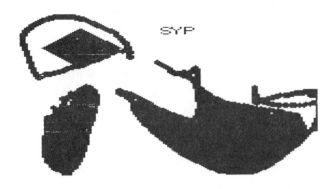

*A ship drawn and labeled on **Color Me** by a four-year-old.*

A good way to review software is to watch how children use it.

tually using the software, for example: speed of loading, number of keys needed, whether unused keys are toggled (inactivated), technical quality, or amount of control by the user. Unfortunately, hands-on trial of software is more difficult than it sounds. Many computer stores do not have facilities for trying the software they sell.

Teachers should not rely on the promotional blurbs when evaluating software as the manufacturer's description is often inaccurate or promotes one aspect of the software, while failing to mention parts that the teacher may find more salient. For example, in the advertisements and reviews of **Color Me**, it is described as a computerized coloring book in which children can select predrawn outlines, and fill them in with desired colors. "A computer coloring book with 25 high-resolution pictures. Pictures are designed with various degrees of difficulty and include familiar objects and animals. Each picture is titled in large capital letters for word and subject recognition. Select from 32 color pots for use in a combination of colors, textures and graphics" (*Software Reports*, 1986, p. FA2).

Coloring books are not recommended by most early childhood educators, as they undermine the children's faith in their ability to draw, they put undue emphasis on product, and they stifle creativity. From the producer's descriptions, and the reviews in *Software Reports: The Guide to Evaluated Educational Software* (1986), I would not consider **Color Me** an appropriate program. But in trying out **Color Me**, I discovered that the coloring book feature is only one aspect of the program. This software also contains an excellent graphics program that allows for free drawing, using a variety of colors and line qualities. There are also options for typing letters, filling in parts of the drawing, and a method for printing the picture that can be used independently by the children.

If possible, try out the software with children before purchase. Children often find ways to use software that adults had not considered. Watching children use software allows you to assess its ability to hold interest, whether children can use it independently, and other possible ways that children may find to use the software. Reviewing software with children is particularly important for teachers who have not yet had much experience working with children and computers together because these teachers have fewer previous experiences from which to draw when reviewing programs.

How Do You Find Software to Evaluate?

Finding software to evaluate is not always easy. Teachers need to explore the resources in their area to discover potential sources for software to review.

In many cases, talking to other teachers who are using computers is the best place to start.

Computer and Software Stores. Many computer stores are not equipped for previewing software. Even those that are often carry only a small amount of software for young children. Sometimes, arrangements can be made with stores for a representative to bring software to a school for review. Other stores will order pieces to be previewed. It is wise to call around to find a merchant who is willing to provide these services in exchange for your patronage. If stores are unwilling to provide such services to a single school or teacher, getting together a group of schools for a preview may make such an effort more appealing to the merchant.

Schools and Libraries. Another way to find software to review is to visit other schools in the area. Schools using computers with young children usually have a collection of children's software. Visiting a school also gives teachers an opportunity to see how the children use the software. Discussing programs with teachers who are using them provides many insights into the software. In many cases, teachers or children will have (1) found unique ways to use certain software and (2) discovered some of the values and flaws that are not readily apparent in an initial review of the software. In many areas, public schools or libraries have special facilities for reviewing children's software.

Parents. In many cases, parents will have purchased software to use with children on home computers that teachers can borrow and preview.

Conferences and Workshops. New software is often exhibited at educational or computer conferences. Many workshop presenters bring software to demonstrate during their talks.

Software Producers. Many of the software companies allow programs to be previewed, usually for 30 days, and returned if not found appropriate.

INPUT FOR TEACHERS:

SOFTWARE GUIDES

Some books evaluate educational software. They include descriptions of the programs and information about the publisher, price, copyright date, manufacturer's recommended user age, and computers for which it is available. They each include lists of software producers and their addresses. These can be an excellent source for finding what software is available. Before reading the reviews in these books, it is important to read the criteria that each uses for evaluating software in order to know how much weight to give to that evaluation.

1987 Survey of Early Childhood Software by Warren Buckleitner. High/Scope Educational Research Foundation, 600 North River Street, Ypsilanti, MI 48198, (313) 485-2000. A yearly guide to early childhood software. The 1987 guide reviewed 229 programs designed for use with children aged 3 to 6 years. Each program is described, including a listing of possible educational goals. The High/Scope Software Evaluation Instrument is used to review the programs. Three major areas are considered: user friendliness, content, and instructional design. Scores for subparts of each component are also provided. The scale does not consider the effect of previous experience on ease of use.

Software Reports: The Guide to Evaluating Educational Software (Fall 1987) Trade Service Corporation, 10996 Torreyana Road, San Diego, CA 92121, (619) 457-5920. A biannual guide to educational software preschool through college. The fall 1987 guide reviews close to 2000 programs. The software is evaluated based on documentation, ease of use, content, instructional technique, and educational usefulness. It is important to realize when looking at the reviews in this guide that the reviewers are not considering ease of use for a young child and that many of the evaluation criteria are looking for software that "teaches the child something."

T.E.S.S. Educational Software Selector by EPIE Institute. (1986-1987). NY: New York College Press. This guide rates a few pieces of software, but it mainly provides ratings and reviews from other sources.

Remembering What You Saw

It is important to review software in a systematic way. After looking at four or five pieces, they all seem to blend together. Spencer and Baskin (1986) suggest using a holistic approach. When trying the software, initially consider your overall reaction. Record these first reactions. Then review the software more analytically, considering the aforementioned characteristics or other specific qualities of importance to you as a teacher. If your overall reactions were favorable, but the evaluation of specific characteristics is weak, consider which qualities influenced that first reaction. Did the positive reaction stem from adult-oriented parts of the program, or does the software have some hidden virtues that the analysis did not highlight? In the same way, if the initial reaction is more negative than the more detailed analysis, try to determine what is creating the disparity.

SUMMARY

Wise selection of software is crucial because software intensifies the chameleon-like nature of the computer. Hands-on review of software is essential for selecting appropriate programs. When reviewing software, the developmental level and previous computer experiences of children must be considered. Teachers should consider the following characteristics when reviewing software: Can children use it independently? Can children control what happens? Does the software allow for trial-and-error experimentation? Is the software and content appropriate for this age child? Will it hold the children's interest? Is it expandable? And is the software technically well made? Teachers must evaluate individual pieces of software as a part of a total software collection. If "ideal software" existed, it would be much easier for teachers to select software. But software does not exist in a vacuum. Its value depends to some degree on both the classroom curriculum and philosophy, and the developmental level and previous experiences of the children.

4

How Can Children Use the Computer If They Can't Find the Keys? Methods for Developing Computer Skills

We have looked at how to select computers, how to set them up in the room, and how to choose appropriate software in order to make computer use an independent, child-directed activity. Now we must look at what skills and knowledge the child needs in order to use a computer successfully. The types of skills required vary somewhat according to the kind of computer, the peripherals, and the software being used. But there are some skills that children need for most independent computer use (Paris, 1985):[1]

1. The child must be able to turn the machine on and off.
2. The child must be able to select and load the desired software.
3. The child must be able to find the needed keys on the keyboard.
4. The child must be able to strike the selected keys accurately and with a single keystroke.
5. The child must be able to select the desired part of the program from a menu.
6. The child must be able to follow and begin to design multistepped *procedures*.
7. The child must be able to follow picture directions, because for many programs picture clues are used to help children proceed through the program. The picture clues are either part of the program itself, or added by the teacher to use as an aid in deciphering the written parts of the program.

[1] In "Skills and Concepts of Successful Young Computer Users," Paris discusses a study done with 43 children ages 4–7 attending the University of Delaware Computer Camp. She found that by the end of camp all children who where successful computer users demonstrated seven skills which the staff had anticipated would be necessary for computer use. The following list contains all of her skills, except the ability to use a hand controller, which is specific to the use of that peripheral. I have added a seventh skill which Paris did not address—the ability to follow picture directions.

Jumping from letter to letter on a floor keyboard strengthens motor skills as well as computer skills.

Meaning? PROCEDURE

When applied to computers, **procedure** means a short sequence of instructions that can be called up to perform an operation. This can be a subpart of an existing program, or it can be written by the user. In noncomputer terms, a **procedure** is a series of steps required to accomplish a goal. The children begin to build skills in following and designing noncomputer-related procedures to prepare them for following and designing computer procedures.

Additional skills are required for specific types of computer use. If children are using peripherals such as the mouse, touch pad, or joystick, they must learn to match the movements of the mouse, stylus on the touch pad, or joystick to the desired movements on the monitor. When using a printer, the child must learn how to get the printer to print and how to advance and remove the paper. Individual types of software also may require certain skills. For example, **Logo** requires children to know left from right. To use **Bumble Games**, children must have some knowledge of graphs, as well as the skill needed to read and plot points on a graph.

Paris (1985) stresses that computer skills cannot be learned independently of computer concepts, as ''skills learned without an understanding of their potential uses are meaningless'' (p. 2). The successful users in her study all possessed some knowledge about computers. According to Paris, children who have both skills and concepts about computers are more in control of the computer. They are better able to manipulate and experiment with the computer, rather than merely passively learning from it. Chapters 5 and 6 examine in greater detail each of the seven skills she describes, as well as some activities that support the development of these skills. Chapter 10 explores the development of skills to support

specific software or hardware. And appropriate computer concepts and supporting activities are presented in Chapters 7-9.

ARE WE HURRYING CHILDREN TO EXPECT THEM TO LEARN THESE SKILLS AT SO YOUNG AN AGE?

It is clear from Paris's study and from watching children use computers that they can obtain the skills needed to use the computer successfully. Do children have these skills before using the computer, or must the skills be developed specifically for computer use? Although children may possess some of these skills before using the computer, there are many skills that they do not possess. Some skills are more difficult to develop in advance of computer use. For example, a child needs to turn a computer on in order to develop the skill to do so.

But other skills may be developed through off-computer experiences. Using machines that have more than one switch may make turning on a computer an easier skill to master (e.g., helping parents turn on a washer that requires selection of the heat of the water, the delicacy of the cycle, and the size of the load). In the same way, selecting and loading a program and selecting from a menu are things that a child is unlikely to encounter without using a computer. A child with experience using a typewriter may have developed some keyboarding skills. If the typewriter being used is electric, single keystroke skills may also be present. Children may develop skills for decoding pictures and following multistepped procedures from noncomputer experiences. Therefore, the children in your classroom may already have as many as four of these skills or as few as none before beginning to use the computer.

If many children do not yet have the skills necessary for successful computer use, might it not be better to wait until children are older? As Elkind decries in *The Hurried Child* (1981), today's children are being pushed to accomplish things younger and younger. Society often wrongly equates earlier with better. Why add computer pressure to the hurried-child phenomenon? Why not have children wait until they have the needed skills before beginning computer use? This question seems to imply that lack of needed skills prior to engaging in an activity makes that activity inappropriate.

New Activities Often Require Development of New Skills

If one were to agree that children must have needed skills before beginning an activity, then a child would never be ready to use a keyboard, nor would an adult, because no one can learn to locate keys on a keyboard without experience using a keyboard. Not only would you eliminate computers from the curriculum, but also, if previous skills were a requirement for including activities in the preschool classroom, much of the current curriculum would have to be banned. Most activities done for the first time require the child to build new skills or to revise previous skills to fit a new situation.

Children do not know how to use a saw until they use it. They need to learn to move the saw back and forth, to keep the saw in the groove, and to press down while moving the saw. These skills are needed in order to use the saw, but they can only be developed while using a saw. Therefore, if children are to be successful sawyers, they must first explore and practice, and perhaps encounter some frustration until they have developed enough skill to use the saw to their own satisfaction.

New skills are easier to develop if the child has had experience with a similar type of material. For example, the more kinds of blocks used, the easier it is to discover the rules and to develop the motor skills needed to manipulate a new type of block. A child who has used Legos, or some other type of stacking block that requires pieces to fit correctly, will find Towerifics, an H-shaped stacking block, easier to learn to use than a child without similar previous experience.

Because children have had fewer experiences than adults, many activities will be new to them and require skill development. In looking around the pre-

school, there are numerous activities that require skill development: getting onto a swing, pumping a swing, sliding down a firefighter's pole, squeezing a baster to make it suck in water from the water table, mixing paint to make new colors, making a jacket stay on a hook in the cubby, getting a puzzle to go together, using a paper punch, rolling a piece of playdough into a snake, and so much more.

One would not eliminate woodworking from the preschool curriculum because children do not yet know how to use a saw. Nor would we eliminate any of the other activities because new skills must be developed. Instead, we expect the child, with help, to develop the needed skills to engage in these activities happily and successfully. In the same way, a child using a computer for the first time may not have the skills to find letters quickly, but as long as children have the interest, cognitive ability, and developmental prerequisites for obtaining these skills, they can become successful computer users who are in control of the machine.

Support for Developing New Skills

What kind of help should and do teachers give to children who are attempting new tasks and developing new skills? To help a child master a new task, the teacher needs to analyze the task to see what steps it involves. Many tasks are really more complicated than they seem. Hainstock, in *Teaching Montessori in the Home* (1968), discusses what is involved in washing hands. She divides hand washing into 12 steps: (1) roll up sleeves, (2) fill sink, (3) place hands in water, (4) rub soap on hands, (5) put soap back in soap dish, (6) rub soapy palms over back of each hand, (7) rub each finger from base to tip, (8) rinse soap off with water, (9) drain sink, (10) dry each finger, (11) dry hand, and (12) hang up towel.

Dissect the Task into its Component Steps. The teacher can **dissect tasks** in the same way that Hainstock dissected hand-washing, evaluating the steps to see whether the children are already able to do them or will need some help. The teacher can then consider whether the children can manage the

Washing your hands is more difficult than it seems.

New tasks, like sliding down a pole, require some perceptual understanding.

sequence of steps when done altogether. If the task appears to be too difficult, the teacher can help the child be successful in a number of ways.

Ask the Child To Do Only Part of the Task. The teacher might modify the task by asking the child to only do part of it. For example, most 3-year-olds cannot tie their own shoes, but they can help the teacher by pulling the ends of the laces tight once a loose knot has been formed.

Provide Ways To Think about the Task. Teachers can help children with new skills by providing ways for thinking about the job. A child who is trying to slide down the firefighter's pole for the first time may not have any idea of how to begin. The teacher may talk the child through the task. "Once you climb onto the railing you must reach out toward the pole with one hand, then the other, now jump your feet over to the pole." New tasks like this one often require some conceptual understanding of what is happening, as well as the actual physical skill to carry out the task. For example, the child who is sawing must understand that pressure on the saw is needed, as well as being able to apply the pressure.

Modify Task To Fit Child's Skills. Teachers can also support children who are learning new skills by modifying materials to make the task more accu-

rately fit the child's skills. For example, velcro can be added to doll clothes if children have difficulty manipulating the buttons and snaps on such small clothing. By changing the type of fastener used, the child can successfully dress the baby.

Modify the Action Required. Teachers can help support children who are learning new skills by modifying how the child does the task to make the required actions fit the child's skills. Sometimes, children do a task the "grown-up way," when a shortcut, or another method, would make the task easier. A child passing out the napkins for snack may constantly be dropping the pile when pulling napkins off the top of the stack to place on the table. The teacher might suggest that the child place the stack on the table so that the top napkin can be removed more easily.

Offer Opportunities To Practice the Task. Teachers can offer opportunities to practice the new task, as well as opportunities to be involved in activities requiring similar skills. If the children are doing a water-mixing activity using eye droppers for the first time, teachers can place basters in the water table, providing additional opportunities to practice the same skills needed for the eye droppers.

Avoid Tasks That Are Too Difficult. To ensure that children are successful when tackling new tasks, avoid including tasks that are too difficult. If tasks attempted by children tend to be too hard, leaving them feeling frustrated, incompetent, and unsuccessful, then these children are less likely to want to try new activities. They may resist working through the initial difficulties encountered in other new tasks.

PROVIDING SUPPORT FOR CHILDREN WHO ARE DEVELOPING COMPUTER SKILLS

Teachers can provide the aforementioned kinds of support to children who are developing skills for computer use. Let's look at some examples of how each of these methods can be used to support successful acquisition of computer skills.

Teachers Can Modify a Computer Task by Asking the Child To Do Only Part of the Task

Much of the software on the Commodore requires a lengthy loading procedure. On **Astro-Grover**, for example, a child must type

load "CBS",8[Return]run[Return]

in order for the program to load. As an adult, with moderately good typing skills, I find that I often have to type this sequence more than once to get it correct. A child would be much more likely to make an error, thereby having to attempt to type this repeatedly. Even if the child was accurate the first time, typing the whole sequence would be a long process. A solution is to have this software preloaded, with a big STOP sign in front of the disk drive so that children know not to unload the program when they finish.

Teachers Can Help Children by Providing Ways To Think about a Computer Task

Children using **Facemaker** often have trouble moving from the "making the face" part of the program to the "moving the face" part of the program. To make the face, children must press the "1." The computer then moves to the making part of the program. When the face is complete, children must press "2" for the computer to proceed to the moving part of the program. The following example shows how a teacher can help a child to think about the task.

Brittany presses "1" to make a face, then gives the computer the necessary commands to construct the face. When her face is finished, she presses "S" to make the face smile. Nothing happens. She presses "T" to make the face stick out its tongue. Nothing happens.

Brittany: Teacher, this program doesn't work!
Teacher: What number did you press to tell the computer you wanted to make a face?
Brittany: "1."
Teacher: Do you still want to make a face?
Brittany: No, I want to move the face.
Teacher: How do you let the computer know that you are ready to move the face?
Teacher: (If Brittany still has trouble at this point, the teacher can refer to the rebus guide on the disk sleeve.) You typed "1" to get it to make a face (pointing to

the "1" on the rebus card). What number do you think you type to let the computer know you want to move the face? (pointing to the number "2" on the rebus card).

The teacher is helping Brittany to figure out that she needs to push "2" to run the second part of the program. She is also making clear the concept that this program has two parts and that part one will only run when you push "1," and part two will only run if "2" has been entered.

Teachers Can Modify Materials To Make Computer Task More Accurately Fit the Child's Skills

Because children find it difficult to learn to locate the whole alphabet at one time, it is wise to begin with software that only requires the child to locate a few keys. For example, **Magic Crayon** only requires children to find the letters of their name, the arrow keys, the [Return] key, and "C" to select different colors with which to draw. By selecting a program in

---

INPUT FOR TEACHERS:

SAMPLE DIALOGUES

Dialogue is used in the text and in many of the activities both to illustrate what might happen between child and teacher and to show what the activity might look like in action. Obviously, individual teachers will phrase their comments and discussions in the way most appropriate to their teaching style and their class of children. The sample dialogue communicates the feeling of an activity or interaction more easily than does a description. The dialogue used should be seen as illustrative and not prescriptive.

---

which the child needs only to locate a few keys, the teacher is modifying the material to fit the skills of the child.

Teachers Can Modify the Required Actions To Make a Computer Task More Accurately Fit the Child's Skills

Magic Crayon also provides a good example of how to modify what the child does to make the task more appropriate. After children have selected the desired color, they are asked, by text on the screen, to press the "X" to register their choice. Children find this hard to remember because they do not read the written directions and there is no logic to using an "X." (In many pieces of software, the letters used to give commands are the beginning sound of the command, thus providing a logical reminder of what to type [e.g., children type "C" in **Magic Crayon** to get color.])

Teachers can modify what children do to register their choice of color in **Magic Crayon**. Color selection can also be designated by striking the **[Return]** key (although this information is not provided anywhere in the program or documentation). For children who have used other computer programs in which **[Return]** "tells their computer to process their command," this is logical, and with little assistance, they can remember to register their choice by pressing **[Return]**.

The beginning of **Facemaker** asks children to answer two yes-and-no questions before beginning the program. However, one child discovered that these questions could be skipped by pressing the "1" when the questions appear on the screen. This moves the program to the face-making sections, bypassing the need to respond to the questions.

Teachers Can Offer Many Opportunities To Practice the New Computer Skills

When selecting sets of software programs to offer simultaneously in the classroom, the teacher can look for programs that all reinforce the same skills.

> ## INPUT FOR TEACHERS:
>
> ## A NOTE OF CAUTION
>
> I have suggested many ways that children can be helped to develop skills. These are never to be used as enforced activities. These are suggestions of ways that teachers can support children who want to succeed in self-selected tasks but who need assistance scaling the hurdles during their first attempt.

For example, software might be chosen that uses [Return] to register commands or that uses the joystick. By selecting software that reinforces similar skills, the children may find these skills easier to master. Once these skills are acquired, additional software with other demands can be added. Teachers can also provide many off-computer activities to help reinforce skills needed on the computer. Many such activities are described in the remainder of the book.

Teachers Should Avoid Computer Activities That Are Too Difficult

Begin with software that is easy for children to master. Sometimes, the easiest pieces are not the most desirable ones when considering other characteristics. (This is discussed in more detail in Chapter 3.) As children become more skilled with the computer, the difficulty of the software can be increased, but it is important to ensure that all software is usable at some level by the less proficient users.

SHOULD CHILDREN BE HELPED TO DEVELOP THESE SKILLS BEFORE USING THE COMPUTER?

With the increasing number of computers in schools has come an increasing number of publica-

tions, teacher's guides, and ditto-master books to help teachers train children to use computers. Many of these have tabletop paper keyboards, large posters of computers, and other materials to enable a teacher to teach about the computer before the child uses one. These materials claim to develop needed computer skills. This is totally backwards. It is like saying we will discuss making playdough snakes while looking at models and practicing with simulations, so that children will have the skills to use the playdough effectively. Preoperational children learn through manipulation of real objects. They find abstractions difficult. Why take a computer, which is already a somewhat abstract instrument, and make it even more abstract? Besides, without the excitement and wonder of a real computer, there is little to motivate a child to want to develop computer skills. These same kinds of activities are appropriate when used in conjunction with computer use, although they are totally inappropriate used as an introduction to the computer.

Although special "computer skill activities" should not be planned before computer use, this is not to say that some parts of the normal curriculum may not also help to develop these skills. Children may learn some keyboarding skills through using a classroom typewriter. They may learn to follow picture clues during cooking experiences. They may learn to understand the meaning of an arrow when exploring the ways that Native Americans marked trails or through a unit on signs. Learning about machines can acquaint children with both the computer's switches and the need for people to operate machines.

WHY SPEND SO MUCH TIME ON COMPUTER SKILLS?

One might ask, "Why spend so much time on computer skills? Might there not be a more productive use of the teacher's and child's time?" If the skills discussed were applicable only to the computer, this would certainly be a valid question. At first glance, one might say that keyboarding has limited applicability. This skill is only useful for computer or typewriter use. But this is not true. In learning to find keys on the keyboard, children are involved in visually matching letters, discriminating among various letters, and talking with peers and teachers about the letters. Helping children develop skill in using the keyboard also provides an excellent opportunity for them to learn to recognize and name letters.

The remaining six skill areas also offer children the opportunity to develop in areas broader than just the computer. In learning to manipulate switches to turn off and on the computers, children are developing skills that can be used on a variety of machines in their environment. A main part of selecting software and selecting from a menu involve being able to use rebus pictures to decipher the available choices. This skill, along with the ability to follow pictorial directions, allows prereading children to be more independent in their environments. They can use the pictures in their environment, such as the pictures of men and women on rest rooms, to make appropriate choices. They can "read" directions that teachers have prepared around the classroom to indicate how to complete an activity. Many cooking activities use pictorial directions, and many teachers use pictorial job charts to assign classroom responsibilities.

Helping children to develop their ability to follow directions and to develop memory are both often goals of early childhood programs. Activities aimed at helping children to follow steps in computer programs will enable them to follow more complex directions in all areas, as well as exercise their memory. Small-muscle development is another common goal in early childhood programs. Developing single keystrokes helps children to refine their small-muscle skills. This refinement will aid them in noncomputer activities as well.

SUMMARY

Independent use of computers requires that children develop certain skills. These skills can be developed while using the computer through both on-

and off-computer activities. They should not be "taught" to children before computer use; they should be developed gradually, as children become involved with simple computer activities. Seven skills have been pinpointed as important for most independent computer use. Children must be able to do the following:

1. Turn the machine on and off.
2. Select and load the desired software.
3. Find the needed keys on the keyboard.
4. Strike selected keys accurately and with a single keystroke.
5. Select the desired part of the program from the menu.
6. Follow and begin to design multistepped procedures.
7. Follow rebus-picture directions.

Additional skills may be required for specific types of computer use.

Teachers can use a variety of techniques to help children develop these and other skills. Teachers can do one or more of the following:

1. Dissect the task into its component steps.
2. Ask children to do only part of the task.
3. Provide children with ways for thinking about the task.
4. Modify the materials to better fit the children's skills.
5. Modify the actions required of the children to better fit their skills.
6. Provide opportunities to practice the skill and practice similar skills.
7. Select tasks wisely to avoid activities that are too difficult.

This chapter has highlighted certain skills that enable children to be successful independent computer users. These skills should not be taken as a prescription. The teacher should not say, "I must train my child to do all of these skills, and then I will allow them to use the computer." Instead, they should be seen as a guide to help teachers understand what is needed to use a computer independently and help them to develop appropriate ways to support individual children in their classroom as the children interact with computers. Teachers may discover that certain of these skills are not needed for the types of computer use in which their children engage, or they may discover other equally important skills that should also be fostered.

5

Activities To Help Develop Skills for Computer Use

Acquisition of certain skills facilitates independent computer use. Teachers can support these skills in a number of ways. In this chapter, the following four skills are discussed in more detail:

1. The child must be able to turn the machine on and off
2. The child must be able to select and load the desired software
3. The child must be able to find the needed keys on the keyboard
4. The child must be able to strike the selected keys accurately and with a single keystroke.

The remaining three skills that were mentioned in Chapter 4 are discussed in Chapter 6. The components of each skill are described, and a variety of methods and classroom activities for supporting development of each skill is presented.

It is important to realize that these skills are not a rigid hierarchy, nor are the activities required for all children. Instead, the skills and activities are presented as a framework for looking at the children in your classroom and providing activities most appropriate to those children. The teacher determines which children need support for developing which skills. The following activities and methods of informal instruction, or similar ones that the teachers devise, can help children to develop needed skills. These activities must be used in tandem with actual computer experience.

Development of many of the computer skills have value in other areas of development as well. Children who are working on activities either on or off the computer who develop *keyboarding* skills may also be (1) increasing their ability to discriminate and match letters of the alphabet, and (2) making connections between lowercase and uppercase letters, depending on what the activity is. As each skill is discussed, the noncomputer benefits of that skill are explored.

Children develop the skills for independent computer use.

Meaning? KEYBOARDING

Keyboarding describes the process of finding needed keys on the keyboard.

TURNING THE COMPUTER ON AND OFF

Obviously, if the children are to use computers independently, they must be able to turn the machines on and off. This task can be broken down into four subskills that must be mastered in order to complete the task of turning the computer on and off.

Subskills Required for Turning the Computer On and Off

Knowing the Components of the Computer System. First, children should know which components of the computer system need independent sources of power. Children (and adults who have not used computers) often do not realize that computer systems contain a series of independent components, and thus the parts may need to be turned on and off separately. The fact that each computer system is designed differently adds to the confusion. For the Apple II series, a single switch on the box housing the keyboard, CPU, and memory turns on all the components except the monitor, whereas on the Commodore and Atari, the disk drive must be turned on separately and the parts must be turned on in a certain order. The IBM also has a single switch that turns on all the components except the monitor, but in this system, the switch is located on the box housing the CPU, memory, and disk drive, rather than on the box housing the keyboard.

Knowing the Correct Sequence of Steps. Children must also learn the order in which to turn on the parts of the computer, an order that varies from system to system. For the Apple, the disk should be

loaded before the system is turned on, whereas for the Atari and the Commodore 64, the disk drive must be turned on before loading the disk and before turning on the box housing the CPU, memory, and disk drive.

Locating the Switches. A third requirement for turning the computer on and off is to locate the switch on each machine. Switches are often hidden on the sides or backs of machines or underneath covering panels on the front, in an attempt to make the machine look more streamlined and attractive.

Being Able To Operate the Switches. Children also must know how to work the switches. Some computers have **toggle switches** (the kind that rock back and forth when you press on one end or the other, as opposed to the lever switch that you can grasp in your fingers and move). Toggle switches may be new to children, and all switches are harder to use if they are tucked away in the back of the computer, where they are difficult to see. To turn the computer off, the child must be able to remember the order of the turning on procedures and then reverse them.

Fostering Children's Skills in Turning the Computer On and Off

Seven methods were described in Chapter 4 for providing support to children who are developing computer skills. These methods are used to organize ideas and activities for developing skills in turning the computer on and off.

Provide Children with Ways To Think about Turning the Computer On and Off. Teachers can help children to understand what is involved in the process of turning the computer on and off by encouraging children to attend to the steps. This can be done through discussion, questioning, instruction, observation, and experimentation. While helping a child, the teacher might say, "First you put the disk in the disk drive, then you turn on the monitor so that we can see the picture on the screen, next

INPUT FOR TEACHERS:

ASKING QUESTIONS

In many parts of this book, questions are recommended as a way of getting children to focus on relevant points. It is important to realize that there are many different ways of questioning; some provide supportive guidance, whereas others are threatening "tests of knowledge." In the preceding example (about turning the computer on), the teacher could use the question, "Which part of the computer gets turned on first?" to help the child focus on the task. If the child seems unsure what to do, or has begun by typing and getting no result, the question may remind the child that there is more than one step and that the first one must be done first. If this reminder does not enable the child to recall the steps, the teacher can then provide additional help. For example, "Let's see what the first step on the loading poster is" or "Let's find the switch with a '1' on it." Questions should never be asked if the teacher feels that the child does not know the answer. Questions should be stated in a thoughtful, pondering manner, suggesting this is something to think about, rather than as a quiz of knowledge.

you turn on the keyboard so that you can type your commands into the computer." This teacher is helping the child to be aware of the multiple steps for turning the computer on and to understand that each step activates a separate part of the system.

A child who has had more experience with the computer needs less assistance with loading. Instead of telling the child the steps, the teacher might use questions to help the child focus on the sequence of steps. "Which part of the computer gets turned on first? What is the next part? Is there any other part that needs to be turned on?" This teacher is getting the child to recall information and to think of the various parts needed to operate the computer. If picture or number guides are available, the teacher can refer to these in discussing the steps.

Encourage children to help their peers start the computer. Stress "telling," not "showing," friends how to turn it on. Verbalizing the steps clarifies the process for the helper as well as for the child being helped. This type of peer support is common to computer use in many classrooms (Borgh & Dickson, 1986; Wright & Samaras, 1986).

Depending on the kind of switches on the computer, children may also need some help with how to use the switches. Children can be encouraged to "try to get the switch to work." When the child has been successful, the child can be asked to explain what was done. If a child becomes frustrated, the teacher can explain that one side of the switch is pushed to turn the machine off, the other side to turn it on. Children can help friends to understand how the switches operate.

Children often are confused by the need to reverse the steps for turning on the computer in order to turn it off. Teachers can discuss how the steps must be done backwards to turn the computer off. The same techniques used to help the child understand the process of turning on the computer can be applied to understanding the reversal of this process.

Modify Computer Materials To Fit Children's Skill Level. Even after turning on a computer a number of times, it is still easy for both children and adults to forget the order of the steps. This problem is compounded if more than one computer system is available. The user must remember which sequence of steps goes with which system. Such confusion may exist even if there is only one computer at school. Children with previous computer experience may confuse the procedures for computers used outside of school with those for the school's computer.

Providing an easy reference guide to remind children of the steps is extremely helpful. The parts to be turned on can be labeled, in order, with numerals. For the Apple II system, a "1" can be placed on the disk drive, a "2" on or near the monitor's power switch, and a "3" on or near the keyboard's power switch. A poster or chart near the computer can display each part in order:

1. The disk drive with a "1" on it
2. The monitor with a "2" near the power switch
3. The keyboard with a "3" on its power switch.

Children often have difficulty locating and using switches that are tucked away in the back or on the side of machines because their bodies are not long enough either to reach or to see the switches. Careful attention to how computers are positioned is important. Make sure that the printer, disk drive, or other materials are not blocking any needed switches. For example, tables are sometimes nested one on top of another in order for the keyboard to be at a better height for the child. This is fine as long as such nesting does not make any switches hard to find or operate.

Modify Required Actions on the Computer To Fit Children's Current Skills. In the earlier discussion of turning on the Apple II, a specific set of steps are listed. Those readers who are familiar with the Apple II system may have been surprised at the steps because the order of two of the steps can be changed with no detrimental effects. That is, the disk drive should be loaded first,[1] but it is irrelevant whether the monitor or keyboard are turned on next. I found it hard to remember which step had to be in a special order and which did not. To simplify this process and to ensure that the disk was loaded first, each step was assigned a specific place in the sequence.

Provide Opportunities To Turn the Computer On and Off and Practice Similar Tasks. The best way for children to learn to turn the computer on and off is to do it. Children should be asked to do this as soon as computer use is begun. At first, the teacher will need to give more help, but gradually, the teacher will move to asking questions, then to giving reminders about a step missed, and finally to providing no help at all.

Teachers can provide opportunities to use other machines requiring multiple steps to start. In the preceding chapter, the washing machine was mentioned as offering such opportunities. The washer does not have the multiple power switches that the computer has, but it does have a series of dials that must be set. A tape recorder also requires multiple steps for its use. The child must load the tape, press the "play" button, listen, press the "stop" button, press the "rewind" button, and then eject the tape to remove it.

Teachers can look around home and school to see what other types of machines with multiple steps are available and safe for children to use. The steps for using these machines can be numbered just like the steps for turning on the computer. If a poster depicting the steps is available near the computer in your room, make a similar poster to explain the steps for turning on the washer, blender, VCR (videocassette recorder), or tape recorder. (Obviously, use of such machines **must** be supervised by a teacher and must include a discussion of the need for adult permission and assistance before using these machines at home.) Learning to operate the machines in their lives is also valuable for children apart from supporting computer learning. Such skill adds to children's independence and bolsters their self-concept. It is important to stress the ways to use machines safely. Children should understand that no electrical machines should be operated at home or at school without adult consent, even if they know how to use it.

Other computer-related activities can reinforce the steps for starting computers. In doing group activities such as **If You're a Facemaker Monitor** (p. 156), the teacher can began by pretending to turn on a poster of a computer. The children can tell the teacher which parts to turn on first, second, and third. The "computer" can then be "turned off" at the end of the activity, with the children helping the teacher to reverse the loading process. Activities such as **Easel Computer** (p. 141—in which the child pretends to load a disk before starting the computer) could be adapted so that the children turn on all parts of the computer in sequence and turn them off when done. In **Build a Computer** (p. 143), children

---

[1]The disk drive needs to be loaded first for automatic start-up, which is desired when children are using the computer.

are constructing their own computers with blocks, and switches can be added to the appropriate machines, as can numerals near the switches. Teachers may want to incorporate these kinds of reminders for proper loading into other activities periodically if children seem to need reminding of the steps. Less frequent users may find such reminders helpful.

Earlier, it was suggested that numerals be added to the computers near each switch so that children would know in which order to turn the computer on. This assumes that the children can read numerals and are able to follow them in sequential order. The picture poster showing the steps may be easier to use, as children can look at the sequence of illustrations and not necessarily have to read the numerals. But this assumes that children know that they must read from left to right when looking at the picture directions. Providing opportunities to use numerals to identify what is to be done first, second, and third may make the numerals a more useful guide. And providing practice following pictorial directions will make the chart more usable. (Practicing with pictorial directions is discussed in more detail in Chapter 6.) Even harder than following the numerals and pictures in forward sequence is remembering to follow them backwards when turning the machine off. When appropriate, the numeral following activities should also be done in reverse order as well.

Provide Opportunities To Practice Using Switches. If children have had little experience with switches, opportunities to use a variety of switches can be provided. Using machines in the classroom such as a vacuum, Dustbuster, blender, or lamp can provide experience with switches. Also, old machines that no longer work, such as an old electric broom, hair dryers, or electric razors, can be added to the house area for playing pretend. (Be sure to check all machines for potential safety hazards. The working machines should be plugged in by the teacher. The nonworking machines should have tape wound around the plugs and sockets covered with childproof caps to discourage attempts to plug them in.) A variety of switches can be attached to a flat board for the children to manipulate. Learn-

---

INPUT FOR TEACHERS:

GOALS FOR ACTIVITIES

In designing activities for use with young children, it is important to make them as open-ended as possible. Each child learns in different ways and has different needs and different interests. Open-ended activities allow children freedom to explore the activity in their own ways. Teachers should set some general goals for the activity. But the goals that are actually reached will depend on each child. The teacher should evaluate each activity afterwards to see which of the possible goals were met. Good early childhood activities encourage development in a wide range of areas. The activities in this book have many computer-related goals, but each also supports some general child development goals as well. The symbols in front of the goals indicate whether this is a computer-related goal ☐ , a child development goal, ⋏ or both.

---

ing to operate a variety of switches increases the children's independence in many noncomputer activities. If your computer uses toggle switches, you might want to look for some machines with this type of switch. Some flashlights have toggle switches, and children enjoy using them. Encouraging discussion of which switches children should use, and which they should not use, and how they determine which is which, will provide a valuable safety lesson.

Avoid Tasks That Are Too Difficult. If you have access to more than one type of computer, it is wise to begin with only one kind of system in the room. Once children have learned the steps to operate this system, a second type can be introduced. The children should become aware that each system has its own procedure for turning it on and off. If you locate the new kind of computer in a different part of the room, the children may more easily grasp the idea that the machines are different.

ACTIVITIES TO BUILD SKILLS IN TURNING THE COMPUTER ON AND OFF

FIRST, SECOND, THIRD

Why?

🏃☐ To provide practice doing sequential activities in the order marked by numerals 1, 2, and 3

🏃☐ To provide practice reversing sequences and using numerals as a cue in doing this

🏃☐ To provide practice in reading picture directions

🏃 To increase visual awareness

🏃 To encourage gross-motor development

What Is Needed?

A bulletin board and push pins

Three cards, with the numeral "1" on one card, "2" on another, and "3" on the last, pinned on the board in numerical order

Picture cards of body parts (foot, hand, head, nose, hips, elbow, shoulder, etc.) pinned near top of the board

Blank cards and a marker

How?

Tell the children, "I am going to see how well you can follow directions. Wiggle your fingers. Wiggle your toes. Wiggle your hair. Wiggle your belly button. That is great. You can follow single directions. Now if I give you two directions, can you remember them and do both? I will tell you both directions, but don't start until I say 'go!' Wiggle your nose, then wiggle your elbow. Go! What part did you wiggle first? What part did you wiggle second?"

Practice two-step wiggle directions a couple of times.

"Do you think you can remember three body parts to wiggle in order? To make it easier, I will put up some pictures to remind you. First, wiggle your foot." (Pin the foot on the board under the "1.") "Second, wiggle your elbow." (Pin the elbow up under "2.") "Third, wiggle your head." (Pin the head up under "3.") Continue giving three-part directions. The children can pick the body parts from the ones you have displayed. You can draw additional parts on the blank cards, as needed. The children can also pick a different motion to do with the three body parts. Once children can easily follow the sequence, place the numerals on the board randomly. When this is mastered, try doing the actions first forward and then backwards.

Making It Your Own:

Use action cards (jumping, hopping, turning, and so on) rather than body parts to move.

Use cards of objects or of body parts that children can sequence in the order to be touched.

This activity can be done over 2 or 3 days if it moves too quickly for your class of children as it is described.

Using a pegboard, let the children arrange pictures during activity time for themselves or peers to follow.

OBSTACLE COURSE BY THE NUMBER

Why?

♣ ☐ To practice doing sequential activities in the order marked by numerals 1, 2, and 3

♣ ☐ To provide practice reversing sequences and using numerals as a cue in doing this

♣ To encourage large-muscle development

What Is Needed?

A slide
4 tires laid out in a line
A barrel or a cloth-and-wire tunnel
3 sign posts, one next to each piece of equipment, with a pocket for holding a number card on each side
6 cards, two with each numeral—1, 2, or 3. Place pairs of the same numeral in the front and back of each sign post
A starting and finishing line made with rope or chalk

How?

Arrange the three pieces of equipment in the same area of the yard. Place the three signs facing the starting line. Let each child begin at the starting line and go through the obstacle course using the equipment in the sequence indicated by the numerals on the signs. After children have done the course a few times, have them go from start to finish 1, 2, 3; then back from finish to start following the signs in reverse order: 3, 2, 1.

After the children have become familiar with the course, let them change the cards in order to go through it in a new order.

Making It Your Own:

Use any three pieces of equipment that fit the children's needs and materials available. It is best not to use house-shaped climbers because children tend to want to stay and play in them rather than moving through to the next obstacle.

Increase the number of steps to match the skills of the children and the number of steps needed to operate your computer.

1, 2, 3, 4 . . . ORANGE JUICE

Why?

🏃☐ To practice following directions in numerical order

🏃☐ To practice deciphering and following pictorial directions

🏃 To exercise small-muscle skills

What Is Needed?

4 jars with easily screwed-on lids
A pitcher of water light enough for children to use
A larger pitcher of water, for refilling the smaller one
A large empty pitcher into which to pour the orange juice mixture
A shallow bowl containing orange juice concentrate
A plastic 1-cup measure with a spout, clearly labeled with tape at the 1/2 cup mark
A 1/8-cup measure
A picture recipe with one step on each card:
　1. Add water (filled to 1/2-cup tape mark)
　2. Add concentrate (in 1/8-cup measure)
　3. Shake
　4. Put in pitcher
A rectangular table pushed against the wall
Tape

How?

Tape the numbered recipe cards on the wall behind the table, in numerical order and spaced evenly. Put out the needed materials at each spot beneath the appropriate numeral. Place the jars at the first step and the lids at the third step. Have children wash their hands before beginning activity. As the children come to the activity, ask which step should come first. How do they know? The children then follow the recipe.
1. They pour water from the pitcher into the measuring cup, then into the jar.
2. They add orange juice to the jar.
3. They screw the lid on tightly and shake the jar.
4. They pour the juice into the pitcher for snack.
Teachers can discuss with the children whether this sequence can be reversed, contrasting it with the steps for turning on the computer. Serve the juice for snack.

Making It Your Own:

If teachers are concerned about their children's ability to screw the lids on, children can put the ingredients into a tall container for hand mixing instead.

Other simple cooking projects with 3-4 steps can be substituted for this one. Making juice popsicles, spreading cheese or peanut butter on crackers, mixing other kinds of juice, or making fruit shakes are some possible alternatives.

If your computers all have a three-step turning on and off sequence you might want to look for recipes with just three steps. For example, (1) spread peanut butter on cracker, (2) dip in wheat germ, (3) put cracker on tray.

Glasses can be substituted for the pitcher in Step 4 so that children can drink their juice immediately.

Going Beyond:

If the children are quite good at following numbered steps, you may want to have the four steps on small tables scattered randomly. Children will need to search for the numerals to know which step to start from and move to.

YOU TURN ME ON

Why?

☐ To practice using toggle switches

⚀ To encourage constructive social interaction

⚀ To allow for creativity

What Is Needed?

2 or 3 tables large enough for 2-3 children to fit under each

Blankets to drape over the tables (if possible, push tables against wall or shelves and secure blanket under back legs to minimize slippage)

4-6 flashlights with toggle switches

How?

Encourage children to decide whether the space under the blanket-covered tables is a cave, house, tent, or something altogether different. The children can then play under the blankets using their flashlights.

More guidance and suggestions may be needed, depending on the particular group of children and their ability to pretend.

Making It Your Own:

If children have had experience with power blackouts, the tables can be houses. The flashlights can provide the emergency lighting. Children can be encouraged to visit back and forth.

Additional props can be added, such as blankets, pillows, books to look at in the habitats, or other materials to complement the play.

Other themes that could be suggested are rabbit dens, living on the moon, bears in the winter, camping, or clubhouses.

Going Beyond:

Children could use flashlights to search around the room for objects or pictures.

Children could use flashlights to create dancing fireflies to the "Flight of the Bumblebee."

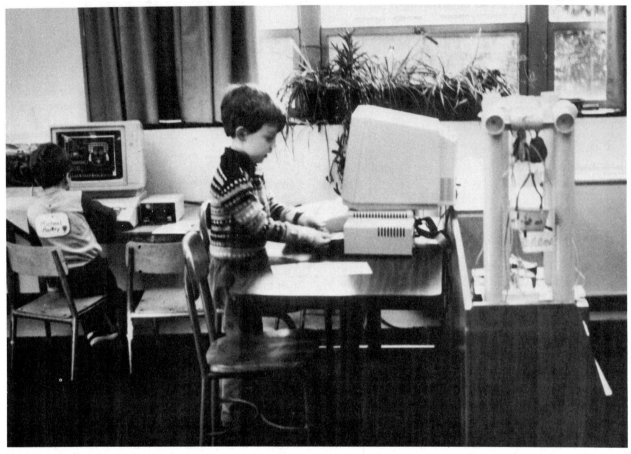

Children can select and load their own software.

SELECTING SOFTWARE AND LOADING DISKS INTO THE DISK DRIVE

Subskills Required for Selecting and Loading Disks

If children are to use computers independently, they must be able to select and load their own software. Selecting software is easy for an adult who can read the labels on the disk. Children will need to develop other methods for recognizing the disks they want. Children must also realize that each disk has its own set of commands for the computer. Many children learn that loading the disk is part of the turning-on process without realizing that the correct disk must be loaded in order for the computer to display the desired program. Once a child has located the needed disk, it must be loaded into the disk drive. Children must learn to hold the disk only at the label, to avoid getting fingerprints and dirt on the exposed part of the disk. They must also know which side of the disk to turn face up when loading, and they must have the motor coordination to insert the disk into the slot. The last thing that the child must know in order to load the disk independently is when during the turning-on process to load the disk. (This part of the loading skill was addressed in the previous section.)

Fostering Children's Ability To Select and Load Disks

Provide Children with Ways To Think about Loading Disks into the Computer. Initially, teachers will have to demonstrate either with the whole class or individually how to hold and load the disk, emphasizing that **where** you hold the disk is extremely important. Depending on the children's previous experiences, you might compare holding a disk with holding a photograph or a record, discussing what would happen to these if they became covered with dirty fingerprints. Holding the disk by the label also ensures that the correct side is face up for loading because the disk drive cannot read upside-down disks.

Teachers can reinforce correct handling by reminding children that there is a special place for holding. Praising children for correctly handling the disk (e.g., "I like the way you remember to hold right on the label") reinforces the desired behavior. Nearby children are also reminded that it matters how the disk is held.

Teachers can help children realize the need for choosing the correct disk if a particular program is desired. When a child approaches the computer initially, the teacher can describe briefly the programs available and ask which the child wants to use. "Do you want to make a face with **Facemaker** or draw your own picture with **Magic Crayon**? To make a face, you need to find the **Facemaker** disk—the disk with the face on it." It is important for the teacher to use the software's name so that children can recognize software names when mentioned in later activities. Because children do not read the titles, they are unlikely to know names unless teachers use them. When doing activities such as **If You're a Facemaker Monitor** (p. 156), which are related to a specific piece of software, teachers can say the name of the software and display the picture symbol used on the disk sleeve. If teachers have an introductory group time during which activities for the day are described, the picture symbol for each program can be displayed when the name of the software is mentioned, or children can be asked which symbol to look for to find each of the mentioned programs.

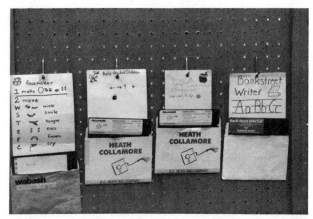

Children can easily select desired software from this display.

If children seem arbitrarily to select disks without looking, the teacher might inquire, "What are you going to do on the computer? Is that the right disk? How do you know?" When children randomly pick disks only to discover that the computer is not "doing the right thing," they quickly realize the significance of choosing the correct disk. If the child cannot resolve the problem alone, the teacher can discuss which program was wanted, what is on the screen, and which program that display represents. Then the child can check to see which disk was used. Helping the child to focus on the relation between the disk used and the display on the screen highlights the significance of finding the right disk for that child.

Modify Materials To Fit Skills. Adding a simple pictorial symbol to each disk and disk sleeve also promotes independent computer use. Taping an index card onto the disk sleeve provides a place for the name of the software, a pictorial symbol and any needed rebus directions. A hole can be punched in the top of the index card to display the software on a pegboard. Children can easily see which software is available and carry the software and directions to the computer without difficulty.

Such displays also encourage children to grasp the disk by the label for loading. If a pegboard is not

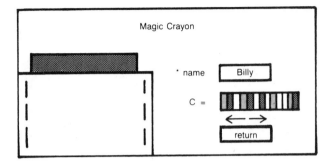

available a bulletin board could be used, or file folders can be made into disk holders. Cut one side of the file folder so that it is 4 inches tall. Staple the two parts of the file folder together at each side and down the middle to make a pocket to slide the disk into. The rest of the folder can be used for directions.

If many pieces of software are available, less-frequent users sometimes have trouble locating a specific program among the many options. Posting a name and symbol over each hook so that each piece of software has a permanent location can often alleviate the problem because children are made aware of the symbols when returning, as well as when selecting, the software.

Provide Opportunities To Select and Load Software and Practice Other Similar Tasks. The

more often that a child selects and loads software, the easier it becomes. Children will become independent more quickly if teachers give the minimum help required. A teacher who asks a child which disk is desired, then waits to see if the child succeeds before asking more questions or offering more help, is allowing the child to practice the skills at his or her highest level. If the child seems confused, the teacher might ask, "What picture do you think is on the disk for your program?" Again, the teacher encourages the child to do as much as possible. In this way, the teacher can continue to ask questions or offer support when the child is uncertain, without offering unneeded support.

If the child finds it hard to insert the disk into the disk drive slot, activities such as post office, in which similarly shaped objects (letters) are inserted into a narrow slot (mailbox), could be added to the classroom.

Activities involving the selection of a desired tape for the tape recorder, record for the record player, or tape for the VCR might help children to understand that the tape or disk selected will affect the output from the machine.

Avoid Disk-Selection and Disk-Loading Tasks That Are Too Difficult or Confusing. Disks that

have to be turned over to be used, such as **Charley Brown's ABC's** from Random House, are extremely confusing to children. Children have been taught specific loading procedures that these disks violate. I recommend avoiding this type of disk if possible. If not, have the teacher load the disk. The teacher will need to discuss the differences in how this disk is loaded, stressing that you should not remove a disk while the system is on. If the teacher feels that the children can manage the two different loading sequences, special provisions will need to be made. These disks would have to be marked in a special way to signify their difference. It would be best to wait to introduce these disks until children are proficient with the normal loading sequence.

For some double-sided disks, different parts of the program are on each side of the disk, and the user must load the disk with the correct side up. In **Peanuts Maze Marathon**, simple mazes are on one side and more complex mazes are on the other side. The desired side can be marked with a colored star or other symbol. The children load the disk with the star side up.

It is best to start with just two or three programs when the computer is first introduced, to facilitate locating desired programs. If more than one computer system is in use, the computers can be color coded (e.g., with green labels for loading one and blue labels for the other). The software can be color coded to match the machine. (This is helpful to teachers as well as to children.) To further minimize confusion, display the software for each machine in a separate location. If the computers are in different parts of the room, locate the software for each near the appropriate system.

ACTIVITIES TO SUPPORT DEVELOPMENT OF SKILLS FOR SELECTING AND LOADING SOFTWARE

PICK A MOVEMENT

Why?

- ☐ To develop the concept that the tape (or disk) that is selected affects the output from the machine

- 🕴☐ To practice making choices based on picture symbols

- 🕴☐ To practice following a numbered sequence to run a machine

What Is Needed?

A tape recorder with
"1" where the tape goes in
"2" (green) on the start button
"3" (red) on the stop button
"4" with an arrow on the rewind button
"5" on the eject
A chart showing the steps for using the tape recorder
3 story tapes, each with a picture representing its story
3 books to go with the tapes, each marked with a picture matching the one on the corresponding story tape

How?

Place the books on display together and the tapes on display at a different spot, both within reach of the tape recorder. The child selects a book, then selects the corresponding tape. The child loads the tape recorder, listens to the story, rewinds the tape, and returns the book and tape to their original spots. If needed, a teacher can help the child to (1) realize that the correct tape can be found by attending to the picture symbols and (2) follow the numbered steps in order.

Making It Your Own:

Instead of story tapes, provide three action tapes. Each tape could tell a story of a different animal—a cat for a walk, a bear in the woods, and so on. Children enact the animal's part as the story unfolds. Teachers can make up their own stories to fit a special unit or interest of their children. Favorite songs from movement records can be taped.

LEARNING TO LOCATE NECESSARY KEYS ON THE KEYBOARD

Looking at Keyboarding Skills

Independent computer use requires children to locate desired keys expediently. Young children need not be touch typists, nor is this even a desirable goal for them. But a child who can find needed keys without too lengthy a search is able to use the computer with less frustration. Children more quickly find keys that they use often. The letters in their names, the [Return] key, and keys needed for favorite programs are spotted faster than keys less frequently used.

Children who can identify letters and numerals, and create an image of that symbol in their heads when it is named, are likely to find it easier to locate keys on the keyboard. If you are searching for an "S" to make the face on **Facemaker** smile, scanning the keys for that letter is easier if you can visualize the "S" in your head. Children who can keep the image of the needed letter in their heads can compare the letters they see to the letter in their head until they come to a key that matches the imagined symbol. Although recognition of the letters is helpful, it is not necessary. A child can refer to the "S" on the rebus guide or on the screen when searching for the "S" on the keyboard. This child need not be able to identify letters but must be able to match them. If a child is not able to match letters, then computer programs that require some use of letter or number symbols will probably be frustrating.

Keyboarding skills also include recognition of common uses for function keys. The [Return] key often tells the computer that the child has "made a choice." In **Bank Street Writer**, **Facemaker**, and many other programs, the [Return] key is pressed to confirm choices on the menu. The [Shift] bar and the arrows are often used to move the cursor. The [Delete] key and the left arrow are often used to erase.

Methods for Fostering Children's Keyboarding Skills

Asking Children To Do Only Part of the Task. Many of the CBS programs for the Commodore are excellent for young computer users, but the loading procedure requires typing a 14-key sequence of keys correctly, including holding down the [Shift] key while typing two of the needed keys. Many children get discouraged and give up during the difficult loading sequence, never making it to the simple programs. Teachers can remedy this problem by having these programs preloaded, thus negating the need for finding the keys and typing them sequentially and correctly in order to use the program. The same problem may occur if you wish to use part of a program aimed at an older audience. **Talking Screen Text Writer** and **Terrapin Logo** each have pieces that are appropriate for younger children, but they involve complex loading procedures that require selection from and movement among a series of written menus.

For most young children, using a word processing program to enter a whole story is too difficult. Instead, the teacher can type what the children narrate, and then the children can type in their own names at the beginning or end of the story. Some children may want to enter other letters and words as well. Teachers can modify the activity to meet individual needs.

Providing Children with Ways To Think about the Keyboard. Teachers can help children to focus on the function of certain keys. After typing her name to enter **Magic Crayon**, Julia is unsure what to do next. The teacher can ask, "Which key do you press to let the computer know that you have finished typing your name?" This teacher is getting the child to recall her previous experiences with the program. If Julia is unsure, the teacher can ask, "Which key do you press on **Facemaker** to tell the computer you have made your choice?" The same technique can be employed to acquaint children with the functions of the other keys.

Some children are confused when they try to understand how the arrows shown on a horizontal plane on the keyboard translate into vertical movement on the screen. The teacher can help by discussing how the child has made the arrow move. A conversation with a child using **Magic Crayon** might sound like the following one.

Teacher: How did you get your line to go up like that?
Child: I pushed the arrow.
Teacher: Which arrow makes it go up?
Child This one.[2]

The teacher can do the same thing less obtrusively by merely commenting while watching the child work. "Oh, that arrow makes the cursor go up." Activities such as **I Command You To Draw** (p. 159) encourage children to think about the relation between the arrows and the resultant movement on the screen. A variation could be developed in which children press on a horizontal arrow keyboard to command movement of a magnetized car through a metal maze of streets, or any type of magnetized character through any setting.

It is sometimes suggested that it would be easier to teach children the keyboard if it was in alphabetical order. Koala markets an auxiliary keyboard called **Muppet Keys** with alphabetized keys. For adults first learning to use the computer, this might be an advantage. They would know to look near the middle of the keyboard for "M" and toward the bottom right for "W." Children do not know the alphabet in the same way. When 4-year-olds search for a "P" on the alphabet poster that displays the alphabet in order, or the location of the "K" on a sequential alphabet puzzle, they seldom use the alphabet as a guide. Children are more likely to do random scanning. Some children recite the alphabet, moving along from letter to letter. These children often get so involved in reciting, they go right past the desired key without noticing. For the children who can recite

the alphabet, alphabetical order is some help in locating a desired letter. But rarely does a child employ the adult method of using knowledge of the alphabet to determine in what section of the alphabet to search for the key.

For these reasons, alphabetical order only offers young children little to moderate assistance in locating letters, not warranting the additional expense for an auxiliary keyboard. Because the help provided by alphabetized keyboards is limited, it would seem to be better to encourage children to use a normal keyboard, so the letter location skills they learn can be applied to later typewriter or computer use.

Modifying Materials To Fit Skills. If children find it difficult and laborious to recognize and match keys, teachers might want to add stickers to the needed keys to make them more obvious. If children have trouble locating the **[Return]** key a red dot might be added, as well as a red dot next to the word *Return* on all rebus cards. The red dot will help distinguish the **[Return]** key from the other function keys. When using a program that employs 4-8 keys, these specific keys can be highlighted with lettered labels so that the keys will stand out from the rest of the keyboard. For **Facemaker**, labels can be put on the "C," "F," "S," "T," "W," and "E" keys. The children will then know that any highlighted key will make the face move. This procedure will also make it easier for children to locate a specific key because only 6 must be scanned, instead of the whole keyboard.

Highlighting special keys can also help more advanced computer users to master more difficult tasks. If children have quite good keyboarding skills, the teacher may wish to have them load the CBS software independently. To simplify the task, the keys for each word in the loading sequence could be highlighted in a different color. The loading directions on the disk sleeve could be written in the same colors as on the highlighted keys. When children see that the word "RUN" is in red, they need only scan the three red keys on the keyboard to locate the letter "R."

[2]As mentioned earlier, such questions should only be used as a way of encouraging children to think more closely about what they are doing. They should not be used as a test and should be discontinued if they are perceived as such by the child. The teacher is trying to gently guide the child. Test questions intimidate.

Modifying Required Actions To Fit Skills.
Many times, it is possible to achieve the same result on the computer through different steps. On **Magic Crayon**, the printed directions on the screen advise users to type ''X'' to register their choice of colors. A child in my class discovered that **[Return]** would also register this choice. The **[Return]** key is easier for children to remember if they have used other computer programs employing the **[Return]** key to enter their commands.

Encouraging children to work together can ease the task of finding needed keys because each child is likely to know the location of their own special keys—most children learn the keys in their name first. But working together can sometimes create problems. When one child is more skilled, the other may not be given a chance to locate keys. A wise teacher encourages helpers to provide assistance only when asked. Teachers who invite children to call on each other for help, and who model appropriate helping behavior, are less likely to have children gloating about their superior proficiency.

Children should be encouraged to help each other. (Photo courtesy of Robert Cohen)

Providing Opportunities To Locate Keys on the Computer and Practice Similar Skills. The best way to learn the keyboard is to use it often. If a child enjoys watching the tear roll down Stickybear's cheek when using **Stickybear ABC**, the child is likely to learn the location of the ''C'' key so that the desired picture will appear. The more opportunities children have to use the computer, the more likely they are to reinforce the keyboard knowledge developed in previous use.

Children can also build keyboarding skills when using typewriters and through a variety of activities that use simulations of the keyboard. The simulated keyboard activities are not advised for precomputer use, as they offer little motivation, but many children who enjoy using the computer or typewriter will transfer this excitement to activities using keyboard simulations. Typewriters are fascinating to children and are an excellent way of developing keyboard familiarity before computers are introduced.

For children who are weak in letter recognition or matching skills, wide varieties of activities using let-

Using the typewriter develops keyboarding skills. (Photo courtesy of Robert Cohen).

ters can be helpful—puzzles incorporating letters, alphabet books, recognizing their names and friend's names (as a way of being excused from group time), alphabet cookie cutters for use with playdough or sand, and the many other alphabet-related activities found in preschools and kindergartens. It is important to stress that I do not advocate formal teaching of letters in the preschool; rather, I suggest that letters, along with the many other materials, be a part of the environment. Activities involving letter recognition, matching, or manipulation can be available for those children who are interested.

Avoiding Keyboarding Tasks That Are Too Difficult. To make keyboarding easier, the first programs used should necessitate locating a relatively small number of keys. (The listing of software in the appendix designates which keys each program employs.) In this way, children can learn a few keys for the first program. As they become more accustomed to the keyboard, programs with more difficult keyboarding requirements can be added.

ACTIVITIES TO DEVELOP KEYBOARDING SKILLS

MAKE YOUR NAME

Why?

☐ To practice locating the letters of their name on the keyboard

⚑ To learn, or reinforce, the spelling of their own names

⚑ To facilitate small-muscle development

What Is Needed?

A bulletin board with a large keyboard displayed
A push pin at the top center of each key
3 cards showing each of the letter keys with a hole punched at the top to fit over the push pin
A long empty space above the keyboard, with a row of push pins along the top for hanging letter cards (the space can be "displayed" on a monitor)
A basket of cards with each child's name near, or attached to, the bulletin board

How?

The children "type" their names by removing the letter cards for their name from the keyboard and placing them in the correct order on the long empty space.

Making It Your Own:

Have children work in pairs, verbally spelling their own names for their partners to "type."
Use the bulletin board keyboard for programming the **Facemaker Face** as in **Program Your Face** (p. 164)
Have children call out random letters for partner to "type."
Use the keyboard to complement a current theme or skill. If the class is learning to make patterns, the children can pick out two or three letters with which to type a pattern. For example,
A D A D A D A D, or
T Y Y T Y Y T Y Y, or
J H G J H G J H G.
Use the tops of styrofoam hamburger boxes for keys

Going Beyond:

For children beginning to use **Logo**, the bulletin board keyboard could be used to plan a procedure.

MAKE YOUR NAME
(Continued)

Children can use the letters on this bulletin board keyboard to spell their names.

NAME JUMPING

Jumping out names.

Why?

☐ To practice locating the letters of their name on the keyboard

🕴 To reinforce the children's knowledge of the spelling of their own names, or to help them learn the spelling

🕴 To encourage large-muscle development

What Is Needed?

A floor keyboard (a replica of a computer keyboard, with letters large enough for children to jump on them. Can be construction paper letters with each row connected by a covering of clear contact paper, or a large piece of canvas or a shower curtain with the keys drawn on)

A card with each child's name written on it

How?

The children "type" their names by jumping on the needed letters on the floor keyboard in order. If children are unsure of how to spell their names, the name cards can be used. Children can also type each other's names.

Making It Your Own:

Children can spell their names for classmates to "type."

Going Beyond:

Children can jump on the **[Return]** key at the end of their name to indicate that they are done. This can be used to reinforce the use of the **[Return]** key if that is needed in the class.

Children can type full names or other words, depending on their skills.

A game such as twister can be played so that they have to touch each of the named letters. So if a child's name is John, first a foot is placed on the "J," then another on the "O," then a hand each on "H" and "N." If the child has a long name or one with letters that are far apart, other children can help to cover letters.

KEYBOARD BINGO

Why?

☐ To practice locating keys on the keyboard

🕴 To exercise small-muscle skills

What Is Needed?

A card with a model of a keyboard for each child
A bowl full of plastic chips to cover keys
A box with cards for each letter on the keyboard
Children who recognize letters

How?

One child or teacher is the caller. The caller picks a letter from the box and names it. The players cover the named keys. Players yell "bingo" when a whole row is filled. (Note that the game is not competitive. All the children should yell "bingo" at the same time.) A new child becomes caller. Play continues until the next row is full. A new caller is picked. Play continues in this way until all the keys are covered.

Making It Your Own:

If the children are only using a few keys for the current programs in use, color those keys red. Only place cards in the box for the red keys. Children call "bingo" when all red keys are covered.

Going Beyond:

Add the number keys and the function keys.

OFFICE

Why?

☐ To gain familiarity with the keyboard

☐ To provide practice with single keystroke

🏃 To provide opportunity for dramatic play

What Is Needed?

3-5 typewriters—electric if possible. (Older typewriters that have been replaced by newer models often can be found at school system supply warehouses. Universities, typewriter stores, rummage sales, and businesses often sell used typewriters remarkably cheaply.)

Staplers

Pencil holders with pencils

Envelopes and paper

Stamps (the kind that come with book club or magazine advertisements are great)

Boxes for finished work

Date stamps and ink pads

A Rolodex holding the first name of each child (the type that sit flat are better than the hanging circular Rolodex)

How?

Set up the preceding materials like an office with a number of desks and work spaces. Encourage children to work in the "office." They can "type letters," print name cards (if they are comfortable typing names, type addresses on envelopes, and compose "reports").

Making It Your Own:

Adjust the materials and setup of the office to resemble either the office at your school or other offices the children may have seen.

Going Beyond:

Visiting the school office before this activity, to see what the secretaries do will add to the richness of the play.

Older children might be offered a job board with jobs to be done. The jobs might include a picture of an addressed, stamped envelope, a pattern to type (e.g., a f a f a f), the alphabet to type, numerals from 1 to 9, or other similar jobs.

Instead of having an office, consider another type of dramatic play that could incorporate a typewriter: a house with a desk for doing work, a newspaper, a book printer, and so forth.

MOVE A FACE

Why?

☐ To reinforce the word "command"

☐ To practice finding the keys needed for **Facemaker**

🕺 To exercise facial muscles

🕺 To encourage social interaction

What Is Needed?

A small table and chair

A floor keyboard (with the bottom of the keyboard near the front of the table)

A cardboard box with the bottom and top cut out to look like a monitor; monitor should be secured on table

2 rebus cards for **Facemaker** with the letters for moving the face and pictures to illustrate each letter (place one inside monitor, the other near the floor keyboard)

How?

One child sits in a chair with her or his face inside the monitor. The other child gives the monitor commands by jumping on keys to move the face. The jumper calls out the letter jumped on. The child in the monitor makes the appropriate face. The children can trade places after a while. (The calling out is important, as the jumper's feet may be covering the letter. If the child in the monitor wants to see the key, the jumper can be asked to move to the side of the letter key.)

Making It Your Own:

To include more children, have two or three monitors instead of one, or have children take turns "typing" the commands.

Adapt to reflect other programs.

If children have trouble finding keys, make the 6 keys for **Facemaker** a different color than the others.

Going Beyond:

If the class has been discussing programming, the children can program the face. Add a pegboard with a row of hooks and a pile of "T," "W," "C," "S," "F," and "E" cards with holes punched in them. The cards should have the rebus representations of the motions as well as the letters. One child jumps the commands, another child enters them on the pegs, a third child is the monitor. After the program is written, the jumper presses the **[Return]** key. The monitor then follows the program, doing each command in order.

KEYBOARD PUZZLE

Why?

- To become familiar with the locations of keys on the keyboard

- To facilitate eye movement from horizontal to vertical plane

- To encourage small-muscle development

What Is Needed?

3 file folders serving as game boards, with a completed keyboard drawn on the top and a keyboard with blank keys on the bottom

A set of four light blue strips, each duplicating one row of the keyboard

A set of eight light yellow strips, each duplicating half of one keyboard row

A set of 26 light pink pieces, each showing an individual letter key

How?

Set up the keyboard folder so that half rests on the table and the other half leans against a block or the wall. The child uses the vertical keyboard as a guide for placing the light blue strips correctly on the blank horizontal keyboard.

For more skilled children, use the yellow or pink pieces. All three puzzles could be put out, and children can select the one that they wish to use.

Keyboard puzzles can help children learn key location.

BAG A LETTER

Why?

☐ To help children locate keys on the keyboard

🏃 To encourage cooperation

🏃 To encourage large-muscle development and hand-eye coordination needed for throwing

What Is Needed?

A floor keyboard (with bottom toward wall keyboard)
A keyboard poster on the wall (reachable by children)
4 bean bags
Self-stick note paper
A strip of paper from which self-stick notes can be easily removed, mounted near wall poster

How?

One child tosses the bean bag onto the floor keyboard and calls out the "bagged" letter. Another child covers that letter on the wall keyboard with a self-stick paper. Continue until all the keys are covered. Remove papers, and place them on a strip near the poster for the next game. Change roles and play again.

As the game progresses, encourage children to aim for the letters that are not yet covered.

Going Beyond:

Have the children try to "bag" the letters in alphabetical order. Only cover the wall keyboard when the bean bag lands on the "correct" key in the alphabetical sequence.

LEARNING TO USE A SINGLE KEYSTROKE

Why Children's Computer Use May Be Enhanced by Learning to Use a Single Keystroke

For many pieces of software, it is important to strike the desired key quickly. If the finger lingers on the key, the computer will register the continued contact as a series of keystrokes rather than a single one. If Karen does not yet realize the importance of quick key strokes, she may find the result of typing her name looks something like this—KKKKKKKKKaaaaaarrrrrrreeeeeeeennnnnn. To master the skill of using a single keystroke, children must understand the need to strike the key only once, know the importance of striking the key quickly, and have the fine-muscle coordination to implement this knowledge.

Methods for Fostering Children's Skills in Using a Single Keystroke

Providing Children with Ways To Think about Single Keystrokes. The teacher can help children to understand the need for a single keystroke in two ways. First, the teacher can describe how to strike the key: "Tap it quickly." The teacher may demonstrate a quick finger stroke, or hold the child's finger and type the key swiftly. Second, the teacher can explain that the computer is not as smart as people. It cannot see or tell how many times your finger has touched the key. If you leave your finger on the key, the computer interprets that you are pressing it again and again. If you leave your finger on "K," the computer will think you want it to display more and more "K"s until you remove your finger. This information can be offered when children have let their finger linger on a key creating an unexpected result.

Providing Opportunities To Use Single Keystrokes on the Computer and Practice Similar Skills. Using software that requires single keystrokes will help children realize the need to touch the key only briefly, as well as providing opportunities to practice this skill. For some software, the length of keystroke is irrelevant. If a child is using **Bald-Headed Chicken** with the keyboard, a prolonged keystroke will merely move the cursor further. When the child is first trying to acquire the skill to employ a single keystroke, it might be helpful to present a variety of software that makes this skill necessary. If only one piece requires a precise keystroke, it may take the child longer to realize the need and develop the required skill.

Children can also develop both the concept and the skill to employ the single keystroke when using other machines that also require a quick touch. An electric typewriter is an excellent opportunity for such practice. Its similarity to the computer keyboard makes it especially appropriate. Calulators and electronic games also offer similar practice.

Avoiding Tasks That Are Too Difficult. Some software, such as **Primary Editor**, will only respond to distinct keystrokes. The computer will only recognize one command from that key no matter how long the child's finger remains on the keyboard. Providing software of this type will negate the need for single keystroke skill. Although software of this type should certainly be considered, it should not replace software that does necessitate discrete keystrokes. Many excellent pieces of software require single keystrokes, and to use them, children must develop this skill. Because it is a relatively easy skill to acquire, avoidance of software requiring it is not usually necessary.

SUMMARY

Teachers can use a variety of formal and informal methods for helping children to develop skills in turning the computer on and off, locating and loading desired programs, using a single keystroke, and locating the needed keys on the keyboard. By considering what is involved in each of these skills, teachers can develop a variety of ways to support their development. The activities and suggestions here are meant only as a springboard. Teachers should revise and modify these activities to meet their needs and the needs of their children, as well as generating their own unique activities.

6

More Activities for Developing the Skills Needed for Using the Computer

This chapter looks at the last three skills that enhance independent computer use:

1. Selecting from a menu
2. Generating and following procedures
3. Following pictorial instructions.

SELECTING FROM A MENU

Characteristics of Software Menus

Within a computer program, the user is often offered some choices. The list of choices presented on the screen is called the menu. The user may be asked to select an item on the menu by moving the cursor to the desired option. Some programs begin with a menu. For example, **Kindercomp** has six different activities. In order to begin using the program, one of the program options must first be selected. Menus are also incorporated into some programs. For example, in **Magic Crayon**, the children use a color menu—a rainbow selection of colors—to change the color of the "crayon." Many programs include a variety of menus at different spots for making different choices. For example, in **Facemaker**, there are eight menus: one with which to choose the part of the program, one from which to choose the type of feature desired, five that show the choices for each of the different features, and one from which to select ways to move the face.

Menus are an integral part of most computer programs. Thus, to use the computer independently, children must be able to understand and select from the menus. Children are already well versed in the skill of making choices. They are constantly making choices. In a preschool classroom, children might be deciding which bead to put on the necklace first, where to ride on their tricycle, or which of the dress-up clothes are best for the Daddy.

Children build concepts about computers while using them.

When making choices from computer menus, the options are limited. For example, when using **Juggle's Rainbow**, the only things that can be made are a windmill, a rainbow, or a butterfly. **Kindercomp** includes six possible activities, but the child cannot choose to write a story, compose music, or animate a face since these are not on the menu. To do these things, other software must be used.

No matter what a child does, the choices are limited. When choosing which bead to thread first, the child is limited by the colors and shapes of the beads. When riding a tricycle, the boundaries of the play yard define the options possible. When choosing "daddy clothes," the child must select from the apparel the teacher has provided. As with other materials, children may need to alter their intent to fit the available options. If a suit coat is not available, a similar piece of clothing can be substituted. If the preferred nose does not appear on the **Facemaker** menu, a second best will have to do.

For children making a necklace or dressing up, the options are clear: they can use the beads in the basket and the clothes in the wardrobe. But sometimes the choices on a computer are less clear to children. Many programs, such as **Kindercomp,** display the menu as text, thus making the menu inaccessible to nonreaders. Some children memorize the number needed to bring up their favorite choices (Hess & McGarvey, 1987), but other children find the incomprehensibility of the menu confusing without teacher help or teacher-made rebus menus. Some programs provide picture menus. **Juggle's Rainbow** begins with a menu of four pictures: "1" a rainbow, "2" a butterfly, "3" a windmill, "4" a question mark.

But even picture menus can be confusing. The one described for **Juggle's Rainbow** initially confused both teachers and children. The "1" allows the user to make a rainbow, "2" lets the user make a butterfly, and "3" enables the construction of a windmill. We all assumed that pressing "4" would allow us to make a question mark, but instead, a written list of program adjustment options appears. To get the menu back, the "4" must be pressed again. Because the need to press "4" is explained

in writing, most children cannot determine how to get out of the directions once they have stumbled in.

What makes selecting from a computer menu more difficult than selecting from a basket of beads or a wardrobe of clothes is that it is a more abstract process. The child is not selecting from the actual objects but rather from a list of pictured objects that can be used to request the computer to produce the requested object. It is the difference between selecting a soda from a shelf in the refrigerator and pushing a button displaying a picture of the soda on a soda machine. In the first case, the child selects the soda desired; in the second case, the child pushes a picture to produce the soda. The second process is more abstract.

Skills Required for Using a Software Menu

In order to use a piece of software independently, the children must be able to decipher the menu. Children also must learn how to indicate their selections. There are many different ways to register choices. In **Facemaker**, the child uses the spacebar to move the cursor to the desired feature, then presses **[Return]** to enter the choice. In **The Bald-Headed Chicken**, the arrows change the choice displayed on the menu. In this program, the menu is like a View Master, which displays one picture at a time until the choices rotate back to the beginning. The "apple" key, or the button on the mouse or joystick, enters the selection.

Independent use of software depends on learning the rules that govern selection from its menu, as well as on deciphering the menu. For some programs, such as **Color Me**, the menu is quite complex, offering many different kinds of options. Children can use these without understanding all the choices, as long as they can learn to find the choices they need. **Color Me** wisely combines picture and words on the menu. Nonreaders can get cues from the pictures, and readers can find clarification for the symbols in the written words. For some programs, such as **Print Shop** or **The Bald-Headed Chicken**, the children must go through a number of steps to locate

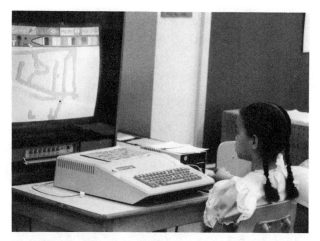

*The **Color Me** menu is displayed at the top of the screen.*

the menu they need. (This is discussed in more detail in this chapter's next section, on procedures.)

Developing Skills Related to the Use of Software Menus

In Chapter 4, seven methods were described for providing support for children who are developing computer skills. Some of these methods will be used as a framework for discussing the development of skills in selecting from a menu.

Ask the Child to Do Only Part of the Task. For complex programs such as **Terrapin Logo**, which has many different options and a series of written menus that must be negotiated before moving the turtle robot, the teacher can preload the program. Programs such as **Color Me** and **Koala Pad**, which have a complex menu always displayed on the screen, can be simplified by helping children to learn only the choices that they wish to learn.

It is interesting to watch different children use these programs. Maura was content to move the cursor around with the mouse. After 2 days of use, she also periodically changed the drawing color. Dan, on the other hand, wanted to discover everything the program would do. He discovered the fill

option by mistake. His cursor entered the menu area and changed the draw option to the fill option. Now, when he pushed the button on the joystick instead of drawing, it would make ever-increasing diamonds of color until the whole area of the drawing was filled. Dan also discovered that when he pushed the button on the mouse again, the diamond would stop spreading. After these discoveries, Dan systematically explored all the menu options. He did not seek teacher help; in fact he would often stop working if he thought he was being observed by a teacher. He would occasionally call a teacher or peer to witness a new discovery but not for advice.

The fact that children use the software in different ways indicates that such pieces provide the opportunity to satisfy a wide variety of interests and needs. The possibility of using these programs to meet differing learning styles should be prized. Teachers should not attempt to teach each child to use each part of the menu, but rather to assist the child to use those parts that he or she desires to use.

Provide Children with Ways To Think about Menus. There are a number of ways in which teachers can provide children with a verbal description of menus and how they work. First, when a program is introduced to the class, the teacher can mention the activities that are possible by referring to the rebus card needed to "read" the menu. As a child is looking at the program, the teacher can assist at the appropriate level, giving information, asking questions, or commenting on what the child has done. Each of these formats allows the teacher to describe what is happening.

The following illustrates the way in which a teacher might help a child to use **Juggle's Rainbow**. At the beginning of the program, the teacher can comment "I see you chose the rainbow from the menu. The disk drive must be moving to that part of the disk to get you the rainbow you wanted." On the other hand, if the child seems confused about how to select a picture, the teacher might ask, "Which kind of picture do you want to make?" If the child is still unsure, the teacher can say, "Do you want to make a rainbow, a windmill, or a butterfly?" pointing

INPUT FOR TEACHERS:

DESIGNING ACTIVITIES FOR SPECIFIC PIECES OF SOFTWARE

The **Create a Creature** activity on page 100 was designed to complement a particular piece of software—**Creature Creator**. The selections for body parts are the same as the selections offered in the program. By modeling an activity after a particular piece of software, the teacher can offer children more chances to become familiar with the choices offered by that program. Because a computer is an expensive commodity, most schools have a limited number, and thus children often need to wait for a turn to use it. Off-computer activities that complement particular software give children the opportunity to "be involved with" new software while they are waiting to use the computer. These off- computer activities will also provide another forum for developing the skills. **If You're a Facemaker Monitor** (p. 156) and **Program Your Face** (p. 164) both help children become familiar with the movement choices available on **Facemaker**. Both these games also allow children to practice the letter keys needed to select desired movements from the menu. **Program Your Face** (p. 164) and **Program an Obstacle Course** (p. 166) both provide opportunities to practice using the **[Return]** key to indicate that a choice has been made. Teachers should develop similar activities, when necessary, to help children in their class learn the choices and the way to register choices for specific pieces of software. Chapter 10 discusses in more detail activities to support specific software.

The "moving" menu in **Facemaker** requires reading unless a rebus guide is provided.

For example, "This program uses the **[Space bar]** key to move the cursor through the menu, just as **Facemaker** does." The teacher can also encourage the child to experiment by trying procedures learned in other programs. "How do you tell the computer you have made your choice in **Magic Crayon** or in **The Bald-Headed Chicken**? Do you think one of those ways will work for this program?"

Modify Materials To Fit Children's Menu-Using Skill. Providing rebus picture menus to supplement a written menu makes many programs usable that otherwise would be too difficult. For example, **Facemaker's** menu of "ways to move the face" is written in text. The child who cannot read can learn that each of those letters makes the face move, but the child cannot make the face do a specific motion without memorizing the symbols. A teacher-made picture menu depicts of the parts of the face that moves next to the appropriate letters will enable the child to choose the desired motion.

to the appropriate pictures while talking. If the child knows which picture but is unsure how to register the choice, the teacher might ask, "What number is near that picture? What do you think would happen if you press that number?"

Sometimes teachers can encourage children to compare the different programs, helping them to focus on the process they are using to obtain an end.

Provide Opportunities To Use Menus and Practice Similar Skills. Children already have countless opportunities to make choices. However, they might need additional practice making choices from a limited field, understanding pictorial menus, understanding the choices on specific software, making choices from an abstract menu rather than from real objects, and registering their choices in the appropriate ways. Using computers and negotiating real computer menus will obviously reinforce these skills. Off-computer activities can also help children to develop these skills. Activities such as **Program an Obstacle Course** (p. 166) and **Robot Orchestra** (p. 168), in which children must make choices from a small number of options, reinforce the need to work within the limits of the menu.

Avoid Menus That Are Too Difficult. When evaluating software to use in the classroom, the teacher must consider the clarity and usability of the menu as well as the value of the rest of the program. Even if most parts of a program are simple and appropriate for the level of the children in your room, the software is useless if the child cannot comprehend and/or use the menu. For some programs, rebus menus can be added, but for programs containing multiple menus or extremely complex menus, it may be impossible to design rebus menus that are clear for young children. This is discussed in greater depth in Chapter 10.

ACTIVITIES TO BUILD MENU-READING SKILLS

SODA MACHINE

Why?

☐ To practice making selections from a menu

↟ To participate in an activity that requires social cooperation

What Is Needed?

18 empty soda cans, 6 each of three varieties

A cardboard box with the back open, large enough for a child to stand in. On the front, mount one of each type of can so that half of the can is inside the box and half is outside. Beside each can, insert a slot. Under each slot inside the box, place a small box or basket to catch the coins. Also on the front of the box, cut a hole for dispensing the soda purchased.

30 cardboard coins

A chair inside the box, if desired

2 boxes for cans: one inside the machine for sodas to dispense, one outside for returning empty cans

2 small boxes for holding coins: one inside the machine for used coins, one outside for coins with which to buy soda

Select from the "menu" to get a soda.

How?

One child is the customer and another child is the soda machine operator. The customer chooses the desired soda from the three displayed, then drops a coin into the slot under the selected soda. The operator checks to see which can is above the box containing the coin. The operator hands a can of that type of soda out the can-dispensing slot.

Used cans can be placed in the box next to the machine and be restocked inside the machine as needed. Used coins can be recycled from inside the machine to the can outside so that children can get money to buy sodas.

SODA MACHINE
(Continued)

Making It Your Own:

Change what the machine dispenses to art supplies, McDonald's food, cardboard snacks, or something to better fit your classroom.

Use the machine to dispense a choice of real food or drinks at snack time.

Use the machine as a jukebox to play the chosen record or tape.

Use the machine to dispense animals for cots at nap time. Because you are unlikely to have multiples of the same animals, the animals can be displayed in 3 windows. When one is selected that one is removed and dispensed through the slot. Another animal is then put in the window.

Going Beyond:

To make the process more abstract, a picture of the soda can, rather than the actual soda can, could be displayed.

CREATE A CREATURE

Why?

☐ To practice selecting from a menu

🏃 To work together cooperatively with peers

🏃 To develop motor skills

What Is Needed?

3 "menus" for selecting **Creature Creator** parts. Divide each laminated menu into four parts, with a small box at the top left of each part. One menu would show four faces from **Creature Creator**, one would show four bodies with arms, and one would show four types of legs.

A crayon

Tissue, for rubbing crayon marks off menu

A "creature post"—a dowel rod set in a box of sand or other heavy weight, with three cubes mounted on the rod so that they rotate: the top cube should have the four faces, the middle one four sets of bodies and arms, the bottom four sets of legs—these should match the body parts on the menus

How?

One child marks the menus. The child looks at the faces and selects one by making a mark in the small box at the left of that face. The child shows the menu to a second child who rotates the head cube so that the selected face is toward the child who is marking the menu. This process is then repeated with the bodies and legs. When the creature is completed, the menus are checked against the finished creature. The menu can be erased by rubbing it with a tissue. The children can change roles and play again.

The creature post is being turned to the body marked on the menu.

CREATE A CREATURE
(Continued)

Making It Your Own:

Instead of using a "creature post," make a flip book. Have four pages for heads, four for bodies, and four for legs.

One child marks the menu, and the other child flips the book to the correct pages.

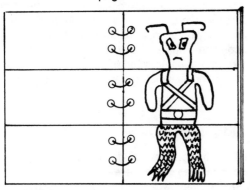

Use other software instead of **Creature Creator** as a base for this game.

Going Beyond:

Make a cube post that shows one person in different positions. Have six or seven cards of each position. Write a program of leg movements. Press [Return], then make the cube-post person dance by moving the legs in the order shown on the program.

TACO BY THE MENU

Why?

♠ ☐ To provide practice deciphering rebus pictures

☐ To provide practice in selecting from a menu

♠ To allow children to compare a variety of food tastes and textures

♠ To use small muscles

What Is Needed?

A bowl of browned ground beef with a spoon
A bowl of tomato pieces with a spoon
A bowl of sour cream, or yogurt, with a spoon
A bowl of cheese with a spoon
A bowl of green pepper pieces with a spoon
A bowl of mushroom slices with a spoon
A bowl of shredded onions with a spoon
A bowl of shredded lettuce with a spoon
A baking sheet
4 laminated menus with 8 boxes
4 crayons
A basket of taco shells
Paper for writing names to identify each child's taco on cookie sheet
An oven
Tissues
Small paper plates

How?

Place the bowls of food around a table. At one end of the table, offer menus and crayons. Have children wash their hands. They can then use the spoons to place a small amount of the food they wish to sample on their plates. Teachers and children can discuss the tastes and textures of the foods. Children then take the menu and use a crayon to mark the foods they want in their taco. They then take a shell and walk around the table filling it with the foods marked on the menu. When the shell is filled, it is placed on the cookie sheet next to a slip of paper with their name on it. Children can then use a tissue to wipe the menu clean for the next child.

The teacher can put the cookie sheet in the oven at 350° to bake until it is warm (about 5-10 minutes). Children who wish to make extra tacos can make second helpings, or make one for a teacher or classmate who does not want to cook. The cook can ask the noncooker what ingredients to mark off on the menu.

Making It Your Own:

Adjust the ingredients to complement your objectives and the tastes of the class.

Use similar menus for other cooking activities: fruit salad, green salad, trail mix, pizza, fruit kabobs (fruit on a skewer), or other simple projects that require few steps, and allow choices.

Going Beyond:

For children who are ready to read numerals, offer a recipe for fruit salad or fruit kabobs, with a picture of a different kinds of fruit in each square of the menu. In the bottom of each square, list a 0, 1, 2, and 3. The child circles the numeral that shows how many pieces of that fruit are wanted.

TACO BY THE MENU
(Continued)

Menus and food waiting for a cook.

TACO BY THE MENU
(Continued)

Mark the Menu.

Making the taco.

Eating the taco.

TREASURE HUNT

Why?

☐ To provide practice using a menu

🧍☐ To provide practice reading rebus pictures

🧍 To develop small-muscle skills

What Is Needed?

A baby's Busy Box

A menu depicting each compartment—the character above and the opening device that is inside below

A can with a set of five cards each depicting one of the characters

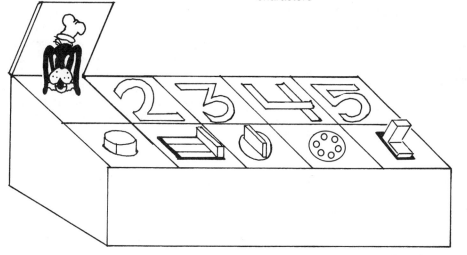

busy box

menu

can of cards

TREASURE HUNT
(Continued)

How?

The child picks a character picture out of the can and uses the menu to decide which part of the Busy Box must be used to find the selected character. The teacher can explain that the child must "look at the menu to see what must be pushed, dialed, or moved on the Busy Box to find the character they are looking for." The child should then try the Busy Box to verify the answer.

Going Beyond:

Hide small objects in the Busy Box, e.g., a penny, a button, a paper clip, and a bead. Have a menu showing the devices for opening each part of the Busy Box (i.e., a dial, a switch, or a sliding box). In each box of the menu, attach a piece of velcro. Provide pictures of each object on a separate card with velcro on the back. Use velcro to adhere each object picture into the square showing where it can be found—that is, if the paper clip is in the compartment opened with the dial, then place the picture of the paper clip in the menu box with the dial. Have a second set of object pictures in a can. Children pull a picture from a can. They are to find that object in the Busy Box by looking at the menu and opening the correct section. A child can hide the objects in the appropriate parts of the Busy Box, or put them in new places, moving the velcro pictures to show where the objects are now hidden.

FOLLOWING AND BEGINNING TO DESIGN MULTISTEPPED PROCEDURES

Types of Procedures

"Procedure" has two meanings, and both apply here. In computer terms, a *procedure* is a series of steps within a program (Galland, 1983). For example, if children are using **Logo**, they can program a series of commands, which, when followed in sequence, draw a square. The children can then label this procedure (or series of commands), and the computer will run the procedure when the child types in the label. There is some dispute as to whether young children should be taught to use **Logo** (Barnes & Hill, 1983). It is true that kindergarten children and first graders can learn to use **Logo**, but often, the amount of teacher time required keeps computer use of this type from being an independent activity. When this skill was originally stated as a goal for the CAPP participants (Paris, 1985), the children were not expected to develop the skill to generate program procedures, but rather to be able to follow procedures and begin to "think procedurally." Being able to think of the required steps to reach a goal is the beginning of procedural thinking.

Procedure also has a noncomputer meaning. A *procedure* is "a series of steps followed in a regular definite order" (Webster's Seventh New Collegiate Dictionary, 1967). Children using the computer need to be able to follow procedures even if they never intend to program. To load the computer, the child must follow the correct procedure. To make selections from the menu, children must follow a procedure. In fact most computer use requires children to work within the procedures for the specific hardware and software being used. Children can also create procedures in the noncomputer meaning. As children become familiar with a program, they may have a particular intent in mind. Bree and Mary Beth decided they would program their **Facemaker** face to move in a pattern, like the patterns they were making elsewhere in the classroom. They decided which two motions were wanted—wiggling ears and sticking out tongue. They planned how the pattern would be made. Bree would type the "E"s for ears, and Mary Beth would type the "T"s for tongue. They then followed this procedure they had developed to make their pattern. These children are not developing procedures in the strict computer sense of the word, but they are learning to think procedurally, a prerequisite to problem solving and eventual computer programming.

Developing Skills for Following and Beginning to Design Procedures

In order to follow a procedure, the child must first realize that the correct order of steps is important. If the procedures for turning on and loading the computer are not followed, the desired program will not appear on the screen. Once the need to follow the sequence is understood, the child must also have the ability to move through the procedure in the prescribed manner.

Provide Children with Ways To Think about Procedures. Teachers are constantly helping children to understand the need to follow the correct procedures. When asking children who want to use the computer "What do you do first when . . . ?" the teacher is reminding children that a sequence of steps exists and must be followed correctly. When the computer does not work as it should, the teacher can help a child to retrace the steps taken and then try again, paying particular attention to the appropriate order of the steps.

Modify Materials To Fit Children's Procedural Skills. Rebus guides for turning on and off the computer, moving through a menu, or getting the **Print It** card to work all assist children to follow procedures and to more successfully use the computer independently. These rebus guides both help the children to know the appropriate steps and make it clear that a specific procedure is required. Teachers can develop pictorial guides for any procedures that children need help following.

Provide Opportunities To Follow and Generate Procedures and Practice Similar Skills. Any direction-following activities help develop children's skills in following procedures. Cooking activities in which children must follow a recipe are excellent for developing this skill. After all, procedures can be thought of as precise recipes. Single-serving recipes are most appropriate because they require each child to follow the procedure from start to finish, as in **Pizza Parlour Procedure** (p. 109) and **Taco by the Menu** (p. 102). If the activity to be attempted is simple and familiar to the children, they can be encouraged to help plan the needed steps and then follow the procedure they have generated, as in **Plan the Planting Procedure** (p. 114) and **Peanut Butter Planning** (p. 115).

Avoid Tasks That Are Too Difficult. When reviewing software, consider how complex each required procedure is. It is also important to consider the compounding effect when many simple procedures are combined together in one program. Carefully select software that will not overwhelm the children in your class. Often, by introducing only some of the software's options at one time, a potentially more complex piece can be simplified.

For example, to enter and draw with **Magic Crayon** is relatively simple. Children must type their names, then press **[Return]**, wait for a minute, and then use the arrow keys to move the cursor and draw on the screen. **Magic Crayon** also lets children save their pictures. To save, the child must press "R" for remember, type a name for the picture, press **[Return]**, press the **[Esc]** key, and then the "Y". This procedure is quite complex. But **Magic Crayon** can also be used without introducing the possibility of saving. When a child is ready to manage the longer saving procedure, or when a need arises to save a picture (as when free-play ends before the picture is completed), then the teacher can introduce the child to saving. The rebus directions for saving can be placed on the back of the disk sleeve or on another card, making it available for the children who are ready to learn it. Placed on the front, such directions might confuse the children

---

INPUT FOR TEACHERS:

SINGLE-SERVING RECIPES

Cooking is a valuable activity for young children. It can support many aspects of development. Children strengthen motor skills when cutting, mixing, measuring, pouring, and chopping. Children expand concepts about the physical properties of objects and how they change. Children develop self-help skills that can be used at other times. Cooking is usually considered an "adult" activity. Children feel proud of their ability to be helpful and successful in an "adult" activity. Cooking activities often introduce new vocabulary as well as provide a cozy working environment that fosters general conversation.

If the cooking activity is planned so that six children are working together adding ingredients to one bowl, most of each child's time will be spent waiting. The child is likely to feel restless and bored. The sense of success and general conversation are not likely to be promoted in this atmosphere. Each child will only have a small amount of time in which she/he is physically involved, thus motor skills will not have much chance to develop.

On the other hand, if single-serving recipes are used, each child will be involved all the time, and the activity is likely to promote the development of the total child. To let each child work on an individual recipe, it is important to select relatively simple recipes. Two excellent projects are salads or soups; the children chop and add ingredients, but the exact proportions are irrelevant. These two cookbooks contain single-serving recipes.

Cook and Learn (Veitch & Harmes, 1981) has 160 single-serving recipes. It also has an excellent reference section that contains such information as how many teaspoons of egg are in a large egg.

The No-Cook Cookery Cook Book (Stangle, 1976) has many single-serving or small portion recipes.

---

still working on the simpler procedures. Ways of adapting specific pieces of software to the skills of your children are discussed more in Chapter 10.

ACTIVITIES TO DEVELOP SKILLS IN FOLLOWING AND GENERATING PROCEDURES

PIZZA PARLOUR PROCEDURE

Why?

🧍☐ To practice following step-by-step procedures

🧍☐ To practice following directions with substeps

🧍 To generate positive feelings about self, through preparing one's own snack

🧍 To compare tastes and textures of a variety of foods

🧍 To see the changes in the ingredients from raw to cooked form

What Is Needed?

English muffins, toasted and cut in half
1 bowl of pizza sauce with a spoon
1 bowl of pepperoni pieces
1 bowl of mushroom slices
1 bowl of green pepper pieces
1 bowl of cheese
Picture directions at each step
2 wipe-off menus for selecting toppings—a laminated piece of cardboard with four blocks showing pepperoni, mushrooms, green pepper, and cheese with a small square in the corner of each box to check choices
2 crayons
Tissue for erasing menus
A cookie sheet
An oven
Paper strips to mark pizza
2 small plastic plates
2 pencils

How?

Set the steps out along a table in order, assembly-line fashion. The picture direction for each step should be next to the ingredients.

1. A hand putting the muffin on the plate (The container of muffins and a pile of plates should be placed by this picture direction.)
2. A hand putting 3 spoonfuls of pizza sauce on the muffin (The pizza sauce should be placed by this picture direction).
3. Someone marking a menu (The menus and crayons should be placed by this picture direction.)
4. Children placing items from their menu on pizza (The pepperoni, green pepper, mushrooms, and cheese should be placed by this picture direction.)
5. A hand wiping off and returning the menu to the table at Step 3 (The tissues should be placed by this picture direction.)
6. A hand writing a name on the paper slips (Paper and pencils should be placed by this picture direction.)
7. A hand putting the pizza and name on the cookie sheet (The cookie sheet should be placed by this picture direction.)

The children begin at Step 1 and follow the directions for each step until all seven steps are completed. The children may need help from the teacher the first time they follow the steps. Teachers can encourage the children to try to decipher the pictures. The children should be able to make a second pizza more independently. Some of the children who have already completed a pizza can assist the children who are just beginning. This will encourage those who are done to "read" the picture directions again. Children can taste the toppings before deciding which to add to the menu.

After the pizzas are completed, the teacher can put them in the oven to cook at 400° until the cheese is bubbly, about 10 minutes. The pizza should cool a bit before the children eat them.

PIZZA PARLOUR PROCEDURE
(Continued)

Making It Your Own:

Use other simple recipes in a similar assembly-line fashion.

With older children, the first step could be to toast the muffins.

Going Beyond:

If a microwave is available, the child can make the pizza on a paper plate. The last step could be to program the microwave and cook the pizza. This could be used as a part of a lesson on the many different things computers can do, or to discuss the concept that a computer is a machine that can be programmed with a series of commands.

NECKLACE FACTORY

Why?

♀ ☐ To practice following multistepped directions

♀ ☐ To practice following rebus picture directions

♀ To provide an opportunity to exercise small-muscle skills

♀ To explore how colors mix to form new colors

What Is Needed?

Red, blue, and yellow food coloring

Pasta in a variety of shapes that can be strung, such as wagon wheels, rigatoni, or extra large macaroni shaped noodles

Yarn with one end tied to a piece of pasta, the other wrapped with tape

Wax paper

Plastic cups

Vinegar

Water in a large bowl or bucket

A small pitcher (1/2 cups)

A spoon

Directions cards with pictures showing
1. Puting on smock
2. Filling cup 12 full with water
3. Adding 6 drops of food color
4. Mixing
5. Adding pasta to water, and removing it to waxed paper with spoon
6. Threading noodles on yarn
7. Hanging necklace up to dry

Plastic smocks

A drying rack or line

How?

Fill water bucket with approximately 16 parts of water to every 1 part of vinegar. Place the bucket at Step 1, with the plastic cups and a small pitcher for scooping water out of the bucket to pour in the cup. The child should fill cup half full. At Step 2, the child adds 6 drops of food color. The child can experiment with mixing drops of different colors instead of using all six drops of a single color. The child mixes until the color is evenly distributed in the water. The child then selects pasta to drop in the water. Children can experiment with how the length of time in the water affects the intensity of the colors. The pasta can be laid on waxed paper until all are dyed. The child then strings the pasta onto the yarn and hangs it up to dry. Plastic smocks are recommended. Cloth smocks can absorb liquid, wetting clothes underneath. This should be avoided, as food coloring can stain clothing.

NECKLACE FACTORY
(Continued)

Making It Your Own:

Many early childhood educators question the use of food stuff in activities in which the product is not eaten, given the number of hungry people in the world. Others feel that food can be used if it ends in a usable product such as a necklace. For teachers that hold the former view, this activity could be modified. Various shapes of manila paper can be substituted for the pasta. Children can punch holes in the paper with a paper punch, then lower the paper into the dye. To keeps hands out of the water, a partially unbent paper clip can be hooked into the hole.

BOOK BINDERY

Why?

⚓☐ To practice following a series of picture directions

⚓ To increase language fluency

⚓ To increase small-muscle development

⚓ To encourage children to "write," using words, letters, or random marks, depending on their level

What Is Needed?

4 tables
4 station signs showing steps in pictorial form:
1. Illustrating the book
2. Writing the book
3. Printing the cover
4. Binding the book by stapling it together.
Crayons and paper at Station 1
Pencils at Station 2
Folded construction paper and markers at Station 3
Staplers at Station 4
Some previous class discussion of how books are made and bound

How?

Set up the dramatic play area as a book bindery. Children illustrate the book at Station 1, write the words at Station 2, decorate the cover and print the title and author's name at Station 3, and staple the book together at Station 4. Children can either take their books through each step or stay at one step, delivering their part of the book to the next station for other workers to complete. It is important to encourage children to write in their own way. Some children will make real words, others arbitrary letters, and others will still be making random marks.

Making It Your Own:

Change the medium used for illustrations, depending on the types of illustrations the class has explored. If children's writing is just beginning, you might want to combine the illustrating and writing station to encourage children to move more freely between drawing and writing. If the class has discussed or visited printing presses, then letter stamps and ink pads can be added to the writing station. (Note: this will decrease the children's own writing at the station.)

Going Beyond:

For an older group, you might want to combine the bindery with a book store or a library. Once books are finished, they can be delivered.
For an older group, you might add steps for numbering pages and making a title page.

PLAN THE PLANTING PROCEDURE

Why?

🏃☐ To practice following multistepped procedures

🏃☐ To begin thinking of activities in terms of a sequence of steps and be able to generate the steps needed for completing a simple task

🏃 To practice "reading" picture directions

🏃 To encourage use of richer and more descriptive language

What Is Needed?

Styrofoam cups
Corn kernels
A bucket of dirt
A bowl of water
Newspaper or trays to cover table
Paper and marker to make signs for each station
Children with previous experience planting
A variety of different sized bowls, scoops, and shovels

How?

Explain to the children at a group time that today you have some corn for them to plant, but you did not have time to write down the directions. Enlist the children's help to decide what must be done to plant the seeds. Get out the things they name as they name them. If they say "dirt," take a bucket of dirt. Follow their directions precisely. If they tell you to put the seed in the dirt, put it into the bucket. Then ask, "But where will you plant your seeds?" If they suggest that you put dirt into a cup, ask what to use to pick up the dirt. Be literal in following directions, to encourage children to state the directions more clearly. If the children say to use a shovel, take out a large shovel. If the children object, then ask why. Ask them to describe a better size. (If the children do not object, put a large shovel in the bucket, and try pouring dirt from it into the cup.) After you have followed all the steps and planted the seed, ask the children to help you make directions so that everyone can remember what to do.

Draw each step that they describe on a separate sheet of paper tacked to the bulletin board. If the steps are not in the correct order, draw them anyway. After the children have listed many steps, you can then go back and rearrange the pictures with the class so that they are in the correct order.

Place the direction sheets and the needed materials along a table in order. Have children follow the directions to plant their seeds.

Making It Your Own:

Use this same process to generate other procedures.

PEANUT BUTTER PLANNING

Why?

♠ ☐ To provide practice in following step-by-step procedures

♠ ☐ To provide practice considering the needed actions and their appropriate sequence for completing a desired task

♠ ☐ To provide practice following picture directions

♠ ☐ To provide practice following numbered steps

♠ To encourage small-muscle development

What Is Needed?

A previous experience making peanut butter
Paper and marker
Peanuts in their shell
Saltines (or other sturdy crackers that will not break easily)
Oil
A blender
Bowls
Paper and marker to make signs for each station
Blunt knives
A tray for completed snack

How?

At a group time, tell the children that the class is going to make peanut butter again and then spread it on crackers for snack. Explain that you need their help planning the activity to ensure that it comes out right. Discuss with the class what you need to have to make peanut butter. As children name the ingredients needed, draw pictures of what they mention on the board. Encourage them to think of what will be needed for the spreading as well as the making.

After the ingredients are listed, ask children to help you make up directions so that everyone will remember what to do first, second, and third. These steps might be planned: shell the peanuts, throw away shells, measure oil into blender, add the peanuts, spread on crackers, and put crackers on tray. If children are having trouble thinking of steps, teachers might ask questions to encourage them to focus on the relevant areas. "What ingredients do we need?" "Do we put the shells and the peanuts in the blender together?" "What do we do with the shells?" These and similar questions can be used if needed.

Set out the cooking project on a long table or counter so that children can walk along doing each step. Have picture directions at each of the steps.

PEANUT BUTTER PLANNING
(Continued)

Making It Your Own:

If you are not a good artist, use premade pictures of needed ingredients ready made to put up on the board so that you do not need to draw them on demand. (Pictures can be cut from magazines or traced from coloring books or cook books.)

Use any simple recipe that the children can generate on their own: making apple sauce, popcorn, or salad, for example.

If children have trouble generating a procedure with the whole class, use this as a small group activity. If the class has more than one teacher, each teacher can take a group. Each group plans their own procedure. If the class has just one teacher, a small group can be planners for the day, and other children can plan another day.

Some teachers prefer this to be a 2-day activity. The class plans one day. The next day, the teacher sets up the activity according to the students' plans. Depending on class schedules and number of teachers, it is sometimes hard to set up in accord with the children's plans after the group time.

Going Beyond:

When children are good at generating the procedure, let them generate one without as much assistance. If the procedure has some errors in it, let the children discover the errors by doing the activity. Help children to modify the procedure so it will work.

FOLLOWING PICTURE DIRECTIONS

Skills Needed for Understanding and Following Picture Directions

In four of the six skills already discussed, rebus picture directions were recommended as ways to modify the skill to better fit the child's level. Picture symbols or directions were suggested to help with remembering the steps for turning the computer on and off, for finding the desired program, for understanding menus, and for remembering a variety of procedures. Pictorial directions and symbols are easier to understand than written words. But learning to understand symbols is a skill as well. The child must realize that the pictures are meant to communicate something. They must understand what the picture represents and what that representation is meant to convey. A picture of the **[Return]** key must be recognized for what it is, and the child must know that this drawing means they are to press the **[Return]** key. Children learn at quite a young age to interpret symbols in their environment. As parents drive by a sign for McDonald's on the expressway, even young children often recognize the familiar logo.

If the pictures are used to show a series of steps, the child must realize that the pictures must be interpreted in a set order, from left to right and top to bottom. Teachers may need to help children learn to interpret rebus pictures in order for these guides to provide the expected assistance. If children understand that the pictures are intended to communicate something, they still may need help understanding the meaning that specific pictures are intended to convey. Often, after a child has been helped once to decipher a set of pictures, those same pictures will be comprehensible when the child later encounters them alone.

Children will sometimes need to decipher symbols within a program. **Color Me** uses pictorial symbols in its menu. Often, children will need to recognize and respond to symbols on teacher-made aids. Whether the symbols are an integral part of the program or on an external aid, the ability to recognize and respond to them is still necessary for independent computer use.

Developing Skills for Understanding and Following Picture Directions

Provide Children with Ways To Think about Picture Directions. When children are having trouble, teachers can refer them to picture guides. For example, if a child is having trouble remembering how the face can move in **Facemaker**, the teacher could suggest that the child look at the pictures on the disk cover. What are these faces doing? The teacher should encourage the child to look at the pictures for information and try to decide what is being communicated.

Modify Materials To Fit Children's Skill Level in Deciphering Pictorial Symbols. It is important to keep evaluating and revising the teacher-made rebus cards. If children seem to have trouble with a particular program or procedure, is there a way that you could make it visually clearer to the child? When I first used **Facemaker** in the classroom, the rebus guide showed each of the ways for moving the face with the appropriate letter to make it move. I found that my children had a great deal of trouble remembering to press "1" for the making part of the program, then "2" for the moving part.

I revised the rebus card, adding a large "1" with a blank face after it. Next to the face are some features that can be selected. This part of the rebus card depicts the "making part" of the program. Under that are some heavy lines running across the card to indicate a separate part of the program. Under the line is a large "2" with the guides for moving the face. Rebus cards should be adjusted to fit the needs of each individual class and teacher.

Provide Opportunities To Use Pictorial Symbols. Many of the activities already described provide opportunities to practice deciphering picture symbols. Many noncomputer activities in the classroom also offer these opportunities. The ability to

old

new

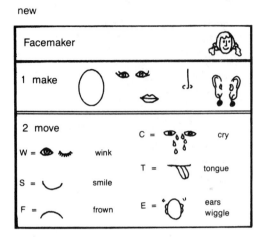

read picture directions will help nonreaders in a variety of situations. Teachers can develop innumerable activities to reinforce this skill. Teachers can design such activities to complement current themes in the classroom. These activities involve simple picture "reading," such as **Pets On Parade** (p. 119), in which the child needs only to respond to a single picture, or **Use Your Body and Make Some Music** (p. 120), in which the child must respond to multiple pictures and do so in the correct sequence.

ACTIVITIES TO DEVELOP PICTURE-READING SKILLS

PETS ON PARADE

Why?

🚶☐ To practice deciphering picture symbols

☐ To encourage small-muscle development

What Is Needed?

Pictures of pets with which the children are familiar: rabbit, fish, gerbil, cat, dog, frog.
A transition time

How?

At the end of a group or story time excuse children by holding up the picture of a pet and calling a child's name. That child must move to the next activity as the pictured pet would move.

Making It Your Own:

Instead of pets use pictures of farm animals, zoo animals, kinds of transportation, or other animals or objects that fit the interests of your class. (Note you must be careful to use pictures of things with whose movements children are familiar.)
If the children can recognize their names, the teacher can hold up a name card and an animal card. The child whose name is displayed can leave in the way that the animal on the card moves.

Going Beyond

If the children can easily follow single picture directions, the child may be shown two cards, one that shows an animal and another that shows a dot near the sky or a dot near the ground. The child will need to move like the pictured animal at a high or low level as indicated by the dot card. Instead of height, the second card can indicate speed, forward or backward, or other conditions for how to move.
Instead of using this as a transition between activities, the children can do it during group time or activity time. The child will pick two cards, one that says how to move and another that is a picture of where to move.

USE YOUR BODY AND MAKE SOME MUSIC

Why?

- To provide an opportunity to read picture symbols
- To practice reading pictures sequentially
- To increase body awareness
- To encourage creativity

What Is Needed?

20 cards with body pictures on them—4 each of the following parts: arms, legs, feet, hands, and mouth.
Blank cards
A marker
A bulletin board and thumbtacks

How?

Have the children clap their hands to make music to accompany the following song. Sing to the tune of "Mary Had a Little Lamb."

Clap your hands, and make some music,
Make some music, make some music.
Clap your hands, and make some music.
Let's make some music.

Try the song again, clapping loudly, softly, and then in other ways that the children suggest. Ask the children, "What other parts of the body can make music?" If feet are suggested, sing

Use your feet, and make some music . . .

Encourage children to use their feet in their own unique ways. The teacher can then suggest that children try ways that other children have discovered. Continue exploring other parts of the body. Suggest that the children compose a song using the different body parts as instruments. "Which part should we start with?" Pin on the bulletin board a picture of the named part. If you do not have a premade picture, draw one. "Which part of our body should we 'play' next?" Continue putting up parts until there are about 8 pictures. (Be sure to make clear that it is all right to play a body part instrument more than once.)

As you sing the song again, point to the pictures in order. The children should use the body parts to make music as you point to them. Sing as you make body music: "Use your body, and make some music."

Making It Your Own:

If this activity is too long for your group to manage in one sitting, begin by using single body parts. After the children have spent a couple of days exploring the parts they can move, then the sequence of movements can be added.

Instead of changing the body parts, make up symbols for different ways to move one body part—clapping, shaking, rubbing, etc. Use picture cards to make up a dance, "Shake your hands, and make a dance."

OLD McDONALD HAD A FARM

Why?

♀☐ To practice using pictorial clues

♀ To use knowledge of animal sounds

What Is Needed?

Pictures of farm animals
A bulletin board and thumbtacks

How?

Sing "Old McDonald Had a Farm" with the children. Pin up a picture of the first animal referred to in the song at the bottom of the board. Hang up a picture of the second animal selected above the first animal—for example, the cow might be sung first and placed on the bottom, the pig is chosen next and placed above the cow. When the children get to the end of the pig line, they will repeat the cow verse.

Old McDonald had a farm, E I E I O.
And on his farm he had a pig,
E I E I O.

With an oink, oink here, and an oink, oink there.
Here an oink, there an oink, everywhere an oink, oink.
With a moo, moo here, and a moo, moo, there.
Here a moo, there a moo,
everywhere a moo, moo.
Old McDonald had a farm, E I E I O.

Continue singing the song. Add each new animal on top of the others. At the end of each new verse, sing down through all the other animal sounds in order. The teacher can point to the animals to help the children remember which comes next.

Making It Your Own:

McDonald can have a pet shop, zoo, band, highway, or other collection of sounds to fit your classroom. My children like Old McDonald to have a school with a Kathy, Kathy, here, and a Mark, Mark there. Photographs of the children can be used, or name cards can be used if the children recognize each other's names.

Old McDonald can have a gym with a sit-up here, and a sit-up there, and a jump, jump here, and a jump, jump there. Other exercises can be added—toe touches, stretches, jumping jacks, or whatever your children can do.

PICTURE TREASURE HUNT

Why?

⚕ ☐ To practice "reading" picture symbols

⚕ To exercise large muscles

What Is Needed?

An outside time
Laminated pictures of 6–10 distinct objects in the play
    yard with holes punched in them
String for attaching pictures around playground
Stickers
A laminated card with holes punched in it, showing a
    picture of a teacher
A START sign

How?

The teacher will place the START sign in a prominent
    place on the play yard. Under the START sign will
    be one of the picture signs. The second picture sign
    will be placed on the object depicted in the first
    picture. Therefore, if the picture under START is of
    the swing set, the second picture will be attached to
    the swing set. The third picture will be placed on the
    object depicted on the sign by the swing set, and so
    on. The last picture should be of the teacher.
The children begin the treasure hunt at START. They
go to the object shown on the first picture, where
they see another picture and go to what it shows.
They go from picture to picture until they come to
the teacher, who gives them a sticker. (Note: this is
not intended as a race. Children will start at different
times and end at different times. Some will want to
run, others to walk. Teachers should not encourage
racing by praising faster children.)
Children can do the course as many times as they
    want, collecting a new sticker each time. Encourage
    veteran treasure hunters to help beginners to follow
    the course.

Making It Your Own:

Make similar pictures for a treasure hunt around the
    classroom or around the school.

Going Beyond:

Once children are familiar with the treasure hunt
    pictures, let them plan their own course. The
    children can arrange the pictures in the order that
    they are to be found, with the first stop on the top of
    the pile, and the teacher's picture on the bottom.
    The children will hang the first picture under START,
    the second picture at the spot indicated by the first
    picture, and so on until all the pictures are
    displayed.

SUMMARY

This chapter has discussed three important skills to be developed concurrent with computer use:

1. Using menus
2. Following and beginning to design multistepped procedures
3. Understanding pictures and following cues.
   Suggestions are given for ways that teachers can support children developing each of these skills. Many possible activities are suggested.

Teachers should adapt these activities to fit their needs and the needs of the children in their classroom. Using the discussion of skills presented and the sample activities as models, teachers can design their own activities to meet the unique needs of their children.

7

What Can Children Learn About Computers?

We have established that there are many potential benefits of using computers with young children. Now we need to ask whether children should learn "about" the computer as well as use it. Are there concepts about the computer that are within their grasp? If so, is it valuable to explore these concepts? Is "the computer" an appropriate subject for study in the preschool, kindergarten, or early elementary classroom? Does the computer belong with more usual topics of study such as the farm, community helpers, families, and transportation? Will learning about computers enhance the children's use of computers? Is learning "about" computers necessary in order for children to benefit from using them? This chapter addresses these questions.

SHOULD CHILDREN LEARN ABOUT COMPUTERS?

Children's most important method of learning about the world is to explore, manipulate, and build concepts about the objects in their environment (Almy, 1967; NAEYC [Bredekamp, Ed.], 1986). Children are constantly creating concepts and theories about the things in their environment (Kamii & DeVries, 1978; Forman & Kuschner, 1983; Piaget, 1964). If children use computers, they are bound to create theories and concepts about computers. Clements (1985b) gives some interesting examples of young children's comments about computers.

> "What happens when you load a program?"
> "Well, what happens . . . this is the mouth [pointing to the tape cassette] and the computer eats the program off the tape. Then it goes through here [pointing to the cassette cable] like a straw, to the computer's stomach. Here's its face. [the TV monitor] like a big eye, and you can look in and see what's in the stomach. . . . Then when you say run, the computer's got the energy to run

Children are fascinated by the inside of the computer.

'cause it ate the program. If you don't load the program, it can't run 'cause there's no energy to . . . . You know what else computers eat? Potato chips. I hear there's lots of chips in these things."
Tony, age 8 (Clements, p. 49)

Tony has taken what he knows about the way people work and used this information to understand the workings of a computer. Tony's conclusions provide a framework within which he can understand the computer, even though it is certainly not an accurate interpretation of what a computer is or how it works. As Clements's example demonstrates, children who are aware of computers are bound to have impressions about computers. Hyson and Morris (1985) found that 4-year-olds with no computer experience still had ideas about computers. These ideas became more accurate and more detailed after the children had used computers in their classroom. So, in answer to the question, "Should children learn 'about' computers?" one must reply that it is impossible to stop them from developing concepts about computers if computers are an active part of their environment. Children will be learning about computers whether we teach them or not. We must ask, "What can children learn about computers? What is *necessary* for children to learn about computers in order to use them? And *when* and *how* should they learn it?"

MUST CHILDREN KNOW ABOUT COMPUTERS IN ORDER TO USE THEM?

We have established that with or without formal instruction, children who are using computers *will* learn about computers. How important is it that they learn "correct" concepts about the computer? Will this knowledge help children to use computers more effectively?

One could argue that because the computer is a complex electronic device, it is important for people who use it to have some understanding of it. But is

this necessarily so? Many people drive cars yet few have an understanding of how the engine works. We are surrounded by complex technology— telephones, VCRs, automobiles, elevators, to name a few. Most people who use them understand little about how they work. To use these machines, like using the computer, you do need some knowledge.

For example, using a car requires knowedge of how to turn on the engine, how to steer, how to change gears, and which peddle to use to stop or go. The driver needs an *operational knowledge* of the car: an understanding of which actions from the driver elicit the desired reactions from the car. In the same way, it is possible to use the computer by gaining an operational knowledge of the computer (how to turn it on, locate the disk, learn the appropriate commands for the program being used) without having any understanding of how it functions, which we will call *functional knowledge*.

Does Functional Knowledge of an Object Enhance Its Use?

But this still leaves a question unanswered. Although knowledge of the computer may not be necessary for children to use it, will that knowledge enhance their use of computers? For the answer, we return to the car analogy. It is true that it is possible to drive a car with only an operational knowledge of the car, but at times, some functional knowledge would be helpful. For example, I always have trouble remembering the best way to start the car in the winter. Should I pump the gas first? Should I hold the pedal down? Do I gun the engine after it starts, let it just kick in on its own, or slowly increase the gas? I have been told the rules for this many times, yet I never remember. So, I use a trial-and-error method to arrive at the best solution. If I understood how a car engine starts and how cold affects this process, then the best method for starting a car on a cold day would be obvious to me.

There are three ways to approach the problem of how to start a car on a cold day:

1. Memorize the procedure
2. Discover the procedure each time through experimentation
3. Have enough functional knowledge of cars so that the correct procedure is obvious.

Knowledge about the car is a viable but not a necessary approach.

Does Functional Knowledge of Computers Enhance Computer Use?

We look now at children using computers to see whether any functional knowledge about computers either is necessary or would expedite computer operation. Regan (4 years old) has been playing with **Magic Crayon** for the last week. She now can use the program independently to draw. The printer has just been added to the classroom. The children make their picture on one of the "drawing" computers, save the picture onto the disk, then take it to the "printing" computer, reload, and call up their picture. Regan makes her picture, turns off her computer without saving the picture, then boots her disk into the "printing" computer. When the teacher tries to call up Regan's picture, there is no picture saved on the disk. The teacher explains to Regan that the computer will not save a picture unless someone tells it to. Regan goes back to the drawing computer to make another picture. The teacher suggests that Regan call a teacher when the picture is completed so that the teacher can help her tell the computer to save the picture.

Over the next 2 weeks, Regan makes and loses many pictures because she continually forgets to save her picture. How can she ensure that her pictures are saved? Will knowing how the computer works ensure that she will remember and be able to save those pictures? As with the aforementioned car analogy, she could:

1. Memorize the procedure for saving
2. Experiment to discover the procedure

3. Learn more about computers so that she will understand that they cannot do anything without a command.

There are two additional approaches to Regan's problem:

4. She could ask a teacher or peer to help her
5. The teacher could make a picture reminder of the steps needed to save a picture.

Acquiring Functional Knowledge Is One of Many Ways To Solve Computer Problems

Will learning "about" the computer be more effective or efficient than the other approaches to Regan's problem? Can it help to support or supplement other approaches? Let us look at each of the five approaches individually.

1. **Memorize the procedure.** Regan could memorize the procedure for saving pictures on **Magic Crayon**. This may not work because so far, her excitement about completing the picture and eagerness to print it have made her consistently forget that she needs to save the picture first.
2. **Experiment to discover the procedure.** Trial and error might help her to remember that she must save the picture, but due to the complexity of the saving process (press "R" for remember, type a picture name, press **[Return]**, press the **[Esc]** key, press "Y," then wait for the red light on the disk drive to go out), trial and error would not help her to discover the steps needed for the procedure.
3. **Have some functional knowledge about computers.** If Regan's understanding of the computer included the knowledge that computers cannot do anything without being given a command, it would be obvious to her that she must tell the computer to save the picture before she turns the computer off. If Regan understood that disks store information and that the red light on the disk drive indicates the picture is being re-

corded, then she would be more likely to wait until the red light goes off before she unloads the disk.

4. **Receive assistance.** A teacher or friend could sit with Regan and help her to save the picture. This would ensure that Regan could print that picture, yet it would not enable her to save another picture unless she again had assistance. Repeated saving with assistance might help her to learn the procedure. On the other hand, unless Regan pays attention to the process she is being guided through, she may be unable to repeat the process on her own.

5. **Follow picture directions.** Picture directions will not help Regan to remember that saving is necessary. But they may be able to help her do the saving independently once she realizes the need to save. The picture directions generally are not clear unless the child uses them with a peer or an adult a few times. So if the adult assistance given is in the form of instruction on how to use the rebus guide, Regan may eventually be able to use the guide in order to save independently.

Functional Knowledge Combines with Other Techniques for Solving Computer Problems

As can be seen from the preceding discussion, each of these five approaches help in some ways. Regan must do some experimenting in order to discover the need to save. But some functional knowledge of computers may help to speed this discovery along. Regan can learn to save without understanding about the computer, but an understanding could help her deal with it more efficiently and effectively. Knowledge that computers need commands and that the red light indicates that the disk is recording might also be transferable to other situations. With this knowledge, Regan may find it easier to learn how to save with **Bank Street Writer** or on other drawing programs. She may notice the disk drive's

red light on when the disk is loading or *"booting"* and be able to generate a broader definition for the red light.

Meaning?   BOOTING

Booting a computer occurs when the instructions from the disk are being copied into the computer's memory. The red light on the disk drive indicates that the computer is booting. The disk should not be removed while its instructions are being read or written by the disk drive. When a computer is first turned on, it is being booted.

Children usually learn through a combination of these alternatives. They experiment to see what the materials will do, draw conclusions based on this experimentation, and often use information from teachers and peers to help integrate what they have discovered into a more cohesive concept (Copple, Sigel, & Saunders, 1979).

USING THE COMPUTER TEACHES CHILDREN ABOUT THE COMPUTER

While in some cases, knowledge may help children to use computers, it is also important to note that the reverse can also be true—use may help children to acquire computer knowledge. Memorizing the procedure, experimenting, and receiving assistance may all provide Regan with the foundations for building concepts "about" the computer. After having the computer repeatedly lose her picture when no "save" command is given, yet remember it when so commanded, Regan may began to see the computer as a machine that can only do something if commanded by people.

Computer Experience Helps Children To Construct Functional Knowledge

Sometimes, functional knowledge of the computer is gained while solving operational problems. As an illustration, let us look at Russell and Sam (both 4 years old) as they each deal with a computer-related problem. Dealing with the operational problem, they gain functional knowledge about the computer.

Russell made a picture using **Magic Crayon**. He saved the picture at clean-up time. The next day, he took the **Magic Crayon** disk to the Apple computer on which he drew his picture the previous day. Someone was using that computer. He would not use the other unused Apple because he wanted to waited until "his" computer was free. I suggested he take his disk to one of the other computers, but he said, "This is the one with my picture in it." I explained that the picture was saved onto the disk, not in the computer, but he did not believe me.

Russell believed that his picture was inside the computer, so he had to wait until that computer was free to get it out. He ignored my explanation because it was too much at odds with his own concept of the computer. He finally revised his concept when we introduced the printer with a separate computer. To print his picture he had to load his disk into the "printing" computer. His picture appeared. This experience, along with a discussion of how he was taking his picture on the disk from one computer to another, helped him to revise his understanding of the computer. He then was willing to use any computer to finish pictures he had saved onto disk.

Sam, a novice computer user, was watching the "art show" on **Delta Draw**. The art show places a variety of previously drawn pictures on the screen.

Sam: I don't want to draw any more. I want to see the boat!
Teacher: We have to tell the computer.
Sam: (Putting one hand on either side of the monitor and staring into the monitor earnestly) Make a boat!

Sam does not yet know enough about computers to know that most will not respond to voice requests. If he understood this concept, he would not have addressed the monitor so earnestly and politely. He will learn that it does not follow voice commands from its lack of response to his request, coupled with its responsiveness to pressing certain keys recommended by his teacher.

Sam would be able to control the computer more effectively if he knew more about it. But he can only gain that knowledge through manipulation and experimentation, perhaps coupled with informal instruction from the teacher.

In the case of both Russell and Sam, some knowledge about the computer would help them deal with the problem, but it is only through dealing with the problem that the children are able to develop the background needed to comprehend that knowledge.

Developmental Level Can Affect Ability To Acquire Some Functional Knowledge

In the preceding cases, it was the child's lack of experience with the computer that made the computer information difficult to comprehend. With more experience, Russell and Sam were able both to solve the problem and to grasp the information. In other cases, the child's developmental level renders the computer information that could be helpful too difficult to comprehend.

Take the case of Timmy (5 years old). He is using **Astro-Grover**, which presents the children with a variety of arithmetic tasks. The program asks him to add 4 and 5. Timmy presses "8." The moon frowns, indicating a wrong answer. He continues pressing the "8," becoming progressively more frustrated. "I keep doing the right thing but the moon keeps shaking its head."

Timmy is still in the preoperational stage. He is not capable of the following logical deduction: "Computers are programmed to always respond correctly to arithmetic problems; therefore, if the moon shakes its head, I must be making an error." Even if Timmy were to agree with the first part of the statement, about the infallibility of computers at this type of computation, his feeling that he is "right" would lead him to believe that the computer must be wrong. For Timmy, more knowledge would not help him with his dilemma. If he were to try another key, he might, by chance, hit the "9" and his problem would be solved, though I doubt that this would shake his faith in his first answer.

The Importance of Functional Knowledge Depends on the Situational Context

We return to our original question: "Is functional knowledge of the computer necessary for, or will it help to expedite computer use?" In answer to the first part of this question, functional knowledge of the computer is not necessary to use the computer; for use children need only have some operational knowledge. Whether functional knowledge will expedite computer use must be answered in a situational context. The situation will determine which one of the four following answers is appropriate:

1. The necessary functional knowledge is too complex for the young child's developmental level.
2. The functional knowledge can be comprehended once the child has had many chances to explore the computer.
3. Children will develop functional knowledge while solving the problem at hand.
4. Functional knowledge will expedite use as the child applies knowledge previously gained to help solve a new problem. Functional knowledge can help expedite computer use in certain cases by giving the child the ability to approach new problems independently.

WHEN SHOULD CHILDREN LEARN ABOUT COMPUTERS?

From the earlier discussion, it is clear that children will begin learning about computers the mo-

ment they begin to interact with the computers. Through exploration, manipulation, and experimentation, children learn what a computer is like and what will happen when the computer is used in various ways. In exploring the machines, the children construct physical knowledge about the appearance of the computer and operational knowledge about the steps to follow when using the computer, and they begin using these to build functional knowledge about the computer. Some of the concepts they construct about the computers will be correct; others will be faulty. At what point should teachers begin teaching children about computers to support this independent learning and to guide children toward constructing more accurate concepts? Should the teaching be formal, informal, or some combination of the two?

Experience with Computers Is a Prerequisite for Learning about the Computer

Knowledge of child development tells us that children of this age learn best through experimenting and manipulating objects, and then putting what they have discovered into the context of previous learning (Piaget, 1964). They do not learn as well from being told or given information by adults. They must discover and create the information on their own. Once they have some experience with the objects, then outside information can be integrated into the framework of understanding they have created. Previous concepts can be adjusted and revised to accommodate new information and ideas (Copple, Sigel, & Saunders, 1979). Children must have some experience with real computers in order for a discussion of computers to be meaningful. They must know through use and manipulation what a keyboard, monitor, disk, and disk drive are in order to gain meaning or value from a class discussion.

Once children have explored a computer, then the teacher's explanation of a keyboard brings to mind a picture of a computer keyboard and the things that they have done with it. For example, when the teacher discusses that the computer will not start without the disk, because the disk tells it what to do, Melissa can remember her annoyance when the computer would not start when she pressed the keys without turning it on or loading the disk. Or when the teacher talks about the parts of the computer that work together, Micah may remember how the teacher jiggled the wires on the back of the monitor when the picture went off because the wires were not connected well. The class discussion can help children to reorganize their information about the computer into a more logical usable framework of knowledge.

Because children need concrete experience with objects first, before they are provided with more-formal learning, the children should have the opportunities to explore and get to know what computers look like and what they can make the computer do before they are given formal instruction such as a unit on computers, group discussion about computers, or activities that help teach concepts about the computer.

During this exploration period, children discover many things on their own. They also receive a good deal of informal instruction from teachers. The teacher uses the correct terminology, teaches children how to load and use the computer, and discusses what the computer is doing, whenever appropriate.

Informal Instruction Can Be Offered along with Computer Use

A couple of examples illustrate this type of informal instruction. Russell (4 years old) is using **Facemaker**. He has constructed the face and is giving it commands to move. This is the second or third time he has used the program. He presses the "W" key and smiles as the face on the monitor winks at him. He continues pressing the "W," looking more and more annoyed. Finally he says, "I want it to wink with the other eye." The teacher explains, "The person who wrote the **Facemaker** program only programmed it [taught it] to wink with that one eye. When you press 'W' it can only do one thing. It's not as smart as you. You can wink with either eye, can't

you? If we knew how to write programs, we could teach it to wink with the other eye just like you."

Russell asks what else it can do. The teacher points out the direction sheet with the letters that move the face and pictorial representations of the actions. Russell makes his **Facemaker** face stick out its tongue and frown.

Russell: Now I want it to sneeze.
Teacher: That is not one of the commands it knows. The programmer did not teach the face how to sneeze.
Russell: Yeah! It's not as smart as me!

Binta is using the computer for the first time. The teacher asks, "What program do you want to use? Do you want to make a face that can move, or draw your own special picture?" Binta chooses the face. The teacher explains, "Then you need to take the **Facemaker** disk—the one with the pictures of faces on it. This is the disk that tells the computer that you want to make a face."

Micah is using the computer and suddenly the screen goes blank. Micah calls for a teacher to help. The teacher looks behind the computer and discovers that the cable from the keyboard to the monitor has become disconnected. She encourages Micah and the other children nearby to look with her at the back to find the loose wire. "This wire takes the picture from the keyboard to the monitor. It has come loose. What should we do so that it can make the picture come to the monitor again?" The teacher reconnects the cable as the children suggest. "Now that the cable is reconnected, your commands can get from the keyboard to the monitor."

In these three examples, the teachers modeled use of appropriate vocabulary, helped children with operational questions, and presented functional knowledge as they helped children to look at what was happening. This type of informal learning in response to children's questions and needs goes on constantly as it does in all areas of the classroom.

The Place of More-Formal Teaching about Computers

A formal unit on computers or a formal class discussion of computers should wait until all the children have had a chance to get to know the computer, and therefore are able to use the information provided. Class study of families always begins with the children's experience of their own families. A unit on the farm has much more meaning after children have been to a farm. In the same way, children need to get acquainted with the computer in order to have some background with which to build concepts.

Children who want it should have ample time to explore the computer. After initial use, children will go beyond to what Beaty and Tucker (1987) call the "meaning stage." This is when the children feel free to experiment with the program. If children are using **Juggle's Rainbow**, and the program asks them to press "above" or "below," they may intentionally press the wrong key just to see what happens. They may try pressing two keys at once to see which will respond first. These children are now comfortable with the software. They know what it is supposed to do and want to explore beyond that. Children should feel comfortable using the computer prior to any instruction about the computer.

The minimum length of time between the introduction of computers for use in the classroom and the formal discussion of computers varies, depending on the number of computers available and the amount of time the children have on the computers. For a guideline, I would say children should have used the computer three or four times for up to 20 minutes at a minimum, and they should be able to use at least one piece of software independently.

For each teacher, the time to begin some formal instruction will vary, as will the way in which this formal instruction proceeds. Some teachers will offer a unit on computers. Others will select a few concepts to look at now and then, as the children's needs dictate. Each teacher must determine which concepts are appropriate for the class at which time.

INPUT FOR TEACHERS:

DEFINING "FORMAL" TEACHING

When I describe "more-formal" teaching, I do not mean to imply that children should all sit in rows, hear lectures, and be held accountable for what they hear. Rather, it refers to the more planned part of the curriculum. Children are constantly learning through chance occurrences. A child finds that some things float in the water table. That child may experiment to discover which objects will float and which will not. Sometimes, the learning is totally spontaneous; at other times, the teacher adds things to the environment that may spark the children's interest and encourage them to investigate. The wise teacher will expand on these chance occurrences with informal teaching using questions, encouragement, and discussion.

Teachers also plan more formally for learning to occur. They plan group time discussion, stories, games, or demonstrations that introduce new ideas to the class or help children to tie together old information. Teachers may prepare a series of activities around a set subject or topic. "More-formal" teaching refers to these kinds of planned activities.

Strong early childhood classrooms will have an intertwining of all three types of learning— incidental learnings from discoveries with carefully set out teacher materials and from more planned group and free play activities. Teachers often plan the more-formal learning around topics and skills that emerge from spontaneous events. Children often continue to explore teacher-planned topics or skills on their own, creating spontaneous learning that supports the more planned events.

WHAT CAN CHILDREN LEARN ABOUT COMPUTERS?

If young children develop concepts about the computer in the process of using computers, educators must determine which concepts children can learn and understand.

Computers Have Many Interconnected Parts

The most obvious place to start is with what the child can see. In looking at the computer, children can discover what parts the computer has, as well as how the parts are connected. Adults can provide the correct words for the parts that the children are observing. Through observing the computer, children can began to build a basic definition of a computer.

Computers Cannot Work without People

When using the computer, children can discover that it cannot do anything by itself. People must turn on the computer, load a disk into the disk drive, and press some keys (or move the mouse, joystick, or touch pad) in order for the computer to respond. Children also discover that computers must be told what to do in certain ways. The way you tell a computer what you want it to do is different for different programs. In **Magic Crayon**, pressing the arrow keys moves the cursor, whereas the spacebar moves the cursor in **Facemaker**, and the mouse (koala pad or joystick) moves it in **Color Me.**

Computers Have Strengths and Weaknesses

As children explore a variety of software and hardware, they begin to see the many different things computers can do, as well as the many limitations of computers. No matter how much children try, they cannot make the face on **Facemaker** sneeze, print a message they have made on **Many Ways to Say I Love You**, or get the Commodore to load more quickly. The software can only do what it is programmed to do. Every piece of software and hardware has certain limitations. Children, through use, discover many things they would like the computer to do that it cannot do.

McDonald's has a computerized cash register.

Computers Have Many Uses

Field trips around the school or community can acquaint the children with the many different uses for computers. Opportunities to see such things as the word processor in the office, the microwave in the kitchen, the computerized cash register at McDonald's or the grocery store, and the "checking-out" computer at the library can help children to expand their understanding of what computers can do.

Computer Hardware and Software Are Made and Repaired by People

When a computer is not working properly, the children can observe the teacher checking to see that the cables are secure, that all the components are turned on, and that the disk is loaded correctly. If the computer still is not working, another teacher or a technician may come to examine the machine. A *programmer* can come to visit the class, bringing a simple program that has been created for the children's use. Amateur programmers can create programs that support dramatic play, such as a program to record books checked out of the classroom library or to simulate a McDonald's cash register. Through such experiences and discussion, children can see that software is made by people, and that the machines are repaired and cared for by people.

Meaning? PROGRAMMER

A **programmer** is a person who can write programs—a set of instructions for the computer.

Computers Process Information

Teachers can help children expand their definition of computers beyond the foregoing physical description to include a basic procedural understanding. Children can see that giving the computer a command elicits a response from the computer. Discussion and other activities can help children to build this into a framework for understanding what happens when they use a computer.

1. They put information into the computer through keys, joystick, touch pad (input).
2. The information is processed by the central processing unit of the computer (CPU).
3. Then the computer creates a display on the screen, prints on the printer, or moves the turtle (output).

Selecting the Appropriate Topics for Your Class

It is clear that there are many concepts about computers that are well within the reach of the preliterate child. These concepts can be organized in many different fashions. The method of organization and the key phrases selected to define each con-

cept have an impact on the way in which the study of computers will proceed. Therefore, each teacher must redefine the following concepts to fit the particular needs of her/his class of children. The following is one of many possible ways to divide and define the topics.

1. Computers are machines made up of parts that work together.
2. Computers cannot do anything unless people give them a command.
3. Computers can remember a whole series of commands called a "program".
4. Computers can do many things.
5. Computers have enormous potential as well as limitations.
6. People enter information or commands into the computer (input), the central processing unit (CPU) processes the information, then it produces images on the monitor screen, prints on the printer, or moves a robot (output).
7. Computers and computer software are made and controlled by people.

It is important to remember that this is neither the only or the best way to organize the learning for your students. Once teachers have selected the topics for their classes and the appropriate timing for presenting these topics, it is important to look at each concept more closely. Each of the preceding concepts should be expanded to indicate the scope of appropriate information.

SUMMARY

Children learn about computers as they use them. They will develop "operational knowledge" about how to operate the computer through actually operating it. In using the computer, children will also be constructing concepts about the computer, or "functional knowledge" of the computer. Some of the concepts that children construct about computers will be accurate; others will not be. Teachers can guide children to more accurate understanding of computers through a combination of spontaneous discussions and more planned activities. Teachers should decide both which concepts to stress and the method for teaching them in accordance with the needs of each class.

In the next two chapters, each concept is explored in greater depth. What exactly can children learn about each concept? What activities help support this learning? Each concept is discussed, and a number of formal and informal activities are presented for introducing and reinforcing this learning in the classroom. Chapter 8 explores the first three concepts.

1. Computers are made up of parts that work together.
2. Computers cannot do anything unless people give them a command.
3. Computers can remember a whole series of commands called a "program".

Chapter 9 explores the remaining four concepts.

4. Computers can do many things.
5. Computers have enormous potential as well as many limitations.
6. Input is entered into the computer is processed by the CPU, which then creates output.
7. Computer hardware and software are made and controlled by people.

8

Helping Children To Learn About Computers

This chapter looks at three concepts that are appropriate for young children to learn about computers: (1) computers are machines made up of parts that work together, (2) computers cannot do anything unless people give them a command, and (3) computers can remember a whole series of commands called a "program." Each concept is discussed, then informal ways for helping children to acquire these concepts are presented, along with activities for free play and group times.

COMPUTERS ARE MADE UP OF PARTS THAT WORK TOGETHER

Although microcomputers are housed in a variety of styles, most have certain basic parts, such as the keyboard, disk drive, and monitor. The specific details vary slightly, depending on the type of computer that the children are using. For the sake of simplicity, this chapter examines only one type of computer—the Apple IIe. You should adapt the discussion to fit the type of computer you use.

Taking a Look at a Computer

There are many things about the Apple computer that children can learn from observation and experience. This computer has three major parts: a keyboard, a disk drive, and a monitor. These parts are connected to each other. The disk drive is connected to the keyboard with a flat grey cable. The monitor is connected to the keyboard with a round cable that easily connects and disconnects. The keyboard and monitor have power cords that plug into the wall, bringing electricity to the computer.

The children can also look more carefully at each part of the computer. The disk drive has both a special place into which the disk can go and a door that

After "programming" an obstacle course, children "run the program."

must be closed after the disk is loaded. The disk drive has a red light that goes on when the computer is searching for, or recording, information onto the disk. Both the monitor and the keyboard have switches to turn them on. The disk drive's light goes on when the keyboard is turned on. The keyboard has many different types of keys. The disk must be loaded into the disk drive in order for the computer to work. Different disks tell the computer different things. If you wish to draw with **Color Me**, you must select the correct disk, and it must be loaded into a machine that has the peripheral being used to run the program.

Children also find it interesting to look at the parts inside the computer. They can see the large green **motherboard** and the card that attaches the disk drive to the motherboard. Children can also see the cards that attach peripherals such as the mouse, joystick, robot, or **voice box** to the motherboard.

Meaning? MOTHERBOARD AND VOICE BOX

The **motherboard** is the main electronic circuit board of the computer. Cards are plugged into this to interface with the computer if the computer is expandable.

A **voice box** is a peripheral added to some computers to provide the capacity to talk. (Other computers have a built-in voice capacity.)

Building Concepts about What They See

Teachers can help children go beyond merely observing to building concepts of how the parts of the machine work together. The disk drive reads the information on the disk and sends it to the motherboard through the connecting cable. The motherboard processes the information and sends the appropriate picture to the monitor through the round cable that connects the keyboard to the monitor. In order for the computer to work, it must be plugged in, the parts must be turned on, and the cables must all be connected. To use a computer, you need all of the parts, and they all must be connected to each other. If peripherals are used, the children can learn that these too must be connected to the computer in order to work.

Learning Computer Vocabulary

While children explore the parts of the computer and how they are connected, they also begin to learn the correct vocabulary for computer parts and processes. Children enjoy mastering the grown-up sounding "computer words." Parents enjoy the precocious sound of their children prattling on about disk drives, CPU, input, and executing commands.

Some books suggest using "cutesy" names for various computer parts. Beaty and Tucker (1987) suggest calling the disk drive a "disk garage." I take exception to this. It reminds me of the adults who refer to a penis as a "wee wee." Most experts (Levine, 1966) recommend that children learn the correct terms for anatomical parts. Levine offers the following advice about sex education. "Use correct terms—an avoidance of proper terminology sooner or later suggests to the child that this is a subject of some mysterious significance." (Levine, 1966, p. 177). Thus, it may be that avoidance of proper computer terminology makes computers more mysterious than they need be. Use of the correct terms also negates the need to relearn terms later and makes it easier for children to communicate with adults and peers from other classrooms about the computer.

This is not to say that children should be asked to pass a test on the correct terms, but rather that the teacher should use the correct terms, so that when children learn to label computer parts, they too will use the correct terms. Many terms can be taught informally when children hear the teacher use the correct vocabulary. Other terms can be introduced or reinforced at group time or during free-play activities. There are many terms that preliterate children can learn to use correctly.

COMPUTER TERMS CHILDREN CAN LEARN

Following are some computer terms that can be used with young children, along with simple definitions of the terms. Do not feel that ALL of these terms must be used. It is not a list of terms to be mastered by all children, nor should the definitions be memorized. The definitions are provided to help teachers find simple ways to describe the terms when using them with children.

boot: Putting the disk that tells the computer what you want it to do into the disk drive.

cable: Round or flat wires that connect the different parts of the computer to each other.

card: The hard green boards that fit into the motherboard to (1) connect the turtle, mouse, disk drive, voice box, or other hardware to the computer; or (2) increase the computer's memory and functions.

command: Telling the computer what you want it to do.

CPU, central processing unit: The "brains" and memory of the computer that process the input to produce the appropriate output.

cursor: A blinking light or box showing either where the image will appear on the screen or the current selection on a menu.

disk: This stores information such as a picture you have made or a whole program that the computer can retrieve and then process.

disk drive: The part of the computer that "reads" from and "writes" onto the disk.

execute a command: Follow a command.

input: Information that is put into the computer by either a disk or commands received from the keyboard, joystick, mouse, or other peripheral.

joystick: A box with an upright handle, which can be used to control cursor movement on certain programs.

key: The squares on the keyboard with symbols, letters, or words that you push to give the computer commands.

keyboard: The part of the computer with keys like a typewriter.

Koala Pad: A flat device with a blank surface; by moving a stylus over the surface, the cursor can be controlled on certain programs.

load the program: The process of transferring information from the disk into the computer's memory.

menu: A list of choices from which to select.

monitor: The screen part of the computer that lets you see the program.

motherboard: The large green board that processes the information given to the computer; other boards are plugged into it to attach them to the computer.

mouse: A square box, with from one to three buttons, which is attached to the computer by a cable; the cursor can be controlled on some programs by moving the mouse on a flat surface.

output: What the computer produces when it is finished processing the information; it may be a display on the screen, a movement of a turtle, print on some paper, or other things, depending on the program.

printer: A machine that can be attached to the computer to print your output onto paper.

program: A series of commands put together; the computer can do all the commands in order. Some programs are short, others are a whole disk of commands that tell the computer what game to play.

[Return]: A key on the keyboard, which is used in many programs to tell the computer that you have finished your entry or made your choice.

run a program: Have the computer execute, or carry out, all the commands that make up a program.

save: Tell the computer to remember either your creation on the computer or some other information by recording it on a disk.

Most vocabulary is taught informally. While the child is using the computer, the teacher talks to the child, using the appropriate terms. For example, "I like the way you remembered to close the disk drive door after loading the disk." The teacher uses the correct term along with an explanation for the child who is unfamiliar with the correct term. "Can you move the cursor—the white square—over to the mouth you want for your face?" Vocabulary can also be taught in a more formal manner. A teacher might have a group time in which a term, such as "command" is introduced, as is done in **Jane Commands** (p. 152). Activity time projects can also be designed to reinforce vocabulary, as in **Program an Obstacle Course** (p. 166), in which children repeatedly use the terms "program," "command," and "run." Activities with other primary objectives can easily reinforce vocabulary as well, with only slight alteration.

Building Concepts about the Computer and Its Parts

Children can learn information about computer parts in much the same way they learn vocabulary.

There is considerable informal learning as children use computers. While using the computer, Binta learned the need for the correct disk (p. 131) and Micah learned how the cables connect the parts of the computer together (p. 131). Children can be introduced to the computer more formally as well. A group time can be devoted to discussing what the computer is and how it does what it does. The beginning of **I Command You To Draw** (p. 159) has an example of such a group time. Free-play activities such as **Build a Computer** (p. 143) can also help children to build concepts about what a computer is.

After children have learned about the parts of the computer in their classroom, they can begin to look at other computers. Do all micros look the same? How can you tell which part is the monitor, the disk drive, and the keyboard? Do they all connect in the same way? Do computers found in other places have the same parts? Where is the keyboard in the bank machine? Does it have a disk drive, or a monitor? How do the parts in the microwave compare to those in a microcomputer? These questions expand on the concepts discussed here. They will be explored in more detail under "Computers Can Do Many Different Things" (p. 176).

ACTIVITIES TO TEACH ABOUT COMPUTER PARTS

COMPUTER EASEL

Why?

☐ To use and strengthen knowledge of parts of a computer

⩓ To allow for creativity

⩓ To encourage small-muscle development

What Is Needed?

An easel
2 six-cup muffin tins
12 craypas (oil based crayons) [markers or crayons could also be used]
A small flat box with a slit in the side as a disk drive
A cardboard disk
Yellow construction paper cut into the shape of a monitor and keyboard with a dark green screen
Blocks or a small table on which to rest the muffin tin
Number circles to show the order in which to turn on the machine

How?

During free play, the children can come up and make a picture on the easel computer. Teachers can reinforce the words for the parts of the computer. The children can load the cardboard disk and push the buttons to start the easel computer, as they would on the real computer.

(**Note:** It is interesting to observe that most 4-year- olds do all their drawing on the screen part of the paper. Many of the drawings resemble the programs that are in use in the classroom.)

Making a picture at the "computer easel."

COMPUTER EASEL
(Continued)

Making It Your Own:

This activity was designed to complement the drawing programs that we were using in the classroom at the time. If you are using a writing program, the same activity might be done with letter rubber stamps and stamp pads.

If you use a tape recorder rather then a disk drive to load your program, adapt the box to resemble a tape recorder.

If your machine loads in a different order, have the labels indicate your loading sequence.

BUILD A COMPUTER

Why?

☐ To use and hear computer vocabulary

☐ To encourage children to look more closely at the computer and use the information they have learned

🕇 To encourage small-muscle development

🕇 To allow children to work cooperatively

🕇 To encourage creativity

🕇 To encourage problem solving

What Is Needed?

Unit blocks
Pieces of cardboard shaped like a monitor laminated or covered with clear contact paper
Heavy yarn or string (to use as cables)
Cardboard disks
Paper cutouts of the keyboard (lamented)
Old computer paper
Cutouts for knobs and switches
Scrap paper
Markers
Masking tape
Colorforms
A computer in the classroom to refer to

How?

Encourage the children to use the blocks and other props to build a computer like the one in the classroom. The teacher can stimulate play by asking questions such as:
"What parts do we need to make?"

"What shape is the monitor? the computer? the disk drive? the printer?"
"Which part is largest?"
"How does the information get from the disk drive to the keyboard? from the keyboard to the monitor?"
Children can use the scrap paper and markers to make the red light, the apple sign, or other details that they need. Children can then use the Colorforms to make a picture on the monitor. (It is best to find Colorforms that in some way resemble the program your children know: for example, a variety of colored lines for **Magic Crayon** or **Delta Draw**, or facial feature Colorforms for **Facemaker**.) Children can also write stories or draw pictures on the printer paper to represent the computer's printer output.

Making It Your Own:

If appropriate Colorforms are not available, the children can use markers to draw on the laminated monitor screen. Drawings can be erased with a damp cloth or sponge.

Going Beyond:

Use a variety of boxes instead of blocks, and let the children make their own computer to take home.
Use the box computers to make a classroom computer store. Make other kinds of computers as well as micros when the class is discussing the many uses for computers.
For older children, provide keyboard sheets with blank keys. Let the children fill in the appropriate letters by looking at the computer or a computer picture.
Instead of using paper keyboards, let the children use letter blocks to add the keys to their block computers.

THIS IS A SONG ABOUT COMPUTERS

Why?

- ☐ To use and hear names for the parts of the computer
- ☐ To reinforce steps for loading the computer
- 🕴 To encourage large-muscle development
- 🕴 To develop listening skills

What Is Needed?

6 cards with pictures of a disk drive
6 cards with pictures of a monitor
6 cards with pictures of a disk
6 cards with pictures of a keyboard
(**Note:** There should be enough cards for each child and each teacher to have one card, with the head teacher having one of each type.)

How?

At group time, give each child a picture card. (For younger groups, seat the children in sections—all the disks together, all the disk drives together, etc.) The teacher sings the following song. The children stand up and sit down according to the directions for the computer part on their card.

This song is sung to the tune of "This Is a Song about Colors" from Hap Palmer's *Learning Basic Skills through Music: Vol 1* (1969).

This is a song about computers, computers.
We use them every day. Load the disk in the disk
   drive, turn the monitor on
Turn the keyboard on the very same way.

Keyboard stand up,
Disk drive stand up,
Monitor and disk stand up.

Keyboard sit down.
Disk drive sit down.
Monitor and disk sit down.

This is a song about computers, computers
We use them every day.
We can draw a picture, or move a face,
Or write a story—this way.

Disk drive stand up.
Monitor stand up.
Disk drive and monitor sit down.

Disk stand up.
Disk sit down.
Keyboard and monitor stand up.

Monitor sit down.
Disk stand up.
Keyboard and disk sit down.

Disk drive stand up.
Disk drive sit down.
Everyone stand up and sit down.

This is a song about computers, computers.
We use them every day.
Before it can work we must give a command
Computers only do what we say.

Making It Your Own:

Change the description of the programs to match the programs used in your class.
Change the computer parts used to stress the vocabulary you are emphasizing with your class.

THIS IS A SONG ABOUT COMPUTERS
(Continued)

Going Beyond:

For an older group, let the children help to make up the verses to describe what a computer does, what it looks like, how you load it, or whatever fits your class.

When discussing the many uses of the computer, substitute the following verses for the current ones. Adjust the uses to fit the kinds of computers you have discussed with the children.

This is a song about computers, computers.
We see them all around.
There are computers in offices, and at the library
And in microwave ovens they are found.

(stand up, sit down chorus #1)

This is a song about computers, computers.
We see them all around.
There are computers at McDonald's, and at the bank.
And computers to take rockets off the ground.

(stand-up, sit-down chorus #2)

This is a song about computers, computers.
We see them all around.
There are computers working robots,
    and in many schools,
And computers that we all can use.

With older children, let them name uses for computers and help make up the verses.

To enable the children to sing the verses, point to pictures of the types of computers as they sing about them.

MEET TIMOTHY TURTLE

Why?

☐ To look inside of the computer and see how peripherals are connected

☐ To use computer vocabulary and understandings of computer parts

☐ To see another use for the computer—moving a robot turtle

🕴 To reinforce practice letter sounds: B, F, R, W and L

What Is Needed?

A microcomputer

A Tasmin Turtle, or Turtle Tot, or another computer-controlled robot, and the appropriate software to control it

A large floor space without carpet

Carpet squares for each child placed around the area where the turtle will walk

A paper or foam head attached to the turtle's ring

Two red legs each with a large "R" attached to the right side of the ring

Two blue legs each with a large "L" attached on the left side of the turtle

Children with experience using the computer

How?

Have the children seated on the carpet squares forming a large horseshoe. The computer table should be at the mouth of the horseshoe, with the back of the computer to the class. Have the power pack for the turtle plugged in with the cable connected. Do not connect the cable to the turtle. Do not have the turtle card connected to the motherboard. Have the turtle in a box under the table.

> Teacher: I have a turtle robot named Timothy. He lives in the box. It does not look like a real turtle. (Take out the turtle.)

> Teacher: How do you think you make it move?
> Children: You give it a command.
> Teacher: (to the turtle) Move turtle! It didn't move.
> Children: Press the keys
> Teacher: (pressing the keys) It still didn't move.

Encourage the children to help you discover that Timothy Turtle must be connected to the computer to receive keyboard commands. Plug the cable (the "turtle's tail") into the turtle. "How do you think I plug it into the keyboard?" With the children, look for a spot to plug it in. Try what they suggest. Suggest looking to see how the disk drive is connected. Take off the top of the keyboard and tilt it up so the children can see inside. Explain that the motherboard is the CPU that processes the input, or commands, that you give it. Discuss how the disk drive is connected to a "card" that plugs into the motherboard. Encourage children to deduce that a card may be needed for the turtle too. Connect the card and plug in the cable.

> Teacher: Now what do I do?
> Children: Press the keys.
> Teacher: It still doesn't work.

Encourage the children to help you realize that the software must be loaded and the computer turned on.

Once the turtle is ready to go, ask the children what key they think you should push to make it go forward. Try the keys that they recommend. If someone suggests the arrow keys, the teacher might point out: "That a good idea. The arrows move the cursor on **Magic Crayon**. That command does not seem to work with Timothy Turtle." Ask the children again what might make the Timothy move forward emphasizing the "F" sound. If the children do not guess "F," the teacher can suggest it. Have the children help you to figure out how to make it go b-b-b-backwards, r-r-r-right, and l-l-l-left. They can also help to make it w-w-w-wink.

Have Timothy Turtle turn around so he has looked at all the children in the class.

Have the Turtle available for the children to use during free play.

MEET TIMOTHY TURTLE
(Continued)

Making It Your Own:

A similar activity can be done to connect other peripherals—mouse, printer, joystick (if it does not plug into a game port), voice box, etc. The children should have had opportunities to use the peripheral before this activity is done. The activity will not have much meaning to the children unless they know what the peripheral is supposed to do. If the mouse is used for the activity, the children should already be comfortable using the mouse. After the mouse has been out of the classroom for a while, bring it back. Do not have the mouse card connected to the motherboard or the mouse cable. Discuss with the children how to get it to work. Load the software and discover that it will not work. Have the cable end prominently visible. As with the turtle, have the children discover the need to plug it in, and to add a card.

Select a name for the turtle, or mouse, with the children. We selected "Timothy Turtle" after reading the book *Timothy Turtle* by Alice Davis (1940). We named our mouse Norman after the mouse whose hobby is art in Don Freeman's *Norman the Doorman* (1959).

Going Beyond:

See Chapter 10 for many activities to supplement use of the turtle robot.

Timothy Turtle is saying hello to the class.

JOY STICK AND THE COMPUTER

Why?

☐ To hear and use computer vocabulary

☐ To use the information they have learned about computers

🯅 To encourage good listening skills

What Is Needed?

A group of children old enough to understand puns (5-year-olds, or late 5's, are usually beginning to enjoy puns)

How?

Read the following story to the class, substituting your name for "Ms. Morris," and the names of the children in your class for the children's names.

It was Joy Stick's first day at school. She was very excited that she would get to use the computer, and wanted to learn everything she could. Ms. Morris told Joy Stick she could work on the **Apple**, so Joy Stick asked Daniel to show her where the refrigerator and knives were. Daniel explained that the Apple wasn't something to eat, but a computer to work on. (Let children explain "Apple" if possible.) Anya and Gene came over and told Joy Stick that a computer is a machine that can remember information that we tell it. It can help us do many things. Janet said it has electronic **chips** inside that helped its memory. Joy Stick couldn't imagine how a bag of potato chips could help her to do things, but she wanted to hear more.

Ms. Morris opened the Apple and Joy Stick was surprised not to find apple seeds or potato chips, but lots of wires and green plastic cards. Ms. Morris closed the top and asked Heather if she would show Joy Stick how to run the computer. Joy Stick said she hadn't worn her jogging suit, or even her sneakers, so she couldn't have a race with a machine. Besides she could not imagine how it could move without any legs. Lily heard that and laughed. She explained that to run the computer meant to (use child's explanation) get it to work. On some of our computers you have to load a **disk** into the **disk drive**. Joy Stick looked around the room and thought all the children were too young to drive. Andy explained that one of the pieces of **hardware** was called a disk drive. Joy Stick was getting confused. She thought this was a school not a hardware store.

Benjamin came over and told Joy Stick that hardware was another name for the machines. Guess what they call the disks that go in the machine? (Child response—looking for **software**.) Evan said, "Would you like to **boot the system**?" Joy Stick went to get her boots to put the disk in. Evan explained that booting the system means (let child explain) putting the disk that tells the computer what you want it to do into the disk drive. Joy Stick's head was about to burst. All of these new meanings for words she had been perfectly happy using before in a different way. Then a list appeared on the T.V. screen, which Michael told her was called a **monitor**. Nikki told Joy Stick that the list was a **menu** and she had to make a choice. Even though they had been talking about apples and chips, Joy Stick wasn't hungry. She said she would rather see what the computer could do than have something to eat. Nikki explained that a menu (child response) lists the different games and things you can do with a **program**. Joy Stick explained that she would really rather use the computer than watch a program on the T.V. Amy explained that a program (child explains) is a group of commands put on a disk that tells the computer the kind of game it should show you when that disk is booted.

JOY STICK AND THE COMPUTER
(Continued)

Kenyatta finished explaining about menus. On **Bumble Games**, you can find the missing space ships and butterflies, or play tic tac toe, or do a dot to dot. Joy Stick was a little unsure of playing a game with a bumble bee, but Beth assured her that he wouldn't sting her. Carlos and Joy Stick decided to play together. Carlos told Joy Stick to give the computer a **command**. She said "I want to play." Carlos explained you need to use the **keys** to give it a command. Joy Stick looked intently at the computer and commented that she could not find the keyhole. Colin explained that the keys are (child's response) the squares with letters on them. You press keys to give the computer commands.

Joy Stick had lots of fun at school that day. She made faces wink and stick out their tongues with Samara on **Facemaker**. With Debra, she learned to draw pictures with the **Magic Crayon**. Joy had had a great time. She had made new friends with both people and machines, but it would take her more than one day to get used to this new language. She promised to return soon and waved good-bye.

Adapted from a story by Barb Draper.

Making It Your Own:

Adjust the story to fit the needs of your class. Use puns from software and computers that you use. Add or omit vocabulary to match the terms your class has learned.

COMPUTERS NEED PEOPLE TO GIVE THEM COMMANDS

Computers can only do things that people tell them to do. Regan's computer did not save her **Magic Crayon** picture (p. 127) because she did not give the computer a "save" command. As Sam discovered when the computer did not respond to his earnest verbal request to "Get the boat!" (p. 129), computers do not understand verbal commands. In fact, one of the things that is often confusing to children is that different programs use different methods for giving the computer commands. **Magic Crayon** uses arrows to move the cursor when drawing, whereas **Facemaker** uses the spacebar to move the cursor through the menu when building the face, and later uses letter keys to give the face moving commands.

Knowing That They Control the Computer Makes It More Manageable

Once children understand that computers are not as smart as people and can only do things that people tell them, then the computer becomes much more manageable. If the computer does something they did not expect, they must figure out what command they gave it. For example, while working on **Magic Crayon**, Kyle accidentally pressed the "?," bringing up the instructions on the screen. His first response was frustration because his picture vanished. Ms. Edwards came to help. She said "Wow! You figured out how to get it to do something different. I bet you pushed the '?' to tell it to give you directions." She helped him to give the computer an "I want my picture command" by pressing the spacebar. Kyle then experimented with the "?" and the spacebar to see if he could do it again. Later, he tried out other keys and discovered that "R" and "P" would also put writing on the screen. With the teacher's help, he figured out what the writing explained after each of these commands. This example demonstrates how computer use can bolster a child's self-concept and feelings of control.

If teachers wish children to see computers as something they can control, rather than something that is mysterious, it is important for teachers to respond calmly when children hit a key that unexpectedly gives the computer a command unknown to the teacher. If the teacher had not known that the "?" key was what gives the command for directions, or that the spacebar was what retrieves the picture, then she could wonder with Kyle about what key he had pushed to command the computer to give him the writing. She and Kyle could experiment with different keys to see if they could discover which one gives the computer the "I want my picture" command.

Finding the Appropriate Commands

It is interesting that children are often much more willing to experiment with random key presses than are adults. We are usually more awed by the computer than are children. Ben (5 years old) wanted to save his picture on **Magic Crayon**. His teacher had just begun using this program and did not yet know how to save. Ben discovered the instructions by himself. He looked at the picture clues, because he was not yet a reader. He experimented with the keys shown on the illustrations until he discovered how to save his picture. Then he taught his teachers and his classmates. Children will make such discoveries in classrooms in which experimentation on the computer is encouraged, but such discoveries will rarely occur in classrooms in which the computer must be used "right way."

Once children understand that computers cannot do anything without a command, and that different programs employ different methods for giving commands, then it becomes a game to discover how to give commands in each new program. Teachers can help children to understand about commands informally while children are using the computer. When introducing children to new software, discuss how the commands are given. "On **Magic Crayon**, you tell the cursor how to move—give it a command—by pressing an arrow to tell it which way to go. I see you are commanding it to go up by pushing the up arrow." Teachers can also help children to notice the differences between programs. If a child is using **Facemaker** and is trying to get the cursor to move to a feature on the menu, there might be a conversation like this.

Teacher: How do you think we command the cursor to move?

Child: Push the arrow?

Teacher: Try it and see. (The child tries it with no result.) The arrow moved the cursor in **Magic Crayon** but isn't giving the "move" command in **Facemaker**. I wonder what the spacebar—the long key at the bottom—would do? (The child tries it and the cursor moves.)

Teachers can also use more formal activities to help children understand the concept of "commands." **Jane Commands** (p. 152) could be used to introduce commands at group time. The concept can be reinforced through a wide range of group time, free play, and informal activities.

ACTIVITIES TO TEACH ABOUT COMMANDS

JANE COMMANDS

Why?

☐ To introduce and use the word "command"

☐ To emphasize that computers cannot do anything unless people give them commands

🕺 To encourage motor development

🕺 To develop listening skills

🕺 To encourage language fluency (when children are giving the commands)

🕺 To use body-part vocabulary

(**Note:** If children do not know body-part vocabulary, the teacher will need to model actions so that they can see what body part goes with the word that is used.)

What Is Needed?

A small felt circle for each child

How?

This activity is done at group time. Have the children stand in a circle. Place a small felt circle on the floor in front of each child. Tell the children that they are each going to be robots, and you are the person who owns them. Robots are a kind of computer. Robots cannot move by themselves. Robots can only move if people give them commands.

Give the robots a series of commands. (Substitute your name for Jane.)

"Jane commands you to put your foot on the circle."

"Jane commands you to take your foot off the circle."

"Jane commands you to put your nose on the circle."

"Jane commands you to put your nose up in the air."

"Jane commands you to turn around."

"Jane commands you to put two fingers on the circle."

"Jane commands you to stand up. I did not tell any robots to take their fingers off the circle. I like the way you stood up with your fingers on the circle because you had not been commanded to move those fingers."

"Jane commands you to put your fingers in the air."

In the first four commands, the children are commanded to do something, and then to stop doing it. Later, the children are commanded to do an action, then do a second action while still continuing to follow the earlier command. This turns the game into a Twister type game. The body parts and actions required, and the complexity of the double commands should be tailored to fit each individual class of children.

After the class has practiced following the commands, pick a child to give commands. Encourage them to use the word "command."

This activity can be continued during free play.

JANE COMMANDS
(Continued)

Going Beyond:

Change the type of commands to fit the needs of your group of children. You can emphasize movement words or spatial relation words instead of, or in addition to, color words.

Instead of one felt circle, give each child a matching set of three different colored circles to work on color names, three different shapes for shape words, or any objects whose names you wish to reinforce.

Tape record commands for the robots to follow.

Let the children tape commands for the robots to follow.

Make robot costumes for the children to wear during activity time. (This will help stimulate children to become involved in the activity.)

When discussing programming, give the children a series of three commands. Touch the circle with your toe, your head, then your knee. Press the **[Return]** button, and see if the computer can remember all three commands. For younger children, put picture cards of body parts on the bulletin board so that the children can see the commands that make up the program.

ROBOT CLEANERS

Why?

☐ To help build the concept that computers can only do something if people give them a command

♀ To practice following directions

♀ To involve the children in clean-up time in a fun way

What Is Needed?

A messy classroom

How?

Pretend the children are robots. At clean-up time, give each child a task. When the task is completed, the robot comes back for another command.

Going Beyond:

Have the children work in pairs; one child gives the command, and the other executes, or carries out, the command. Part way through clean-up, switch roles.

For older children, give them a program of three commands to execute, or carry out, before returning for another program.

If your class has a helpers chart, use this to "program the class" to let each child know what to do at clean-up. Change the chart each day. Children must look at their command for the day when it is time to clean up.

FIND WHAT I COMMAND

Why?

☐ To use the word "command"

☐ To have children give and follow commands

☐ To build the concept that computers cannot do anything unless they are given a command

🏃 To practice using tactile clues for solving problems

🏃 To increase small-muscle development

What Is Needed?

A feely box (a brightly colored box with a hole in one side large enough for a child's hand to fit through. The hole should be covered with cloth or have the leg end of a sock attached around the hole so that the children must reach behind the cloth or through the sock to put a hand into the box)

6 small objects of different shape and texture. For example: a paper clip, a crayon, a piece of cotton, a piece of cloth, a piece of elastic, and a small peg

A basket

6 cards, with a duplicate of one of these objects attached to each card

How?

Place the 6 objects in the feely box. Place the six cards in a basket. One child is the computer. The other child is the person using the computer. The "person" gives the "computer" a command by showing the computer one of the cards with objects attached. The "computer" must follow the command and retrieve the requested object from the box.

Teachers can reinforce the word "command," modeling its use while playing the game or talking to players.

Children can also play the game alone. First, the child selects a command card, then the same child becomes the "computer," following the command and selecting the appropriate object.

Encourage children to feel the object on the command card so that they will know how the object they are searching for in the box will feel.

Making It Your Own:

Select objects that complement the interests of the children in your class and the topics currently being discussed. If you are talking about doctors, fill the box with doctor's tools and objects.

Going Beyond:

If your children are good at feely-box games, make it harder by putting pictures of the objects on the command cards rather than actual objects.

When children are discussing programs, have them use the cards to program the order in which the objects should be found and removed from the box.

Rather than a feely box, have a child-sized box with the "computer" child seated inside. Have two slots in the box. The "person" slides a command card into one of the slots. The "computer" slides the object out of other slot. This variation can be used to help teach and reinforce the concept of input (the command card), CPU (the child in the computer box), and output (the object).

IF YOU'RE A FACEMAKER MONITOR

Why?

☐ To practice the letters used to program the face in the **Facemaker** software

☐ To build the concept that the computer needs to be given a command in order to do something

☐ To use the term "monitor"

🕴 To encourage listening skills

🕴 To practice recognizing the letters T, W, C, S, F, and E, and learning beginning letter sounds

What Is Needed?

A sheet with the letters used to command the **Facemaker** face with a pictorial representation of what command each letter gives.

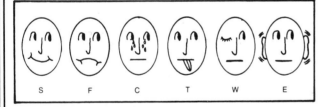

How?

At a group time, tell the children that they are going to be the monitor for your computer. You are going to play **Facemaker**, and they are going to have to follow your commands.

Sing the following song to the tune of "If You're Happy and You Know It."

If you're a **Facemaker** monitor, make a face.
　(Kids make a face.)
If you're a **Facemaker** monitor, make a face.
If you're a **Facemaker** monitor,
If you're a **Facemaker** monitor,
If you're a **Facemaker** monitor, make a face.
"If I type the 'S' key what command will it give you?"
　(Point to the "S" on the picture while saying this, so that children can see what an "S" looks like if they don't know. Children can also see the smiling picture clue next to the "S.")
When I type an "S" smile.
　(Kids should all be the monitor and smile.)
When I type an "S" smile.
When I type an "S,"
When I type an "S,"
When I type an "S" smile.
"You did a great job of following my command. When I typed the 'S' I saw lots of smiling faces on my monitors."
Continue the song, using all of the commands from **Facemaker**. Between each verse, elicit the children's help to decide which letter should be typed to command a certain move, or what move will be made when you type a certain letter.

Going Beyond:

When discussing programming and how the programmer gives the computer commands so that it can do certain things, the class can talk about what commands the programmer who made **Facemaker** taught it. If you were the programmer, what other commands would you teach it to do? Add other motions with an appropriate command letter.

Adapt the song to fit other programs your class is using.

SIMPLE DANCE TO DO

Why?

☐ To build the concept that computers cannot do anything unless people give them a command

🏃 To encourage motor development

🏃 To develop listening skills

What Is Needed?

A record player

The record *Bert and Ernie's Sing-Along* (1975) or another record with the song "A Very Simple Dance to Do"

How?

Explain to the children that they are robots, and that the song on the record player is going to give them commands for how to move. They can execute, or carry out, the commands on the record, but they can only move when the record gives them commands.

Play the song and let the children move with it. Compliment the children on how well they executed the commands.

Making It Your Own:

Select any movement record that is appropriate for your class.

Put the song on tape, and have an area of the room in which children can play the tape and practice following commands during free play.

Going Beyond:

Have the children add their own commands to the song. This can be done during a group time, or children can tape their commands for other children to follow.

When the class is discussing programming, the teacher or children could make three movement tapes with a series of commands. The children can "load" the desired program into the tape recorder. Then they can "run" the program by turning on the tape recorder and following the commands.

I'M GONNA CLAP

Why?

☐ To practice the word "command"

☐ To build the concept that a computer can only do something if people give it a command

⚘ To practice being a member of a group

⚘ To encourage language development (when the children are giving the commands)

⚘ To develop listening skills

⚘ To encourage large-muscle development

What Is Needed?

Children

How?

Sing the following song, substituting the teacher's name for Jane, to the tune of "I'm Gonna Sing When the Spirit Says Sing." Children follow the commands given in the song and join the singing when they are ready.

"I'm gonna clap when Jane commands clap.
I'm gonna clap when Jane commands clap.
I'm gonna clap when Jane commands clap.
And stop when Jane commands stop."

Substitute other actions for *clap*. Let the children choose the action. Sing the child's name in the song as the person who is commanding.

Making It Your Own:

Pick actions that best fit the needs and interests of your class. If the children need practice with body parts, the verse could go: "I'm gonna touch my nose when Jane commands nose." The appropriate body parts could then be substituted for "nose." If the class is discussing transportation, the children could drive different types of vehicles on command.

I COMMAND YOU TO DRAW

Why?

☐ To introduce the word "command" and use terms for the parts of the computer

☐ To emphasize that computers are not as smart as people; they can only understand commands they have been programmed to understand

🧍☐ To practice using arrows to show which way to go

🧍 To encourage motor development

🧍 To develop social skills needed for working as a member of a group

What Is Needed?

Children familiar with **Magic Crayon** software

Pictures of a keyboard, a disk drive, a disk

A large picture of a monitor mounted on a bulletin board or large easel—the screen should be made of graph paper scaled one square to the inch or larger

Colored markers

An arrow floor mat (four black arrows cut from 8″ x 12″ black construction paper mounted between two sheets of clear contact paper or laminated)

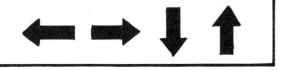

How?

This activity is done at a group time with the whole class. (Or if enough teachers are available, the activity can be done with two smaller groups simultaneously.)

Tell the children you wish to make a picture on the computer using **Magic Crayon**, but first you need to set up the computer.

"What parts do I need to set up my computer?" As the children name the monitor, the keyboard, and the disk drive put up pictures of the appropriate parts. Be sure to use the correct vocabulary.

"Now the computer is all set up. I want it to draw a design for me. Will it draw one if I tell it 'Draw a design?'" Have the children help you to figure out that first you need to plug it in, load the disk, and turn on the computer.

"Now I can tell it to make a design. 'Make a design computer.' Why isn't it making a design? I told it what to do?" Have children help you to figure out that a computer cannot understand when you talk to it. You have to use the keyboard.

"What keys do I use to give the computer a command to draw a design?" (The arrow keys.)

"Now that I know how it works, let's pretend that I am the cursor on **Magic Crayon**. You can be the people who are giving me commands."

Put down the arrow floor mat for children to use when giving commands. Let each child have a chance to touch a few keys to show you how to draw. Use the marker to draw a design on the graph paper. Go one square for each command. To make each child's commands clearer, use a different color of marker for each child. To reinforce the word "command," use it often. For example, "Alex, it is your turn to give a command." or "Jack commanded me to move the cursor up."

I COMMAND YOU TO DRAW
(Continued)

If the children grasp the idea easily, you might try to make a square, box, road, building, or other simple object.

Making It Your Own:

This activity is designed for use with children who are familiar with **Magic Crayon**. You should adapt it to resemble the type of graphic program used in your class.

If used with an older class that is learning **Logo**, then left and right, or forward and backward commands can be used instead of arrows. The children can either give them verbally or on a floor mat with the appropriate keys. If children do not give specific enough commands, then do not respond.

GOOD-BYE COMMANDS

Why?

☐ To emphasize that computers can only do something if people give them a command

☥ To practice following directions

☥ To encourage large-muscle development

☥ To make transition times more fun

What Is Needed?

A group of children to be dismissed from one activity to another

How?

Give each child a command for how to move to the next activity.

"I command you to hop to get your coat."

"I command you to crawl to the door."

"I command you to walk backwards to wash your hands."

"I command you to tiptoe to the bus."

Making It Your Own:

Change the types of commands to fit the needs and interest of the group. Children can be told to move like different animals, vehicles, in pairs, at varying speeds, and so on.

Going Beyond:

Have the children give the commands to each other. Matt can give the teacher a command. Susie will give Matt a command. Leona will give Susie a command, and so on. Each child will **give** a command and then be **given** one until all the children have been excused.

A COMPUTER CAN REMEMBER A WHOLE SERIES OF COMMANDS

What makes the computer unique is its ability to remember and act on a series of commands. For example, when using **Facemaker**, the child can enter a series of movement commands for the face, and then press the [**Return**] button. The face will execute the whole series of commands in the same order in which the child has entered them. The computer will remember the commands (except on the IBM version, which does not have this option) and run the program as often as the child presses the [**Return**] button.

What Is a Program?

Children can learn that a computer can remember a series of commands and that this is called a "program." As mentioned before, if you have entered a **Facemaker** program into the computer, the same program will repeat over and over each time you press the [**Return**] key. The computer always runs the program the same way each time. Children can also discover that the disks they use are called "programs." Discussion can help the child to understand that the information on a disk is called a program because it contains a whole series of commands that tell the computer what to do to get the game that you wish to have. If you are using **Magic Crayon**, the disk tells the computer to put up the title, to show the Spinnaker boy running up the stairs, to ask for your name, and to respond by moving the cursor when you use the arrow keys. If a disk with a different program is loaded, the computer will do different things.

The concept of programming can be expanded when children are discussing the computer's strengths and weakness and its many uses. (See Chapter 9 for a more in-depth discussion of these concepts.) Children can see how the computer's memory makes it a unique machine with enormous potential. They can see how computers can be programmed in different ways to fulfill different functions.

Introducing Programs

Children's first introduction to programming should be through using software that allows them to write small programs or save what they have created. A number of software pieces allow children to create a program by instructing the computer to remember a series of multiple commands. In **Creature Creator**, children (1) use commands to create a creature and then (2) use a grid to enter movement commands for the head, arms, and legs. **Print Shop** allows the child to enter a whole series of commands relating to (1) the type of end result wanted—card, poster, flyer; (2) style and size of font; and (3) style of border. The children enter in all the details, and then press the [**Return**] key. The computer then prints an output that incorporates all of the child's commands. Children can use various forms of **Logo** to do more sophisticated programming. Children can also explore the computer's ability to remember creations by saving on **Magic Crayon, Delta Draw, Many Ways to Say I Love You, Kidwriter, Bank Street Writer, Primary Editor**, or any of the other programs that contain a "save" option.

After they have experienced the computer's ability to save stories, the teacher can encourage children to compare what happens to a story written on a typewriter and one written on a computer. The computer can print the story as many times as you request. It can even remember the story the next day if you have commanded it to save what you have entered. The typewriter can only type the story once. It cannot remember the story the next day. While children are using **Facemaker**, the teacher can ask if they would like the computer to remember a whole series of commands. The children can "write a program"—a list of commands, and then the computer can follow them in order. Similar discussions can introduce the children to programming and saving options on other software. The teachers are doing two things: they are introducing children to computer vocabulary and to the concepts that this vocabulary communicates.

Discussions such as these can take place informally on an individual basis or more formally as part of a group time, as is done in **Program Your Face** (p. 164). Many of the activities that have been used for giving single commands, such as **Robot Cleaners** (p. 154) and **Jane Commands** (p. 152), can be expanded to writing programs. The "robots" in both activities can be given a program of three commands to remember rather than just a single command. Turning command-oriented activities into programming ones reinforces the concept that a program is a series of commands that a computer can remember and execute in order. Almost any activity that involves following a series of directions, such as cooking from a recipe, can be presented as "running a program," as in **Purple Cloud** (p. 171).

ACTIVITIES TO TEACH ABOUT PROGRAMMING

PROGRAM YOUR FACE

Why?

☐ To develop the concept of "program" as a series of commands done in a row

☐ To use the terms "command," "program," and "monitor"

☐ To practice using the [**Return**] key to tell the computer to process the information

☐ To emphasize that computers cannot do anything unless people give them a command

🛉 To develop listening skills

🛉 To develop visual skills

🛉 To practice participating as a group member

What Is Needed?

A pegboard with 8 hooks (or a bulletin board with 8 thumbtacks)

36 **Facemaker** 3″ x 5″ pegboard cards—each with a letter used to command **Facemaker** and a pictorial representation of the command (see illustration below, 6 cards for each command)

A [**Return**] card taped on pegboard (or bulletin board)

A card with the number "1" and one with the number "2" attached to the pegboard (or bulletin board)

A rebus card similar to the one on the **Facemaker** disk holder taped to pegboard

Return

How?

"Do you remember what the computer word is for telling the computer what to do?" "Command." "I am using the **Facemaker** program. I pressed '1' and looked at all the features I could put on my face. I chose the hair and the eyes, the nose, the mouth, and the ears. Now I want to move my face. How do I tell it to move?" Help the children to remember you had pressed "1" to build the face; now you want to tell the computer that you are ready to move the face, so now you must type "2."

Teacher: What command do I give it? What do I type if I want the face to smile?

Child: "S."

Teacher: You are the monitor and must follow the commands I type. (Press the "S" on the rebus card. Try some other single commands.)

Teacher: Now, I want to write a program so that my face will execute a whole series of commands.

Encourage the children to tell you to press the spacebar to get a rectangle on the monitor. Ask the children one at a time to tell you what commands to put in the program. Put the appropriate card on a hook for each command until the 8 hooks are filled. Have the children help you count to see how many commands are in the program.

Ask the children to be your monitor. Press the [**Return**] key to "run" the program. Then point to each command in turn as the children execute the commands in the program. "I really like that; I think I'll run that program again." Press the [**Return**] key again. Take down the commands and continue building programs until each child has a turn to select a command.

PROGRAM YOUR FACE
(Continued)

(**Note:** It is easier to find the command cards as they are requested if you have them sorted into piles or color-coded so that all the frowns are blue, all the tongues are red, and so on.

*"Running" a **Facemaker** program.*

Making It Your Own:

If you have a piece of software other than **Facemaker** that has a programming component, make picture cards and commands to match that program.

Adjust the number of hooks to fit the size of your class and their attention span.

Going Beyond:

Have a pegboard set up for the children to use with this activity during free play. (A basket will be needed for the cards.)

After having done this activity, use it to discuss the limits of **Facemaker**. It can only do 6 motions. "If you were the person writing the program on the disk, what other motions would you program the computer to know? What letter would you use to command that motion?" Make additional cards for the new motions. At free play, have blank cards for children to add their own motions.

PROGRAM AN OBSTACLE COURSE

Why?

- To build an understanding that a program is a series of commands and that programs are written by people

- To practice using the **[Return]** key to tell the computer to process the information

- To practice reading and using picture symbol directions

- To practice left to right scanning

- To encourage motor development

What Is Needed?

A barrel
A balance beam
A pegboard with 8 hooks
A mat
Stairs
12 pegboard picture cards for writing programs—4 with pictures of stairs and mat, 4 with pictures of barrel, 4 with pictures of balance beam
A basket for cards
A **[Return]** card (taped on the pegboard)

Planning an obstacle course "program."

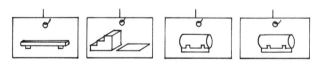

Return

PROGRAM AN OBSTACLE COURSE
(Continued)

How?

The children individually or in small groups select pictures of the equipment and place them on the pegs, going from left to right. The teacher can reinforce computer vocabulary by asking, "What command are you going to add to the program now?" When all the pegs are full, the children press the **[Return]** key to "run the program." The children then follow the program by using each piece of equipment in the order shown by the program command cards.

Children often want to repeat a favorite part of the course an extra time. Help them to move the command cards and thus rewrite the program to allow them to do that.

Going Beyond:

Change the course to include other types of equipment: tires to walk in, hoops to crawl through, blocks or carpet squares to jump over, or whatever equipment best fits the needs of your children and classroom.

Increase or decrease the number of pegs to match the skills of your children.

Increase or decrease the choices of equipment to fit the space available, and the skills of the children.

For children ready for more advanced programming, include symbols for repeat, numerals to indicate the number of times each piece of equipment is to be used, or other symbols that your class has learned.

Instead of equipment, set up color-coded exercise stations. The green card could mean go to the sit-up mat and follow the direction there. The red card might mean go to the jumping jack station and follow the directions there. The actions could be tailored to meet the needs of the class.

ROBOT ORCHESTRA

Why?

- ☐ To build an understanding that a program is a series of commands and that people write programs

- ☐ To practice using the **[Return]** key to tell the computer to process the information

- 🚶☐ To practice reading and using picture symbol directions

  - 🚶 To learn left to right scanning

  - 🚶 To encourage small-muscle development

  - 🚶 To work cooperatively (if done with one child to each instrument)

What Is Needed?

Children who have had several days of free-play to use the instruments

For group time, use:

6 sets of rhythm sticks
6 sets of wrist bells
6 tambourines (increase or decrease the number of instruments so that there is one instrument per child)
A pegboard with 8 hooks
12 pegboard picture cards for writing programs—4 with pictures of rhythm sticks, 4 with pictures of wrist bells, and 4 with pictures of a tambourine.
[Return] card taped to pegboard

For activity time, use:

1 of each instrument on a tray
A basket for the picture cards
The same pegboard, hooks, and picture cards as listed previously

How?

At group time, explain that the children are going to be a robot orchestra. The orchestra will have 3 types of instruments: tambourines, rhythm sticks, and wrist bells. (Have one of each instrument within the children's view.)

Have the children help you write a program for the music that the robots will play. Each child can

A performance of the "robot orchestra."

Return

ROBOT ORCHESTRA
(Continued)

suggest an instrument; the teacher then places that instrument card on the board. When the pegboard is full, count and see how many commands are in the program. Give each child an instrument. Press the **[Return]** key to "run" the program. The children will play their instruments in the order indicated by the program. The teacher should point to the pictures so that the children know what part of the program the robots are executing.

For activity time, place three instruments on a tray. The child can write a program and then execute it by playing the instruments in the appropriate order.

Making It Your Own:

Vary the instruments in accordance with what you have available. (Do not use more than 4 different types of instruments because this will cause each child to have to wait too long to play.)

Begin with giving individual commands, such as ''I command you to play the sticks. I command you to play the tambourine.''

Going Beyond:

For children using **Logo**, add numerals to indicate how many times to play the instrument, repeat signs and parentheses to indicate what parts are repeated, and other programming symbols that the children have learned.

At activity time, set three small carpet samples or chairs in front of the pegboard. Place an instrument on each chair. Have one child program the song for the three-person orchestra to play. This will work better with 5-or 6-year-olds who can work cooperatively.

When discussing CPU, have the children sit on a large green blanket or mat. They will be the motherboard that processes the information. The music will be the output and the commands in the program will be the input.

PROGRAMMING THE PIANO

Why?

☐ To build an understanding that a program is a series of commands that are written by people

🏃 To encourage small-muscle development through drawing and playing the piano

🏃 To practice following a sequence

🏃 To encourage auditory development

Playing a piano program.

What Is Needed?

A piano with one octave of white keys (from C to C) marked with colored paper—use a different color for each note

Three boxes of crayons with the same 8 colors that were used to mark the keys

Paper for programming with a line of vertical rectangular boxes to be colored

How?

The children use crayons to fill in the rectangles, then take their program to the piano. The child then runs the program by playing the colored keys on the piano in the order they are programmed on the paper.

Making It Your Own:

This could also be done on a xylophone.

The xylophone and piano could be used together if the colors on the piano notes correspond to the colors on the xylophone.

If you wish to emphasize left-to-right reading, place an arrow at the beginning of the program to indicate in which direction to go.

Going Beyond:

For older children, let them "compose" their song by playing a note, and then recording what they have played.

For children working on patterns, have them program a pattern to play on the piano.

Planning a xylophone program.

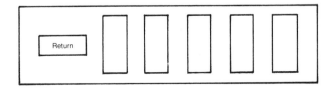

PURPLE CLOUD

Why?

☐ To understand that a program is a series of commands

🚶☐ To practice following a series of directions

🚶 To practice left-to-right scanning

🚶 To practice reading and using picture-symbol directions

🚶 To develop self-help skills

What Is Needed?

A blender

Grape juice in a shallow bowl from which children can scoop

Pineapple juice in a shallow bowl from which children can scoop

Plain yogurt

1 carton of vanilla ice cream, nestled in ice to prevent melting

4 tablespoon measures

A step-by-step picture recipe that is easily visible from a reasonable distance (this recipe is from *Cup Cooking* by Veitch and Harmes, 1981)

A long table with ingredients lined up in a row in the order they are listed on the recipe

A [**Return**] key

How?

Have small groups of children participate at a time. Hands should be washed before beginning. The teacher and the children can look at the "program for making a purple cloud drink," the recipe. Count how many commands are in the program. Discuss the commands if any are unclear. Let each child press the [**Return**] button, then be the computer that "runs the program" by following the directions to make a purple cloud.

Making It Your Own:

Select any simple recipe with 4-5 simple steps.

To simplify for a younger group, use one 1/8 cup measure of each ingredient instead of 2 tablespoons.

Going Beyond:

Use this activity to discuss input (the ingredients), CPU (the blender), and output (the drink).

Return				
2 T	2 T	2 T	2 T	
grape juice	pineapple juice	yogurt	ice cream	blend

FRUIT SALAD PROGRAMMING

Why?

☐ To understand that a program is a series of commands written by people

☐ To read symbol directions

To practice sequencing

To encourage small-muscle development

To let children taste many different fruits

What Is Needed?

A bowl of banana slices, with a picture of a banana

A bowl of pineapple pieces, with a picture of a pineapple

A bowl of kiwi pieces, with a picture of an open kiwi

A bowl of orange pieces, with a picture of an orange

A bowl of apple slices, with a picture of an apple

A bowl of seedless grapes, with a picture of grapes

5 spoons, one in each bowl

3 program holders, each being a piece of cardboard folded over to make 6 small pockets along the bottom

30 small picture cards of the aforementioned fruit, with 6 cards for each type of fruit

A tray with 5 small containers; use each container to hold one of the kinds of fruit cards.

A bowl for each child in the class

A spoon for each child in the class

How?

Have three children wash their hands. The children can then taste one of each type of fruit if they want. The children then decide how they want to "program themselves to make their fruit salad." If they really like pineapple, they might put three pineapple pictures, then an apple picture, then a grape picture, and maybe another pineapple picture.

After the child has created the program, the program can be "run." The child will take one spoonful of the appropriate fruit for each picture on the program holder. When the child is done, the cards can be sorted and returned to the container for the next child.

Making It Your Own:

Select the type of fruit that best fits the season, or the topics of discussion in your class.

Use vegetables to make a salad, seeds to make trail mix, fillings for a taco, or any other easily scooped type of food.

Going Beyond:

At snack time, have the children discuss a three-command program for how they will eat the fruit. The program might be kiwi, kiwi, grape. The child will then eat the fruit in the stated order.

SUMMARY

Children can learn **about** computers as well as use them. They can examine the parts that make up the computer and explore how these parts are connected. Children enjoy using the correct, "adult" terms for the computer's parts and their functions. It is just as easy to learn the correct terms as to learn a euphemism.

Computers can only do things if people give them a command. The command must be given in a form that the computer can understand. Knowing that computers only do what they are told makes the computer more manageable and gives the children a sense of control. A *program* is a list of commands that tells the computer what to do.

This chapter describes many possible activities to help children build three concepts:

1. Computers are machines controlled by people.
2. Commands tell the computer what to do.
3. A program is a series of commands.

These activities should be seen as a springboard for designing activities that fit the needs, interests, and strengths of the children in your classroom.

9

Computers in Our World: Building Concepts About What They Do and What We Must Do

"I can really do this myself!" (Photo courtesy of Robert Cohen)

Computers are an ever-present part of our world today. They control telephone systems, are an integral part of radio and television stations, regulate traffic lights, run trains and subways, calculate purchases, keep track of bank transactions, compute payroll, check out library books, program videocassette recorders (VCR) to record television shows at times we pick, tell our microwaves when and how to cook dinner, allow us to write books such as this, simulate experiences to train us in new skills, and entertain us with games. The presence of computers in our environment is not always obvious, especially to children, because computers look so many different ways depending on their function. A bank machine, a video arcade game, a personal computer and a computerized cash register all have different physical characteristics. From the appearance of these machines it is NOT obvious that they are all computers.

The differences in these computers are not coincidental. Each has been designed to fit a specific need. A McDonald's cash register was designed with a key to enter each item sold there. A bank machine needs fewer keys because once a bank card is inserted to verify the user's identity, the only information to be entered is the type of transaction desired, the user's secret number, and the amount of money involved. Despite the variance in physical appearance, each computer must provide a way for the user to enter information, or **input** into the computer, a **central processing unit** for handling or processing the information, and a way to present the processed information, or **output**. Each computer also has the ability to store specified information.

Although computers are able to do a wide variety of things faster and more efficiently than humans, they also have severe limitations. A computer cannot make decisions unless people have programmed it to make selections based on predetermined criteria. A computer can only accept input in ways decided in advance by programmers. A computer does not feel, and it cannot make value judgments. And although computers as a whole can do a wide variety of things, each individual computer can only do those things that it is programmed to do. A bank machine cannot play video games, a computerized telephone exchange cannot figure out the price of a Big Mac, and a VCR cannot direct an aircraft which is ready to land.

This discussion of computers highlights four additional concepts about computers that are an appropriate focus for young children:

1. Computers can do many different things.
2. Computers have enormous potential as well as limitations.
3. **Input** is entered into the computer, processed by the **CPU** (central processing unit), creating **output**.
4. Computer hardware and software are made and controlled by people.

It is hard to discuss these concepts individually because they are so interrelated. In exploring the uses of computers, children discover their potentials, as well as their limitations. For each computer they encounter, children need to consider

- what it does
- what type of information must be entered
- how the information is entered
- what type of processing occurs
- what type of outcome will result.

In all explorations of the computer by children, it is important to make clear that computers are dependent on people. They are made by people, run by people, and repaired by people. For example, a bank machine cannot work unless a bank worker turns it on and stocks it with money, and a person gives it a command.

For convenience of discussion, each concept is discussed separately, although they overlap each other. Each concept is examined to determine what aspects of it are of interest to, and understandable by, young children. Informal means for helping children to come to terms with these concepts are presented, along with activities to use during free play or group times.

COMPUTERS CAN DO MANY DIFFERENT THINGS

Computers are all around us. We see computers or machines run by computers every day. Many stores have computerized cash registers. Supermarkets use computers to "read" the prices of products, to weigh produce and compute the price for that quantity, to calculate the price of the total purchase, to subtract coupon credits from the total, and to determine and add on the correct amount of tax. These computers also keep track of taxes that the store owes the government, keep an inventory of items sold, and determine what stock should be ordered.

Computerized cash registers are used at fast-food restaurants. Workers enter the items ordered by touching the correct keys. The computer then processes this information. A list of the items ordered is generated, as is the price to charge the customer. If the customer does not pay in exact change, the cash register will determine how much money must be returned to the customer.

These computers also produce other output that is less apparent to the customer. They keep a record of sales. This record can be used to determine total sales, to discover which items are the biggest sellers, to ascertain when business is brisk versus slow, to decide which items must be ordered, and to predict how much food is likely to be sold at that restaurant at a given time. This helps with personnel schedules as well as with ordering.

Some of these functions are a bit abstract for young children. Children are not aware of the need to keep inventory or of the need to schedule workers or food ordered from the wholesalers to best match expected volume of trade. Also, the number concepts of young children are not advanced enough for them to comprehend the mathematical calculations involved in these functions.

What Can Children Learn About the Many Uses of Computers?

If many of the computer's functions are a bit abstract and complex for young children, then what is important and possible for them to learn about the many uses of computers? Although children cannot understand all the functions of the computer at McDonald's, they can see that it is there. They can learn to recognize computers in many different parts of their world. They can see that computers have many different designs. Teachers can help children to understand that people design computers to accommodate specific needs. Children can see how the design of the computer fits its use. Children can explore what kind of input is entered into the computers. They can also discover how the user enters the needed input. Children can observe what kind of output results when each computer processes the input. Children can discuss the ways in which different computers use memory—a characteristic that makes computers different from other machines. The supermarket's cash register stores each of the items entered, then uses its instructions of arithmetic facts to get the final answer. A computer in a library stores who has which books and when they are due, and it outputs overdue notices from this information.

Which uses of the computer are best for young children to explore? The answer to this depends, in part, on what types of computers are convenient for a particular classroom of children to visit and experience. The class discussion of computers should begin with children using real computers. After many such experiences, children can discuss other possible uses of computers that are presented in books, seen in pictures, or described by the teacher or classmates. As with children's development of any concept, the amount of understanding possible from these second-hand presentations depends on the depth of the concepts built from previous first-hand experiences, as well as on the age of the children involved.

Computers in the Classroom

The logical place to begin is with the many uses for the computer in the classroom. The types of uses to be found in each classroom depend on the software and hardware available. Specific items sometimes can be borrowed from parents, other schools, or computer labs for a short period of time. Some of the computer's functions that are possible to explore in the classroom are making pictures, making music, playing games, playing pretend with programs such as the **Explore-a-Story** series that allow children to animate creatures, and writing stories. Whether children write on their own or by narrating to a teacher, they see that the computer can be used to record and print out their stories and ideas.

Children can also explore the computer's potential as a tool. They can write stories on it to bind into books for a class library. They can make banners to announce special events. They can make cards or signs.[1] **Mask Parade** allows children to create masks, feet, or other costume accessories. **Newsroom** and other programs allow the creation of a newspaper.[2] Children also find their own ways to use the computer as a tool. Maura decided to print some of the pictures from **Stickybear ABC** to combine with her own pictures to make an alphabet book for her younger brother. Michael used his computer picture as a blue print for a "bee machine" he was making.

Teachers may also bring in resource people who can demonstrate unique ways to use the computer. Parents are an excellent resource. A questionnaire

---

[1]For younger children, programs such as **Print Shop**—which allows the user to make signs, banners, and cards—may be too difficult for independent use. Visiting children from older grades can act as assistants. Later, kindergartners with lots of computer experiences, or first graders, may be able to use this independently. Even though **Print Shop** may require adult assistance, it is appropriate for occasional use. Although the goal is for computers to be an independent activity in the classroom, occasional uses that require more assistance are allowable if these uses are presented as part of a program to help children see the many jobs the computer can perform.

[2]**Newsroom** should also be used with assistance from an adult or older child. The children could create the stories, and the assistant could type them and format the paper.

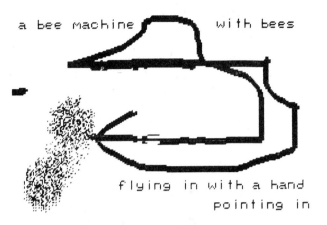

a bee machine   with bees

flying in with a hand
                pointing in

*Michael made a bee machine with **Magic Crayon**.*

sent home about how they use computers on the job can encourage parents to come to school to tell (and show, if possible) the children what they do. Musicians who do composing on the computer could demonstrate what they do and perhaps stay to help the children do some composing. This could be followed up with software for programming music that children can use independently. Another possible resource is a handicapped individual who uses the computer to communicate. This visitor could show the children how the computer enables communication.

Auxiliary hardware can be attached to the computer to allow children to explore additional computer uses. With a **voice box** and the appropriate software, the computer can talk to children and stimulate language. Some computers, like the Macintosh and the Apple IIgs, can speak without additional hardware. Children enjoy typing random letters or names and listening to how the computer says what they have entered. With a **turtle** or other robot, children can learn the computer's potential for controlling the movement of a robot. A **MacVison, Apple video interface**, or other video interface can show children both how the computer can be used to make photographs and how, once the photograph is captured on the computer, the child can change it by drawing on details using a drawing program. Erin was concerned about how she would look when her

loose front tooth fell out. Her dad took her picture with the video camera and the computer. He then used a drawing program to black out the loose tooth creating a picture of Erin as she would look when the tooth fell out.

This is just a beginning list of computer uses that can be explored in the classroom. Each teacher will find additional uses when considering the software and hardware that is available both in the classroom and around the community.

Computers in the Community

Once children have discovered the many uses of computers in their classroom, teachers can help them to explore computers in the community. How do teachers find community computers to investigate with the children? As in the classroom, the specific uses selected depend on what community resources are available nearby. Like the children, teachers have to become more aware of computers in their environment. Teachers should look around on their own to discover the computers resources in their communities, then decide which uses can be understood by young children. Here again, parents can be an excellent resource. A class visit to see the parents' workplaces to see how the computer is used can be exciting and rewarding. Following are suggestions of possible places to find computers. Ways of selecting appropriate computers to explore with children is discussed later in this chapter.

Computers in Retailing. Look for computerized cash registers. Start by looking at places children go often, like fast-food restaurants and grocery stores. Older children can also explore computers used for record keeping—to keep track of inventory, payroll, and schedules. Many gas stations now have computerized pumps that can be programmed to pump a particular mixture of gas.

Computers in Transportation. Computers may be used to control traffic light systems. Travel agents use computers to select, book, and print tickets. Airports use computers to set schedules, assign seats, and assist air traffic controllers. Computer simulations are used to train pilots. Space travel relies heavily on computers for design, for communication, and for directing the spacecrafts. Computers are used for designing, scheduling, and monitoring subway systems.

Computers in Banking. Computers are used at automatic bank tellers and within the bank, both for checking on and recording accounts and transactions.

Computers in Communication. Computers are an integral part of the telephone system. They are used by the post office for sorting mail. Television and radio stations use computers to program broadcasts and commercials. Computers are used for developing animation. Newspapers rely heavily on computers for word processing, storing information, and setting up the paper's format for the day.

Computers in the Arts. Computers are used to compose and play music. They are used as a medium for graphic arts. Computer graphics can also be used to design buildings and sculpture. The artist can use the computer to generate views from different angles, cross sections, and estimates of materials needed.

Computers in Services. Look for computers at the library to check books in and out. Computers are used by police and fire stations to monitor calls, make reports, keep records, and analyze information. Computers are used to assist individuals with handicaps. Weather forecasters rely heavily on computers.

Computers in Science. Computers are used in research. They are used to make simulations, particularly of complex, dangerous, or expensive processes. Computers are an important ingredient in designing new products. Medicine now relies heavily on computers for record keeping and for making diagnoses.

Computers in the Office. Computers, particularly in the form of word processors, have become crucial to the functioning of most offices. They are used for such things as producing and printing letters, organizing mailing lists, and maintaining records.

One More Place to Look for Computers—As Parts of Machines

When looking for computers both at school and in the community, be sure to look inside other machines. When *microprocessors* were invented, more economical new realms of computer use became possible. Not only did this new technology increase the number of homes with computers, it also enabled designers of other machines to incorporate microprocessors into their own inventions. A VCR is a device that can be used for recording and playing television shows. The microprocessors allow people to program the VCR to remember and act on a set of recording directions when the user is not present. When a microprocessor is added to a machine, the machine becomes transformed from an entity that performs a set function to an entity that can be programmed in advance to perform a series of functions in an order specified by the user.

Meaning?   MICROPROCESSOR

A **microprocessor**, or **chip** as it is sometimes called, is a complex electronic circuit placed on a small piece of silicon. These are what makes it possible to have such small computers.

When looking for computer uses to explore with children, consider machines that incorporate microprocessors, such as a VCR, microwave oven, or copying machine. **The Wishing Stone** activity (p. 189) describes using a word processor and a copying machine to make a class book. During this activity, the teacher can discuss the special computer components of the copier. It can be "programmed" to remember a series of commands. The child types in the size of the picture desired (should it be reduced, enlarged, or kept the same size?), the number of copies wanted, and the size of paper on which to print it. Once the program is typed in, the child presses the "start" button, and the copier "runs the program" the child has defined. If possible, lift up the lid of the copier and look inside. Children who have looked into a microcomputer recognize the green computer card that looks like the motherboard and the flat cable that resembles the one connecting the disk drive to the disk card on the motherboard.

Learning More About the Computers That You Want To Study

After you have located a computer that might be of interest to the children, the next step is to determine what the children can comprehend about that type of computer use. There are four important groups of questions to ask about the computer:

1. What can the children actually see the computer doing?
2. How familiar is the activity the computer is doing? If it is not an activity known to the children, how easily can it be understood?
3. Will the children be able to recognize parts of the computer? Will they be able to see the inner workings of the computer as well as its exterior?
4. Can children try using the computer?

Let's examine each of these questions individually.

What Can Children Actually See the Computer Doing? Can the children see how the input is entered into the computer? At the supermarket, they can see the cashier pull the item across the scanner. Can the children see and understand the output produced? At the supermarket, they can see the price flash on the register when the computer has re-

---

INPUT FOR TEACHERS:

PLANNING GOOD FIELD TRIPS

Some advance planning by the teacher can make the difference between a loud, chaotic field trip and an interesting, educational one. The host-(ess) wants to make the trip interesting to the children, but he or she may not know how to describe what is happening at the children's level, or know what sensory experiences will be of interest. By visiting the site first, and talking with the person who will be showing the children around, the teacher can help design the trip to best fit the children's needs. During the trip, help the guide by pointing out things that may be missed, by asking questions to focus both the guide and the children on relevant items, and by interpreting the guide's words at a child's level, if necessary.

If possible, divide the children up into smaller groups, as is done in **A Trip to the Bank** (p. 187). This makes the trip more personal, decreases waiting for turns, and makes it easier for each child to see.

---

corded the input. They can see that if the price does not flash on, the cashier tries to enter the input a second time by rubbing the item across the scanner again. They can also see a second output—the cash register receipt that is produced as an end result of the processing.

As well as being visible, the outcome must have some meaning for the children. At a travel agency, the children will see computers on every desk. They can observe the travel agent typing input into the computer and see the typed output on the screen, but because children cannot read the screen, and they are unlikely to receive a ticket to Disney World, the output has little meaning for them.

Are the Children Familiar with the Computer's Activity? Many computers perform jobs that are unfamiliar to children. For example, police officers

Children can easily try the supermarket computer for themselves.

use computers to help identify cars by tracing license plate numbers. This is a process with which children are unfamiliar. On the other hand, children are well aware of the fact that people must pay for things in stores, and that cash registers are used to add up how much people need to pay. A computerized cash register performs a function that is already familiar to children.

If we hope to teach children that computers can help people by doing many different jobs, then the jobs explored must be ones that children can comprehend in order to understand that the computer is helping. This understanding can come in three ways.

1. The children could already be familiar with the function the computer is performing. For example, most children know that cash registers figure out how much money is owed.
2. The teacher could present stories and/or activities to explain this computer's function before the visit.
3. The function could be one that becomes clear as the children watch the computer working. For example, children may not understand how animation works or the need for remaking the same picture over and over with only a slight variation. But watching an animator draw a picture on the

computer, then change it a little, a little more, and a little more makes the process clearer than any prior explanation could.

Can the Children Recognize the Parts of the Computer? Will the children realize that they are looking at a computer when they see it? Does it have some part that resembles a keyboard where the input is entered? Is it possible for the children to see the connections between the parts of the computer? At the supermarket, can the children see the cable that connects the cash register to the scanner and the scale? Can the machine be opened up so that the children can see the green computer cards that are similar to those in the microcomputer they have seen at school? The more the field trip computer differs from familiar microcomputers, the more important it is that children be able to see some physical evidence—keys, computer cards, or cables—that links this alien computer to the familiar *micros* at school.

Meaning? MICRO

Micro is a slang term for **microcomputer**.

Can the Children Use the Computer Themselves? It is often not possible for the children to actually use the computer they are visiting, but when it is possible, the children's view of the computer as something they can master is reinforced. At the supermarket, each child could purchase a small item for school, and, with the assistance of the teacher or cashier, they could enter the price of the item into the cash register by rubbing the price code across the scanner. At McDonald's, children could key in their own purchases.

Evaluating Which Computers To Explore in the Community

Let's use the previous questions to evaluate the appropriateness of a class trip to a bank money machine.

What Can the Children Actually See the Computer Doing? A trip to the bank does allow the children to observe a computer in action. The children will see people typing in commands and entering a bank card. Then they will see the machine outputting a receipt and some money. They will also be able to see people depositing money and the bank outputting a receipt.

Are Children Familiar with the Function of a Bank Money Machine? Many children have seen their parents using a money machine, giving them a practical familiarity with its function. But often children think the machine "gives people money," without understanding that money will only come out of the machine if the requester has previously put some money into the bank. A story about someone keeping their money in the bank may help children to have a clearer understanding of what a bank is and how a bank machine computer helps the bank to function. (**I Want Some Money Please**, p. 184, is an example of such a story.) Children are not familiar with some of the other uses of computers in banks—transferring funds to other banks, computing interest, and other forms of record keeping and calculations. These should not be discussed, as they would be incomprehensible and irrelevant to young children. Although the children will not be able to grasp all the functions that computers fulfill at the bank, they will be able to see its ability to give out and take in money. A trip to the bank should concentrate on the giving and taking of money and not address the other functions of the bank.

Can the Children Recognize Parts of the Bank Machine Computer? Children will be able to recognize the keys on the outside of the bank machine as similar to the keys on a microcomputer, though the bank has far fewer keys than the micro. When looking inside the bank machine, if this can be arranged with the bank, children will be able to see the green computer cards like those in the micro, and cable like that connecting the disk drive to the micro. Also inside the machine, the children will see the printer typing out receipts in the same way that the printer at school prints output.

Will Children Be Able To Use the Computer at the Bank? It may be possible for the children to use the bank computer. The bank employee may allow the children to use the bank's card to withdraw, then deposit a small sum. If a teacher or a parent has an account at the bank, her or his card could be used in the same way.

A Trip to the Bank Would Be Appropriate. So it would appear that a trip to see the bank computer *would* be appropriate. The children will be able to observe the computer taking in and dispensing money. They will be able to understand the need for a machine to help people withdraw and deposit money. The children will recognize various components of the computer: the keys on the outside and the green computer cards and cables on the inside. The children might even have a chance to use the money machine computer themselves.

Teaching Children about the Computer's Uses

The best way for children to learn what computers can do is to use them to do a variety of things. This use can be supplemented with discussion about what the computer is doing. Teachers can encourage children to compare what the computer is doing to other ways of accomplishing the same task. Both informal and more formal methods can be used to encourage such comparisons. As the child is typing on the computer, you can talk about how fast the computer can make letters. As you are typing a narrated story, you can compare the speed to your speed when writing out their dictations longhand. More formal "lessons" about the computer's use are also possible. The class can compare what peo-

INPUT FOR TEACHERS:

DRAMATIC PLAY

Although the bank dramatic play in **Children's Bank and Trust** (p. 188), and some of the other dramatic play activities suggested in this book, are teacher-structured, this type of dramatic play should be the exception rather than the rule. In general, dramatic play should be the children's opportunity to construct and control the world in which they play. Occasionally however, teachers may use dramatic play as a follow-through for a field trip, or a place to model roles and actions used in a setting about which the children have been learning. Even in this more teacher-structured dramatic play, there should be a lot of flexibility for the children to add their own ideas and to adapt the activity to their own imagination and needs.

ple and computers can do. **This Is a Song about Computers** (p. 144) lists some of the many uses of the computer in the "Going Beyond" section of the activity. Children can help the teacher rewrite the song to include all the uses for the computer that the children have discovered.

Field trips to visit computers are also an excellent way of teaching children about their uses (see **A Trip to the Bank**, p. 187). In order for children to get the most out of a field trip, it is important to have some information in advance. For example, if the class is going to visit a bank money machine, it is important to talk about what it does and what might be seen before the trip (see **I Want Some Money Please**, p. 184). It is important to follow up the trip with classroom activities that reinforce the learning. A trip to the bank could be followed by dramatic play with a bank machine in the classroom (see **Children's Bank and Trust**, p. 188). A trip to the library could be followed with dramatic play involving a computer to inventory or check out books.

ACTIVITIES TO TEACH ABOUT COMPUTER USES

I WANT SOME MONEY, PLEASE

Why?

☐ To introduce children to another use for a computer—the computerized bank teller machine

🕴 To help children understand what a bank is, in preparation for a visit to a bank machine

What Is Needed?

A girl puppet and two adult puppets

Props in a box—a toy rake, pitcher, wooden car, and small sponge that the puppet can use, paper money; 4 small blocks (in scale to make a town for toy train)—tape a drawing of a bank machine to one

A small block or box with a toy train displayed on top

A block to be used as the bank counter

Some play money

A bank card

A box designed as a bank machine with keys, a slot for the money card, and a hinged door for the money drawer (Draw a rectangle on the box with the length running horizontally. Cut along the top and side lines of the rectangle. Pull out the top of the rectangle and fold it along the bottom line. Attach a string just below the top line to use as a handle.)

A low shelf to use as the stage

Setup: Place the box of props behind the shelf. Place the box with the train on top of the shelf to the left hand side with one adult puppet behind the block. Place the bank counter block on top of the shelf to the right with the other adult puppet behind that. Place the bank machine to the left of the bank counter. The teacher stands or sits behind the shelf.

How?

Use the puppets to tell the following story.

One day Lily was walking down the street and saw a train set in a store window.

Lily: What a wonderful train. It would be perfect for my block town at home.

She went into the store to see if she could get it.

Lily: I would like the train set please.
Clerk: It costs $68.00.
Lily: Oh. (disappointed)

Lily really wanted that train set, but she only had 31 cents in her piggy bank. She looked at the train and thought and thought. Suddenly, she had a wonderful idea.

Lily: I know! My parents always go to the bank when they need money. I'll go and get some so I can buy the train.

I WANT SOME MONEY, PLEASE
(Continued)

So she walked over to the bank and waited in line at the counter. Finally, it was her turn to talk to the bank teller.

Lily: I would like $68.00 to buy a train set.
Teller: May I have your **bank card** please?
Lily: What is that?
Teller: The card you get when you put money in the bank. We put it in the computer to find out how much money we are still saving for you at the bank.
Lily: But I never put any money in the bank. I just want to take some out.
Teller: If you have not put any money in the bank, then you cannot take any out. We don't give away money here. We keep money for people so that it does not get lost, then we give it back when the people ask for it.

Lily left the bank and thought some more.

Lily: There must be a way to get some money. My parents get money when they go to work. Maybe I could get a job and earn some money.

So she raked leaves. (Use the rake from the box.) And got some money. (Give her some paper money.)

Lily: This is not enough for the train. I will take it to the bank and get them to save it for me until I have enough. (Have puppet take money to bank.)
Teller: We will keep this money safe for you. Whenever you want to use the money, bring this bank card to the bank so that we can find your money. You can come and get it from me or use the computerized money machine outside. I will also whisper to you your secret code number. When you want money, you need both the card and your secret number. That way, if you lose your card no one else can use it. (Have teller puppet give the girl puppet the bank card and whisper a number in her ear.)

She washed cars (use wooden car and sponge), and got some more money. (Have puppet take it to the bank.)

She sold lemonade (use pitcher), and got some more money. (Have puppet take it to the bank.)

Finally, she had enough money for the train set. She took her bank card and went to the money machine.

Lily: First, I need to put in my bank card so it knows who I am. (Put card in slot.) Then I need to tell it what I want. Bank, this is Lily. I want my money. It isn't giving me my money. What do you think I should do?

(Encourage the children to make suggestions. If they do not suggest using the keys on the money machine, some appropriate questions from you should prompt this idea. You could ask such things as "Do you give the computers at school commands by talking to them?")

Lily: You are right. I need to use the keys to tell the money machine what I want. First I will type in my secret code number. Now there is a sign asking what I want. I'll push this button that says take money out. Now it is asking me how much. I'll press 6-8 for $68.00. It says open the door. (Open door and take out money.) Here is my money and a piece of paper saying how much money the bank is still saving for me. I had better take my card for next time. (Take it.)

Lily walks to the toy store to buy her train.

Lily: I would like the train please. (Hand the clerk the money and pick up the train.)

Lily takes the train home and sets it up in her block town. Then she builds a new building—a bank (use blocks to make a bank), and she makes a bank machine (add bank machine block to bank) so that the people in her town can get their money out of the bank.

I WANT SOME MONEY, PLEASE
(Continued)

Making It Your Own:

Adapt the props in the story to fit those that are readily available to you.

Instead of a puppet show, tell the story using small stuffed animals, feltboard figures, or drawings of objects attached to the bulletin board with moveable paper figures.

Increase the amount of child participation to fit your storytelling style and the discussion skills of the class.

Going Beyond:

After the story, discuss what the bank machine does. What kind of input does it need? (A card and keyboard commands.) What part is the CPU? What does it do? (It checks to see how much money you have and gives you the amount asked for.) What is the output? (The money and a receipt.)

Develop a bank dramatic play to practice the ideas presented in the story (see **Children's Bank and Trust**, p. 188).

Let the children use the puppets during activity time. This will enable the teacher to get a feel for the children's level of understanding.

A TRIP TO THE BANK

Why?

☐ To see another use for a computer

☐ To show again that computers will not do anything unless they are given a command in a language they can understand

☐ To provide another experience with the concept of input/CPU/output

What Is Needed?

Previous class discussion about what a bank is
Transportation to a bank machine
A bank machine to observe
A bank employee willing to show the children the inside of the bank machine
Additional adult chaperons

How?

Take the children on a field trip to see the money machine at the bank. As a group, look at the money machine outside of the bank. Discuss what types of keys it has. Compare it to other computers the children have seen. Watch while a bank employee or teacher puts in a money card and withdraws a small amount of money. If possible, divide the class into two groups. One group can go into the bank with the bank employee to see the inside of the bank machine. The group outside could take turns depositing then withdrawing the $10 from the machine. One child can deposit it, then the other child can withdraw it, and so on.

The children who go to look at the inside of the money machine can look for the familiar green computer boards and for flat cords like the ones that connect the keyboard to the disk drive on microcomputers. Discuss how the person outside the bank enters input into the machine in the form of a bank card, a secret number, and a request for money. The CPU processes the information by checking in its memory to see how much money that person has in the bank. If the person has enough money, the machine will output the money and a receipt showing what the person has done. The children can also search for the money that the machine dispenses. The children observing the inside of the machine will be able to see the money dropping down and being dispensed and the receipts being printed. It is important to stress that the computer keeps a record of how much money each person has. The machine will not give out money if the user does not have money in the bank.

After the inside group has seen how the machine works, the two groups can change places.

Making It Your Own:

If the bank has automatic tellers, or other easily seen and recognized computers inside the bank, let the children explore these as well.

Plan similar trips to visit other computers in the community.

Going Beyond:

Make a classroom bank as a follow-up activity (see **Children's Bank and Trust**, p. 188).

CHILDREN'S BANK AND TRUST

Why?

☐ To explore another use of the computer—as a bank machine

☗☐ To develop an understanding of how a bank machine functions

☐ To practice the words **input, output,** and **CPU**

What Is Needed?

Two large boxes decorated as bank machines, with a slot for entering the bank card and money

A bulletin board in back of the bank machines, with a pocket for each child. Have a child's name on each pocket. Use a separate color for four pockets: 4 red, 4 blue, 4 green, etc.

A bank card for each child with her or his name clearly printed on the card; the card should be the same color as that child's bank pocket

Play money

An envelope for each child containing some money and the bank card. The envelope should match the color of the bank pocket.

Two CPU hats (make strips of cardboard into ring shapes to fit on child's head, decorate with a light-bulb-shaped piece that is labeled ''CPU'').

How?

Encourage the children to become involved in bank dramatic play. One child is the CPU inside of each bank machine. The CPU wears the CPU hat. The other children may deposit their money in the bank by pressing the buttons and entering the money and card through the slot. The CPU takes the card, matches it to a bank pocket, deposits the money in the pocket, and returns the card through the slot.

To withdraw money, children enter their cards through the slot and press some buttons. The CPU takes the card, matches it to the correct bank pocket, and removes some money to slide out the slot along with the bank card.

Making It Your Own:

If children have trouble waiting for their turn to conduct transactions, have the CPU insert a piece of red paper into the deposit slot once the input has been received. This tells the users that the machine is processing the information. (It can be compared to the red light on the disk drive.)

Going Beyond:

For older children, add receipts for the teller to fill out and return with the deposit or withdrawal.

For an older group, add a store nearby so that children can use their money to buy things. Jobs can be available, like stocking the store shelves or sweeping the store so that children can make more money to deposit in the bank.

Banking at the children's bank and trust.

THE WISHING STONE

Why?

☐ To offer practical experience with two forms of computer use: as a word processor and as a component of a copying machine

🧍 To provide an opportunity for creative use of language

What Is Needed?

A computer with a word processing program
A printer
Sheets of 4-1/2″ x 6″ white paper
A copy machine that enlarges
Pencils
An interesting-shaped stone
Colored paper or tagboard for book cover with the title *The Day We Flew* by: (a space for children's names)
A printout of teacher's part of the story placed inside the book cover
A stapler

How?

The teacher and class pretend that the stone is a magic "wishing stone." The teacher begins to read the word-processed story from the book. "One day I was holding the wishing stone as I looked out of the window at a bird flying by. I wish people could fly like birds. All of a sudden the children in the classroom started to fly. Each of the flying children had their own special adventure." Encourage the children to invent a story during activity time about their adventures flying. These stories can then be added to the book.

During activity time, the children can narrate their adventures to a teacher (or other adult), who types it on the word processor. Two copies of the story can be printed out—one for the class book and one for the child to take home. Children can use the half sheets of paper and the pencils to create an illustration to go with their story. If many children want to make up stories at the same time, some can begin with the picture.

The teacher can take the children to visit the copy machine in small groups. Discuss what kinds of commands the copy machine can follow. Have the children try to discover how the input is entered and where the output comes out. If possible, lift the lid and look inside to locate the computer card(s) and cable(s). Let the children enlarge their pictures to the correct size for the book.

Staple together all the stories into a book. Read the book to the class, then put the book on the bookcase for children to read and look at. Discuss the ways in which computers helped to make the book.

Making It Your Own:

Let the children pretend adventures based on their own wishes. The stories could start "One day, (child's name) was holding the wishing stone and wished . . . . "

Make up another stimulus for telling stories that better fits the interest of your class or unit themes being explored.

Use a wordless picture book, such as *Moonlight* by Jan Ormerod (1982) as a stimulus. The children can make up text for the pictures.

Going Beyond:

For older children, let them type their own stories.

Have the children use the computer to make the illustrations as well as the text.

For an older group, make up the beginning of the story with the whole class, letting each child add parts to it.

COMPUTERS HAVE BOTH STRENGTHS AND WEAKNESSES

When people use the computer, they often fluctuate between being ecstatic over its marvelous powers and being annoyed over the many things it cannot do. To be at peace with themselves and the machine, people must learn to accept the computer's limitations as well as its strengths. This acceptance will enable more efficient computer use. If you are aware of the computer's limitations, it is easier to work within its constraints and to find alternative methods for accomplishing tasks, if necessary.

The kinds of weaknesses that users notice varies, depending on their familiarity with the computer and the program. Adults who use a word processor for the first time may be frustrated with their inability to remember how to make the word processor do what they want. Once these adults become proficient users, they begin to see the program's true limitations, such as its inability to format in certain desired ways, or its inability to perform some needed task, such as quickly changing a title from lower case to capital letters.

Children Must Come to Terms with the Computer's Strengths and Weaknesses

Children who use computers must also learn to use its strengths and accept its weaknesses. The things that delight children about computers are not always the same things that delight adults. Children are particularly impressed by the computer's ability to animate pictures and by their own ability to affect what the computer does.

Computers Have Strengths for Children. Like adults, children find that computers enable them to do some things more easily. For young children, printing letters can be a laborious task. Computers offer children the opportunity to produce letters more quickly and accurately than they can do manu-

ally. Children enjoy producing endless lines of random letters on the computer just as they do on a typewriter.

For children who are beginning to write words, word processors offer additional advantages. Christin had been teaching herself to write with a pencil. She had decided that words should be separated so that her readers could tell the words apart. At first, she used a slash "/" to separate words—"Mommy/Daddy/Christin." She found that the slashes were often confused with the letter "I" so she replaced them with dashes—"Mommy-Daddy-Christin." When Christin used the word processor, the space-bar clearly separated words, removing the need for any other symbols.

When using a pencil to write words, Christin found it difficult to gauge the length of words in advance and thus would often reach the end of the paper in the middle of a word. She was concerned that people would not know where the rest of the word was. She tried to make this clearer by adding an arrow pointing to the rest of the word on the next line, but was never really satisfied with this solution. Christin was thrilled when she discovered that the word processor had a solution to this problem. If she was still working on the word when she reached the end of the line, the computer would move the whole word down to the new line, thus automatically keeping her word intact.

Perceived Weaknesses Vary According to Computer Experience. In watching children use computers, it is clear that their evaluations of the machine's weaknesses change with experience, just as adults' do. When children first begin to use **The Bald-Headed Chicken**, or one of the other **Explore-a-Story** programs, they occasionally get frustrated with their inability to move the cursor where they want it to go. "It won't go where I say" or "I want it to get on the box" might be common complaints. At this point, children see the difficulty of controlling the cursor as a weakness of the computer.

With a little practice, children become proficient at moving the cursor, but their proficiency leads

Recently, there has been an increase of research and interest in emergent literacy.[3] Children develop reading and writing skills gradually through interactions with a print-rich environment in much the way they develop verbal language through interaction with an environment full of spoken language. Just as babies "try out" speaking by babbling, preschoolers "try out" reading and writing by imitating what they see done in their environment. Children "write" by scribbling wavy lines across the paper in imitation of cursive. They add strings of letters, some accurate, others invented, to their pictures in imitation of printing. Children incorporate writing into their pretend play by taking notes as they talk on the phone, jotting down an order as they play restaurant, or imitating other ways they have seen adults use writing.

For many children, their desire to write exceeds their physical ability. Children may become frustrated with how long it takes them to make each letter, by their inability to write the letter accurately, or like Christin, with their inability to judge the length of a word in comparison to the remaining space on the line. The computer eases these frustrations. The letters come out beautiful, with less effort, and are placed so that the whole word is on one line. This is not to imply that children should no longer write by hand; they should, and they will. Writing on the computer tends to encourage, not discourage, other writing in the classroom. The computer is merely another tool that children can use when they write.

[3]Some works on emergent literacy are Michael Sampson (Ed.) (1986), *The Pursuit of Literacy: Early Reading and Writing;* Judith Schickedanz (1986), *Beyond the ABC's*; and William Teale and Elizabeth Sulzby (Eds.) (1986), *Emergent Literacy.*

them to discover new problems. At first, Kyle enjoyed making the chicken flap around the screen. He would let it perch in a tree, on the sun, or plop it down in the middle of the pond. He liked to make things vanish by covering them up with other objects or by moving them off the end of the screen. After Kyle had become proficient in moving objects he began to use the program for dramatic play. He had the chicken wander around the screen looking for dinner. (In this program, characters are animated as you move them. The chicken flaps its wings and pecks for food as it moves in the direction you set.) Kyle wanted the chicken to peck at the butterfly when it got there. Although pecking was one of the motions that the chicken did spontaneously while Kyle moved it, the program did not allow him to determine where or when the pecking would occur. Kyle had to settle for having the chicken cover up the butterfly to portray eating.

Lily was also using **The Bald-Headed Chicken**, but she was creating a book. She decided to fill one whole page with chicks. After adding about 8 sets of chicks, a sign appeared saying that no more characters were available. Lily decided to add the additional chicks to the next page of the program. Lily and Kyle both discovered some of the true limitations of the program—that although the characters moved in many fun ways, the user could not control when or where they would move a certain way, and that each screen only holds a set limit of characters. Lily and Kyle needed to decide how to deal with the program limitations they met: Should they change their intent, find an alternative way of accomplishing their goal, or stop using the program?

Computers Are Inanimate. One limitation of computers that children often notice is the computer's inability to respond when spoken to. The computer does follow commands, but the kinds of commands it understands are rather narrow. Because the computer can be so captivating and has so many animated characters, it is easy to see it as an animate object. Although children may know intellectually that the computer and its characters are not alive, sometimes it is easy to forget this.

The kindergarten class had been using a PLATO terminal connected to the University's *mainframe* computer. A favorite program was **Freddie Frog**, with which children could make Freddie jump by touching the screen. One day, the *terminal* was *down* (computer jargon for not working.) A technician came to the classroom to fix it. Mark peered in the opened terminal and asked, "Where's Freddie?" Mark felt that Freddie must be inside the computer.

If you view the computer as an animate object, it is harder to understand its inability to do human things. In coming to terms with the computer's strengths and weaknesses, it is important for children to understand that it is not animate. It is merely a machine that is made and controlled by people. (This concept is discussed in more detail later in this chapter, see page 205.)

Meaning? MAINFRAME AND TERMINAL

A **mainframe** is a large, extremely powerful computer that can be used by many people in many ways simultaneously.

A **terminal** is hardware that connects to a mainframe computer, generally including a keyboard and monitor.

What Can Children Learn about the Computer's Strengths and Limitations?

To make the best use of the computer, children need to recognize its strengths and weaknesses. They can learn to capitalize on the computer's strengths by using it as a tool for those things it does well. If the children want to make a class newspaper with a copy for each child, then the computer, which enables the teacher to take down dictation quickly and allows for multiple copies to be produced, can be a good vehicle for producing the paper. In the same sense, they must realize what it does not do well. If the children want to make pictures for a texture book, these must be made at the art table with materials that can be felt, not at the computer that produces flat, nontextured pictures.

Children need to learn to deal with the computer's weaknesses when they arise. For example, David and Amanda were making a picture on **Magic Crayon**. They were going to turn the whole screen blue by filling it all in with lines. They discovered that the computer would not do this for them. The screen could only hold so many lines. These children needed to decide whether they would print the picture anyway. They decided to print it, then finish filling in the spaces with markers.

The teacher discussed with them how they were "smarter than the computer" because they could solve the problem of filling in the whole screen, while this program could not. They also discussed what they would do to change the program if they were the programmers. First off, they would write the program to let you fill in the whole screen. This type of informal discussion helps children to realize that although the computer can do some things that people cannot do, like draw very straight lines, there are many things that they can do that the computer cannot do.

Teachers can help children to explore the options when a program is unable to accomplish what children want. David and Amanda had a variety of options. Some possible choices were to decide the picture was finished; to begin making a different type of picture; to stop using the computer and do something else; or to complete the picture using other materials off the computer. Children can learn to see the options and select the one they prefer. This ability to select alternatives when your original intent cannot be fulfilled is useful in all areas of life, for it is not just computer programs that have unexpected or unwanted limits. Most activities and materials have limits. A child who is using Lego finds that they have to be put together a certain way in order to stick, and that only a set number of wheel bases and people are available no matter how many may be wanted.

How Do Children Learn About the Computer's Strengths and Weaknesses?

Children learn about the computer's strengths and limitations in the same way that they learn about other objects—as a by-product of using them. Every time they use the computer, they are faced with things that it does and does not do. Informal discussion about these discoveries is very important. Often, teachers can help children to deal with the computer's shortcomings. In Chapter 8, I mentioned Russell, who was using **Facemaker** for the first time. He was excited by the winking at first, but gradually became upset. Finally he announced, "It won't wink with the other eye!" The teacher agreed it would be better if it could wink with both eyes.

"That computer isn't as smart as you are, is it? The person who wrote the program only programmed it to wink with one eye." This teacher is helping Russell to understand what strengths he has that the computer does not have, and also to understand that the program will not do more because the programmer has not designed it to do more. Many of the activities to help teach children the uses of computers also develop the children's understanding of the computer's many strengths.

More-formal class discussions of what the computer can do, as in **The Art Show** (p. 194) and **Recitation Time** (p. 195) help children to pull together the information they have collected about computers.

ACTIVITIES FOR TEACHING ABOUT THE COMPUTER'S STRENGTHS AND LIMITATIONS

THE ART SHOW

Why?

- ☐ To encourage children to consider the computer's strengths and limitations
- 𝄆 To develop an aesthetic sense
- 𝄆 To provide opportunities for language fluency

What Is Needed?

Children's artwork from a variety of graphics programs (if no printer is available, have the computer and disks with stored art)

Children's artwork created with a variety of media.
   [Examples: graphic art made with paint, crayons, marker and/or chalk; three-dimensional art such as clay sculptures, mobiles, or junk constructions; creations with texture such as texture collages, or finger paintings made with paint that retains its shape when dry; and creations with an odor such as those made with scented markers, or paints with aroma (coffee, cocoa, perfume, or cinnamon) added.]

A bulletin board and shelves for display

How?

Have the children arrange the artwork in the museum. They can label each work with the artist's name and the creation's title. If no printer is available to print the computer art, it can be displayed on the computer's monitor. Children, from this class or other classes, can then come to visit the gallery. Other children can be the museum guides showing visitors around. Encourage the children to describe the works of art. What is special about each piece?

Encourage children to compare what is distinctive about the computer art versus noncomputer art. They might notice that the computer art allows straighter lines, more precise filling, and multiple copies (if a printer is available). Noncomputer art can have texture, aroma, blended color, and be three-dimensional. If a printer is not available, the noncomputer art has the advantage of being "take-homeable."

Making It Your Own:

Have a group discussion comparing computer and noncomputer art that is in the museum. Create a written list of the distinctive advantages of each.

Have the children arrange the art by the media used to create it.

Have the children compare the characteristics of various kinds of noncomputer art. Have the children compare the characteristics of graphics made from different computer programs.

Read books about art or museums such as *Norman the Doorman* by Freeman (1959), as a lead-in or reinforcement to the activity.

Take the children on a trip to an art museum or art showing. If a museum or gallery is not available, local office buildings, banks, or public buildings often have small exhibitions that could be viewed.

Going Beyond:

For an older group, let the children help plan the types of art media to be used for creating works for the gallery.

Let the children write (with teacher help) or narrate to a tape recorder a description of the art to be seen in the museum.

RECITATION TIME

Why?

- ☐ To encourage discussion of the computer's strengths and weaknesses

- ☐ To acquaint the children with another use for the computer—talking

- ♟ To encourage auditory memory

What Is Needed?

A poem good for group recitation, such as *Click Beetle*, by Mary Ann Hoberman (in *Random House Book of Poetry for Children*, 1983)

A tape recorder

A computer with a speech synthesizer, a digitizer, and the necessary software to run it

How?

Teach the class the poem. Practice saying it as a group. The class can try reciting it with a variety of different intonations and expressions. Record the class recitation of the poem on the tape recorder. Have the children narrate the words to the poem as the teacher types them into the word synthesizer. Listen to the taped poem and the synthesized poem. Compare the differences. Some points that might be considered are clarity, expression, ability to vary expression, and speed with which the poem was "learned" by the computer and by the children whose voices are on the tape.

Making It Your Own:

Use a song instead of a poem.

Have the children listen to the computer and the tape and guess which is which.

Going Beyond:

For an older group, have the children invent a puppet show or play with a robot as one of the characters. With the help of a teacher, let the children program the computer to speak the robot's part.

COMPUTERS TAKE IN INPUT, PROCESS IT, AND PRODUCE OUTPUT

At the simplest level, the computer can be described as a machine that takes in and processes information in order to produce a desired product. In computer terms, the information fed into the computer is called input. This input is then processed by the computer's central processing unit, or CPU. Output is the end product that results. What makes the computer so special is its ability to process a wide range of input, the speed at which it can process this information, and the wide range of output it can produce.

Young children are not able to understand the mathematical or electronic explanation of how the process works (nor do most adults), but they can understand that they enter input into the computer, the computer then processes this information, and produces the output. Children can explore the various kinds of input that computers can process. Input can be entered by pressing a letter, an arrow, or other keys on the keyboard; by manipulating a mouse or joystick; by inserting a disk in the disk drive; or, on some computers, by giving voice commands.

Although children cannot see the computer processing the information, they can be shown which part of the computer does the processing. They can be told that the computer takes the input the user has entered and changes it to produce the output. Although children do not yet understand how this is done, they will begin to understand that their input is used by the computer to determine the type of output to produce. Children can also see the many different types of output computers can produce. Output can be a picture on the monitor, a printout, motions of a robot, speech from a voice synthesizer, action in a flight simulator, or much more. Children also delight in their ability to master the terms input, output, and CPU to describe their interactions with the computer.

The computer's input/CPU/output sequence is one example of change—an exciting and appropriate noncomputer concept for children this age. A discussion of how the computer changes input to produce output can be expanded to explore many different kinds of change in the child's world. An oven changes the raw cookie dough into cookies. A dryer changes wet clothes into dry ones. A pair of scissors changes large sheets of paper into smaller pieces. Children can explore agents that make objects change from one form to another. This is a topic that is often part of an early childhood curriculum. An exploration of a computer's ability to take input and transform it into output could be the stimulus for a much wider discussion of change and cause and effect. Many of the activities to promote an understanding of input/CPU/output do in fact explore other types of cause-and-effect relationships.

Helping Children To Learn About Input, CPU, and Output

There are many ways that teachers can help children to understand about input/CPU/output. One means of introducing this concept is through presentations and discussions at group times (see **Many Kinds of Processors**, p. 198, and **People Input and Output**, p. 200). These concepts can then be used at appropriate times throughout the day. When exploring the various uses of the computers, teachers and children can look at what kind of input each computer accepts, and how the input is entered. They can look for where the CPU is located, or at least discuss indications that it is processing the input. At the bank, the children will see a "please wait a minute" sign as the machine processes their input. The children can also observe the type of output that is produced.

The activities for learning to understand computer commands and programming in Chapter 8 can also be used for discussion of input because commands and programs are forms of input. In **Program Your Face** (p. 164), children are asked to make a program for moving a face with cards representing facial motions. They then "run the program" by following the commands in order. In this activity the cards can be seen as the input, the child as the CPU that processes the information, and the expressions on the

The soda machine CPU processes the input (money in desired slot) to deliver the output (soda). (Photo courtesy of Nancy Edwards)

child's face as the output. In cooking activities like **Purple Cloud** (p. 171), the ingredients are the input, the blender is the CPU, and the finished product is the output.

An interesting way to help children to understand the idea of "processing" is to compare the computer with other machines that process input. A clothes washer takes dirty clothes and "processes" them to produce clean clothes. A toaster "processes" the input of bread and outputs toast. **Many Kinds of Processors** (p. 198), along with many of the activities in this section, encourage children to explore the idea of machines or people processing input to produce a unique output. Many of the activities for teaching about selecting from a menu and following procedure can also be used to help children learn about input/CPU/output. In **Soda Machine** (p. 98), the coins are the input, the child in the machine is the CPU, and the output is the soda.

These activities should be coupled with either informal or formal discussion of how the computer's processing ability varies from those of other machines. The computer can perform a wide variety of processes, depending on the instructions given most other machines can only process input in one way. The computer can store a whole series of commands, while most other machines can only do one command at a time.

MANY KINDS OF PROCESSORS

Why?

- [ ] To use the terms "input," "CPU," and "output"
- [ ] To introduce the concept of input/CPU/output

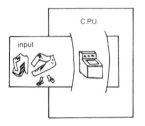 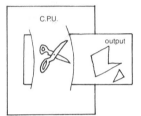

What Is Needed?

A bulletin board

10 "CPU frames," each made from a 4-1/2″ x 6″ sheet of stiff heavy paper or light cardboard with two 4-1/8″ vertical slits cut 1″ in from each side

10 "input/output strips," each made from 4″ x 12″ strips of stiff paper or light cardboard, and each inserted into the slits of one of the "CPU frames" so that the input/output strip runs behind the center of the CPU frame and sticks out at each end

Sets of pictures mounted on the CPU frames and input/output strips

1. A computer on the CPU frame, a keyboard on the left of the input/output strip, and a printer and monitor on the right of the strip
2. A washer on the frame, dirty clothes to the left, clean clothes to the right
3. An oven on the frame, raw food to the left, cooked food to the right
4. A scissors on the frame, a whole piece of paper on the left, a cut up piece of paper on the right
5. A lamp on the frame, a switch on the left, lamp light rays emanating on the right

5 frames and strips with the following pictures mounted on each CPU frame, but no pictures mounted on the strip: popcorn popper, camera, iron, toaster, and sewing machine

A marker

A group time with whole class

Setup: Attach the frames to the bulletin board so that the input part of the each strip is visible, but the output is hiding in back of the CPU

How?

Encourage some informal discussion of the types of machines on the board. Can these machines work all by themselves? What do people have to do to make the computer go? They must enter commands. Tell the children that this is called "input" because it is what you must put into the computer in order for it to work. (If the children mention other things that must be done to the computer—plug it in, turn it on, or put in the disk—then add pictures to illustrate these other input on the strip next to the keyboard.

"When you are playing **Stickybear ABC** and type in a 'C,' what happens?" Encourage the children to tell you what happens—a graphic of Stickybear crying appears. "There is a special part inside the computer that helps it to process (or change) your 'C' into the Stickybear crying. This part is called the central processing unit or CPU; it is like the computer's brain. When you type a 'C,' the CPU thinks about the information that it has stored on the **Stickybear ABC** disk, and it finds that 'C' is telling it to make the crying picture of Stickybear."

"If the computer name for the information you put in the computer is input, what do you think the picture that comes out is called?" "Output." "You give the computer input by typing the 'C.' The CPU takes your input, touching the 'C,' and processes it

MANY KINDS OF PROCESSORS
(Continued)

to produce the output—Stickybear crying." During this presentation, demonstrate input/CPU/output with the bulletin board by sliding the keyboard on the input/output strip behind the computer on the CPU frame so that the monitor emerges from the other side.

Explain that other machines can also "process" input to produce output. Ask children to identify the toaster. What do you put into the toaster? The bread is the input. The toaster is the CPU that processes the bread. What is the output? What comes out from the toaster when it is done?" When the children have said "toast," pull the strip through so that the toast is showing. Have the children review the terms. So the input is the _____. The CPU is the _____. And the output is the _____. Continue in the same way with the other machines, encouraging the children to use the terms as much as possible. After three or four examples, you can ask the children to generate the terms (e.g., "the dirty clothes are the _____").

For the machines with blank input/output strips, have the children tell you what to draw on the input side. Pull the strip through the processor and ask the children what should be drawn on the output side.

Making It Your Own:

Use a selections of machines that are familiar to your children, and that are easy to find pictures of for making the bulletin board.

Divide the activity into two lessons, one defining input/CPU/output, and one looking at machines as processors.

Going Beyond:

Have the children cut out pictures of machines to make their own input/CPU/output frames and strips.

PEOPLE INPUT AND OUTPUT

Why?

☐ To consider the concept of "input/CPU/output" in a more personal context

☐ To practice the words "input," "CPU," and "output"

🕴 To encourage children to think about how they take in, process, and act on the stimuli in the world

What Is Needed?

A bulletin board covered with paper
A large paper person in the middle of the bulletin board
A marker
A group time

How?

Talk with the children about the fact that they can take in information, process it, and come out with output just like a computer. "When you look around the circle, you use your eyes to take in input, or information about who is here today." Encourage class to name the people who are present. "Now I want you to use your brain—your central processing unit—to figure out who is not here." When the children tell you who is absent, ask how they know. Discuss how they took the information they had stored in their memory—a list of everyone in the class, and the input they took in with their eyes—a list of the children here today—to come up with their output—a list of the children who are absent.

Introduce "Chris"—the person on the bulletin board. If Chris came to visit school today, what kind of input might she get? If the children have trouble coming up with ideas, encourage them to think about the input she might get through each of her senses—what would she hear, see, feel, etc. You might also ask what input Chris might get if she went over to the block area, or the art table. To the left of Chris on the bulletin board, write down the input children suggest. (Picture clues can be added next to the words to remind the children of what they said.)

"Chris has gotten a lot of input. Now she is going to use her brain to think about, or process the information. Her brain is her CPU. (Write CPU on or over Chris's head.) What kind of output might Chris produce?" If the children need help to come up with output, look at each input, and think how Chris might react. "We said she might see John playing with the blocks. What do you think she'll **do** then?"

Child: Start building, too.
Teacher: Right! Chris may take the input of seeing John building. Use her CPU brain to process it by thinking: John is building. That looks like fun. I want to build too. The output would then be Chris building.

Continue in this way, writing the output produced on the right side of the bulletin board.

Making It Your Own:

Instead of Chris, use a character that the class particularly likes, such as Big Bird, Charlie Brown, or Garfield.

THEY'RE PLAYING OUR SONG

Why?

☐ To use terms "input," "CPU," and "output" in a meaningful context

☐ To offer practice selecting from a menu

🚶 To provide opportunity to practice small-muscle precision

What Is Needed?

Three records

The record covers for the records

Foil-covered cardboard coins

A CPU hat (a headband decorated with a light bulb with CPU written on it)

A box or puppet theater decorated as a jukebox (three record covers mounted on the front of the jukebox, a slot below each; inside the jukebox, tape a cup below each slot to catch the coin, and a folder above each slot to hold a record)

A record player children can use (inside or behind the jukebox)

How?

One child stands inside the jukebox, wearing the CPU hat. Another child selects a record by depositing the coin in the slot below the cover of the desired record. The CPU child observes which cup the coin is in, removes the record above that cup, and puts it on the record player.

Making It Your Own:

Use tapes instead of records.

To encourage the children to wait until one command is "processed" before giving another command, have only one coin. The CPU returns the coin through an output slot once the record has begun playing.

Construct other types of vending machines, such as a crayon dispensing machine: Children deposit a coin through the slot below the color they wish to use. Instead of coins, children could deposit an old crayon to get a new one.

Make a computerized lumberyard in which the input is a request for a type of block (the form of the request would be insertion of either a coin below the correct type of block or a card with a picture of the block), the CPU is a child in the box, and the output is unit blocks of the kind ordered.

POPCORN PROCESSING

Why?

- [ ] To build an understanding of input/CPU/output
- [ ] To practice using the terms "input," "CPU," and "output"

What Is Needed?

A hot air popcorn popper labeled "CPU"
Popcorn in bowl labeled "input"
A bowl labeled "output"

Popcorn processing.

How?

The children pour popcorn into the popper. Encourage children to tell you what the "input" is. Ask children what is going to be the CPU and process the popcorn. Have children predict what the output will be. Watch as the outcome—popped popcorn—comes out into the bowl.

Note: The popper **must** be closely supervised at all times. The just-popped corn is hot. Also, parts of the popper can become hot, especially if it is used repeatedly.

Making It Your Own:

Use other cooking projects with machines, such as the microwave, eggbeater, or blender, to demonstrate input/CPU/output.

SHAKE A COLOR

Why?

☐ To have a concrete experience with the concepts of "input/CPU/output"

☐ To use the terms "input," "CPU," and "output"

Å To explore how colors mix to make new colors

Å To observe the changes in ingredients when mixed

What Is Needed?

Diluted red, yellow, and blue tempera paint; if made with powdered paint, use 1 T of powder per cup of water
A large bowl of Ivory Snow
4 1/3-cup measures, one in each container of paint and one in the soap
9 small jars with lids (about 2-cup size)
Fingerpaint paper
18 small bowls
A sink and sponge
Smocks
6 large jars

(**Note:** This provides materials for six children to work at the same time. The extra small jars and bowls are to enable the next group of children to begin while the earlier group is rinsing theirs.)

How?

Children place input—1 scoop paint and 1 scoop soap—into jar. (If they wish to mix colors, small scoops of two different colors can be used.) Each jar and child are a single CPU. Once the lid is on tightly, the child processes the paint by shaking it until well mixed. The output—or finished fingerpaint—is then poured into a bowl for painting. If desired, the child can rinse the CPU and mix one more batch before painting. Children can share paint with each other to get more colors. When the child has finished painting, the bowls should be rinsed for the next person. If much paint is left, it can be placed in one of the large jars for later use.

Making It Your Own:

Offer other ingredients that can be mixed with the paint to change its texture, such as sand, hand lotion, or shaving cream

MICROWAVED CHEESE MELT

Why?

☐ To explore a different use of a computer—as part of a microwave oven

☐ To observe how the microwave processes the input to create a different output

☐ To practice the terms "input," "CPU," and "output"

🏃☐ To practice following picture directions

What Is Needed?

Slices of toast,[4] cut in half
Slices of American cheese, cut in half
Margarine
Small paper plates
Butter knives
A microwave oven
Picture directions showing these steps:
1. Put butter on slice of toast
2. Put cheese on toast
3. Put slice of toast on top
4. Put sandwich on plate in microwave

5. Set timer to 2 minutes[5]
6. Eat sandwich

How?

The children follow the picture directions to make and then eat their own grilled-cheese sandwich. During the process, encourage discussion about what the input is—the uncooked sandwich, what the CPU is that processes the sandwich—via the microwave, and what output results—the grilled-cheese sandwich.

Making It Your Own:

Use the microwave for other simple recipes, such as scrambled eggs, cocoa, or pizza muffins.

[4]Toast is used rather than bread because it is firmer and thus easier for children to spread butter on.

[5]The time to cook may vary if your oven has a different heat setting. Adjust the time to your oven.

COMPUTER HARDWARE AND SOFTWARE ARE MADE AND CONTROLLED BY PEOPLE

Computers would not exist without people. They are machines invented and controlled by people. Part of children's interest in using computers is the sense of power and feeling of competence that result from being able to control the computer. The fact that computers can only do what people say helps to demystify what computers do. Children may not be able to understand the intricacies of computer construction or of programming software, but they can understand that (1) people make and fix computers, (2) computers cannot work without people, and (3) software is designed by people.

People Make and Repair Computers

Children learn a lot about how to view the computer by watching how the teacher interacts with it. If the teacher gets flustered and upset when the computer is not working in the expected way, then the children are also likely to get upset by computer-related problems. On the other hand, if the teacher treats a problem matter-of-factly, as something that must be fixed, then so will most of the children. This is an important attitude to foster because problems often arise when using computers. Wires may be loose, the **[Caps Lock]** key may not be down (this is required on some children's programs that run on the Apple II series of computers), or some other problem may exist. Teachers who calmly check the wires and look inside the computer to see whether all the connections are tight will help children to see the computer as something that can be repaired by people.

A computer technician could be invited to visit the class. The technician could either show how the computer is "tuned up" or repair a computer that is not working. Teachers can open the computers to let children look inside. The children can observe when circuit cards are added to attach peripherals, such as a mouse or printer. This helps children to see that

people can adjust the computer to fit their needs (see **Meet Timothy Turtle**, p. 146).

Computers Cannot Work Without People

Computers cannot do anything unless people plug them in, turn them on and give them commands. Children build this concept as they use the computer. Teachers can ask questions such as "How did you get the computer to do that?" which reinforce that it is the child, not the computer, that made the result occur. The activities in Chapter 8 that teach about commands (pp. 152–161) and about programming (pp. 164–172) help children to build the concept that computers cannot do anything unless people enter appropriate input.

Computer Software Is Made by People

Teachers can help children to realize that software is designed and programmed by people. This often comes up informally as children are playing with the computer. For example, Ben was working with **Kidwriter** to make a picture, and he was using each new character to play act the story. He would "fly" the spaceship around the picture. He would make the other objects "get on" the spaceship by covering them up. As he played, Ben decided to move a character that he had used earlier, but it could not be moved. The teacher explained to Ben that the person who wrote the program only taught the computer to understand commands for moving the character currently being added. After this explanation, Ben no longer perceived the computer as a malevolent machine stopping him from doing what he wants, but rather that there was a limitation in the way the program was designed.

Discussions such as this one, about what children would like programs to do, could lead to a class letter to the software company to recommend ways of improving the program.

A programmer (amateur or professional) could be invited to visit the school. For example, a music student came to visit CAPP summer camp to share a simple piano program he had developed for the computer. He talked about what he wanted to do on the computer and how he had given the computer commands so that it would do what he wanted. He showed the children some of the printed program and explained that these were the directions to the computer to tell it how to act like a piano. If you are lucky enough to have a programmer who would like to work with the children, it is fun to develop a program based on the children's suggestions. Because programming is a lengthy process, the children find it boring to watch the whole process. However, they do enjoy seeing how the programmer has adapted an old program to include their ideas.

SUMMARY

Computers are an ever-present part of our world today. We can help children to understand the many different uses of computers, their strengths, and their limitations. Children can learn when to turn to the computer as a tool for assisting them with a task, as well as enjoy it as a fun source of play. Children can see that computers are designed in many different ways to accommodate a variety of different uses. Although the computers may look different, they are all alike in their ability to accept input, process that input in the CPU, and produce some form of output. This process is only possible because people have first designed, then programmed, and then used the computer.

Teachers can use many informal and formal methods for helping children to develop these concepts about computers. It is important to realize that these, and the concepts listed in Chapter 8, are not meant as an all-inclusive list of computer-related concepts. Each teacher needs to consider the needs, knowledge, and interests of the children in each class to decide which of these or other concepts are most appropriate to teach each year.

10

"This Software's Almost Perfect But . . . ": Activities To Support the Use of Specific Software and Hardware

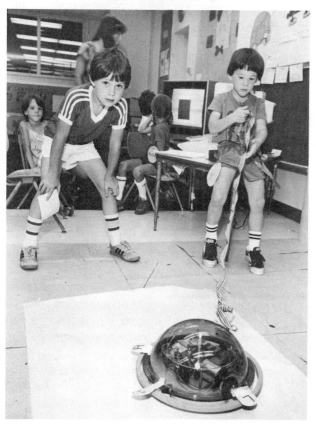

Greta, a "robot turtle" during this activity, is on her hands and knees. She is wearing a large green man-sized shirt that is stuffed with a pillow to make a high-domed "turtle's shell" on her back. A short fat tail is attached to her shirt. Paper armbands adorn her arms. The red band on her right wrist is marked "R," and an "L" appears on the blue band on her left wrist. She is surrounded by cardboard trees and rocks. Small rubber frogs and insects are hiding behind these. One is a few yards to her left.

"Right! Right!" shout Shannon and Margie.

Greta looks at her wrists and turns to her right, toward the red armband marked R.

"NO! NO! LEFT!" cry the children who are "commanding" Greta.

This time, Greta turns left toward the rubber frog that Shannon and Margie are trying to help her eat.

"Forward," they command.

Greta moves forward and pretends to eat the frog.

These children are playing **Feed the Turtle** (p. 212). Although they are 4 and 5 years old, and do not know their left from their right, Greta, Shannon, and Margie are practicing these terms that must be used to direct the real turtle-robot with **Logo** language. **Feed the Turtle** is one of the activities teachers at CAPP invented to help children master a skill that is integral to the use of this software and hardware.

If computers are to be a valuable material for use in the early childhood classroom, then children must be able to use them as independently as they can the blocks, crayons, dramatic play area, or puzzles. Teachers can help children to become independent users of software that might otherwise be too difficult. This chapter discusses two ways in which teachers can support the use of specific software or hardware: (1) Design activities that develop a skill requisite to the using software, as in **Feed the Turtle**. (2) Find ways for children to use the software

Controlling the turtle robot. (Photo courtesy of Robert Cohen)

without having to master an overly difficult skill. Some software contains skills that are too difficult for young children to master—reading, for example. If the teacher can discover a way to circumvent the needed skill, like providing picture clues to negotiate the parts that require reading, the software may then be appropriate for independent use.

These are two ways in which specific pieces of software or hardware can be used to develop activities. There is a third way in which software can stimulate the development of classroom activities. Good teachers are constantly developing new classroom activities and materials to build on their children's interests. At CAPP we found that favorite software often suggested exciting off-computer activities that had no computer-related goals, but that did facilitate general child development goals. This chapter discusses all three types of software-generated activities:

1. Those that help to develop needed skills of specific software
2. Those that help to circumvent difficult skills in some software
3. Those that facilitate general developmental goals.

DETERMINING, THEN DEVELOPING THE SKILLS NEEDED FOR INDEPENDENT USE OF SPECIFIC PIECES OF SOFTWARE AND HARDWARE

Chapters 4-6 discuss a number of skills that are generic to most computer use. In addition to these, specific software or hardware may require additional special skills. Some software requires skills that are too difficult for young children, in which case the software should not be used. Other software either requires skills that can be mastered by young children or allows modification to make it appropriate. If the skill can be learned with experience, teachers can design off-computer activities that help develop the skill.

The first step is an analysis to determine the skills required. Which skills do the children already possess? Which skills can be mastered by children this age? And which skills can be modified to make them accessible to young children? This process is hard to explain in the abstract, but some concrete examples may help to clarify the process. Sample pieces of software and the activities the software has generated are presented. Each includes a discussion of skills required, suggestions for ways to modify the material or the skills, and some methods for supporting the development of needed skills.

The reader should not assume that mention of a specific piece of software is meant as endorsement. The software discussed are programs that have been used at CAPP and whose use has resulted in the development of supporting activities. As mentioned in Chapter 3, each teacher must use his or her own criteria and knowledge of his or her children to select appropriate software.

Activities Generated by Use of the Turtle-Robot

The turtle-robot is a dome-shaped robot connected by a cable to the CPU. The turtle can be "commanded" to rotate left or right, and to move forward or backward by merely typing the first letter of each of these directions. For example, "L" makes the turtle rotate to the left. To use this software, it would appear that a number of skills are necessary:

1. To be able to differentiate the front from the back of the turtle-robot
2. To realize that left and right represent directions
3. To know which way is right and which is left
4. To understand that spatial directions are not static in space but reflect the perspective of the turtle
5. To understand that turning and moving the turtle are two different steps—if you want the turtle to move to its right, first you must press the "R" key to rotate the turtle to the right, then "F" to move the turtle forward.

Children control the turtle with the keyboard.

Let us look at each of these skills individually to see whether they are ones children already have, ones that young children can master, or ones that can be modified in some way to make them appropriate.

Orienting to the Turtle's Front and Back. It can be surprisingly hard to distinguish the front, back, and sides of the turtle-robot. It is a smooth circular dome. The only obvious landmark on the dome is the tail, which is attached near the top but slightly to the back, so the front of the turtle must be the side away from the tail. Determining the turtle's orienta-

tion by the tail can be difficult even for an adult. Adding paper feet and head to the robot make its orientation clearer to the children, as well as giving the turtle a bit more personality.

Knowing the Existence of Directionality and Distinguishing Right from Left. Most children are aware that "left" and "right" are used to designate opposite directions, but few young children, even with practice, are able to regularly distinguish right from left. If children **must** know their right from their left to use the turtle, then the robot would be too difficult for young children to use independently. But children need not know their left from right in order to use the "L" and "R" commands. As is seen in the example of **Feed the Turtle** at the beginning of the chapter, children can maneuver the turtle solely through trial and error. Children can randomly try "R" or "L." If the turtle does not turn in the desired direction, they can either compensate by pressing the opposite command or continue with the original command, typing it enough times to rotate the turtle in a circle until it points in the needed direction.

Modifying the Activity So That Children Do Not Need To Know Right from Left.

Children automatically modify the way they use the turtle to eliminate the need to distinguish right from left. As described previously, they use trial and error to discover the desired direction. Although this random method of getting the turtle to go in the desired direction does work, the turtle can be moved more efficiently if the correct direction can be selected initially. For some children, efficiency is irrelevant. To them, being able to control the robot is the end goal. To them "control" means being the one who decides the kinds of commands to give.

But other children may find the length of the trial-and-error method frustrating. They may see "control" of the turtle as involving an ability to move it more expediently wherever they want it to go. Teacher-made aids can help these children to realize which way is left and which is right. The paper turtle legs can be color coded. The right legs can be red, with a large "R" on each. The left legs can be blue, with a large "L" on each. The rebus directions on the disk cover can show a red "R" for right next to a picture of the turtle with an arrow showing it rotating toward its red right legs. For a younger class, stickers can be added to the letters used to move the turtle. The "L" can be marked with a blue "L" and the "R" with a red "R." The stickers help the children locate which of the many keys on the keyboard are the ones that command the turtle. The colors on the labels help the children to match the keys with the legs, and thus the turtle's directionality.

Understanding That Directions Must Be Given from the Turtle's Perspective.

When children use colored and lettered legs on the robot to determine the necessary command, they need not consider how the perspective changes as the turtle changes. They push blue to make the turtle turn to the blue side or red to make it turn to the red side. Thus, with these guides, children can use the turtle without being aware of the way the directional commands relate to the turtle's perspective. This concept is, however, within the grasp of young children. If you want the children to pay more attention to direction, rather than relying on color, the legs can be color-coded but not the keys, so that the children cannot rely merely on matching the color of the leg to the color of the key. And the legs should not be marked with "L" and "R," again to prevent the children from merely matching without having to view direction from the turtle's perspective. The children can be given armbands that are color-coded to match the turtle's legs. The child can wear a red armband with an "R" on the right arm and a blue band with an "L" on the left arm. This can be used as the two children do in the following example.

David and Michael are using the turtle. They are trying to get it to move to the blue paper pond to the left of the turtle on the floor. Michael stands in front of the turtle, facing the same direction as the robot. Slowly, he turns left toward the pond, leading with his left arm. Then he looks at the "L" on the band. "LEFT!" David presses the "L" key for left, and they both cheer as the robot rotates in the desired direction.

The way David and Michael are using themselves to determine the correct direction helps them to realize the importance of taking the turtle's perspective when giving commands. Off-computer activities such as **Feed the Turtle** (p. 212), and **Fire! Fire!** (p. 214) allow children to practice taking the perspective of others.

Realizing That Rotating and Moving Require Separate Commands.

When playing **Feed the Turtle**, or other games in which the children are following direction commands, children often interpret a

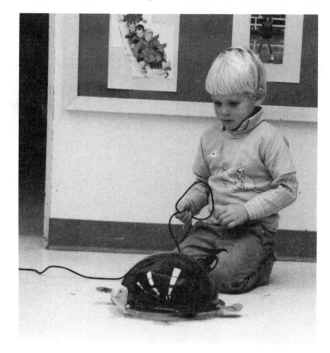

INPUT FOR TEACHERS:

TWO-STEP COMMANDS

Children often find it difficult to understand the separate nature of the rotational and linear movement commands. It is best for the teacher to be the first person to follow directions in these off-computer activities. The teacher can easily mimic the turtle and distinguish rotating movements from linear movements, making two separate actions that require separate commands.

"Timothy Turtle" greets a child.

"right" command as meaning to move right, not just to rotate to the right. Similarly, when they use the turtle-robot, children often expect that a "right" command will cause the turtle to move right, rather than just to rotate in that direction. An understanding of the nature of the commands—that rotation and linear movement are two different requests—can come from two sources.

1. An understanding of turtle commands can be developed by either using the software as it is, or in conjunction with on-computer activities, such as **Timothy Turtle** (p. 146), or **Turtle Tasks** (p. 218).
2. Off-computer activities such as **I Command You to Draw** (p. 159) or **Feed the Turtle** (p. 212) can also help to develop this understanding.

Activities To Teach Turtle-Robot Skills

Timothy Turtle (p. 146) is an activity designed to introduce the children to the turtle-robot.

ACTIVITIES TO TEACH TURTLE-ROBOT SKILLS

FEED THE TURTLE

Why?

☐ To use and following right and left commands

☐ To become comfortable with the commands needed to move the turtle-robot

⚘ To encourage social interaction and cooperation

⚘ To practice giving clear, concise directions

⚘ To practice following verbal commands

What Is Needed?

A green or brown man's shirt with the sleeves rolled up, and a paper or cloth turtle tail attached to the back at about hip height for the children

A pillow

An elastic belt

Blue paper armbands marked L and red bands marked "R" (1 set for each child participating)

Trees, rocks, and bushes made out of painted and cut tagboard (taped to hollow blocks, sign posts, or boxes to make them stand up)

Large rubber frogs and insects

How?

A teacher is the turtle. The elastic belt can be used to hold the pillow on the "turtle's" back. The shirt is then put over the pillow to represent the turtle's shell. The turtle wears a set of armbands and is on hands and knees. The children give the turtle directions for how to move to get to an insect or frog for dinner. The teacher should encourage the children to give directions one at a time and should respond to them exactly. The turtle should only recognize **Logo** directions. Right and left will make the turtle rotate to the right or left. Forward or backward will move the turtle in the direction requested. The children giving directions can use armbands as well if they wish. The direction-givers may need to "take the turtle's perspective," by standing in front of the turtle and facing in the same direction, to determine the appropriate command.

After children understand what the turtle is to do, they can take turns being the turtle.

FEED THE TURTLE
(Continued)

Using arrow pad to "feed the turtle."

Making It Your Own:

Add other props such as some stuffed or rubber "baby" turtles, a pond (made of blue cardboard, or a blue bath mat), lily pads on the pond, or props of your choice.

Instead of a turtle, have the child be a robot, a person walking through a dark cave (a blindfold can be added for darkness), or an animal that needs help to get to a specific place.

Adapt the activity to use arrows instead of right and left. Have a mat with the directional arrows from the computer— one pointing right, one left, one up, and one down. The direction-givers press an arrow on the pad to direct the turtle. (This will help children learn to read the arrow directions used on many pieces of software.)

FIRE! FIRE!

Why?

☐ To practice commands needed for turtle-robot

☐ To practice distinguishing right and left with armbands as aids

🕴 To facilitate cooperation

🕴 To practice giving and following verbal directions

What Is Needed?

A large canvas drop cloth with a series of streets drawn on it

Cardboard boxes decorated as houses and stores

Paper flames with tape to attach to one of the boxes

4 firefighter hats

A set of armbands for each participant, red bands with an "R," and blue bands with an "L"

A table

3 chairs

3 microphones on the table (real ones from tape recorders, or cylindrical blocks or toilet paper tubes made into pretend microphones)

How?

Spread drop cloth on floor. Place buildings along the road. Tape paper flames to one of the buildings. Place the table on the edge of the mat, with chairs on one side so that children look at the mat across the table. All children can wear armbands and hats. Three dispatcher firefighters are at the station giving directions for going to the fire. One "engine" firefighter is at the edge of the city following the directions. The dispatchers can tell the "engine" how to move—turn left, turn right, forward 3 steps, or backward so many steps. The dispatchers can stand in front of or behind the "engine" firefighter to orient themselves if necessary. Once the fire is out, the "engine" can be directed back to the station.

Children can take turns with the various roles. The children can rearrange the buildings in the town and add the paper flames to a different building after each fire.

FIRE! FIRE!
(Continued)

Making It Your Own:

If children have not had much practice giving or following directions, it may work best for a teacher to be the first "engine" firefighter to model how to follow directions and how important specific directions are. This could be done during a group time, with children taking turns giving directions, or during a free-play activity time with a smaller group.

If children are eager to be in the city, let two children drive in the truck together. They will follow the directions as a pair.

Use other dramatic play themes. The children could help someone to negotiate the raised walkway through the swamp without falling off and getting eaten by the alligators. Children can be guided through a maze to find the "treasure." Children can be directing the "substitute letter carrier" through the route to deliver letters. Teachers and children can make up their own characters and destinations to fit the current theme or their own imaginations.

Instead of the children being the fire engine, use a toy fire engine. The city can be drawn on a piece of cardboard.

Going Beyond:

Place a map of the city on the table. The direction-givers can plot the firefighter's moves with a paper fire truck on the map and then give the appropriate directions.

Using the map, have the city firefighter radio to the station the path being used. The station firefighters then follow the engine's path on the map.

(**Note:** some children may get overexcited or scared by the "fire" or "alligator" play; the teacher must be careful to set and maintain the tone for this activity.)

HOKEY POKEY

Why?

☐ To practice using armbands to differentiate left from right

♣ To encourage large-muscle development

♣ To develop skill in following verbal directions

What Is Needed?

A pair of armbands for each child and teacher—a red one with an "R" and a blue one with an "L"

How?

Each child is given the armbands and helped to put them on the appropriate wrist. The teacher also puts on armbands. Begin by asking each child to "raise your right arm, the one with the red band." Practice a series of simple directions raising an arm, waving, touching head, all with the right or left arm. The teacher should follow the directions too so that the child can see which color band she is raising. If some children seem confused, be sure to mention the appropriate colored band along with the left or right direction. After a few minutes of hand directions, ask the children whether they can guess which is their right leg. "Correct; it is the one next to your right arm with the red band." Do a couple of leg directions. Now ask children, "Stretch your right arm into the circle. Stretch it out of the circle. Give it a shake, then turn all the way around. You did a great job at following my commands. I have a command song we can do. You will need to listen carefully to see whether I say "right" or "left."

Sing "The Hokey Pokey."

Put your right arm in
   (put right arm into circle)
Put your right arm out
   (put right arm out of circle)
Put your right arm in
   (put right arm into circle)
And shake it all about
   (shake right arm)
Do the Hokey Pokey
   (put arms over head and shake hands)
And turn yourself about
   (turning around while shaking hands)
That's (clap) what it's all (clap) about (clap).

Repeat the song with the left arm, right leg, left leg, right side, left side, and whole body.

Making It Your Own:

Let the children pick other right and left body parts to use.

If the children tend to be your mirror reflection—raising their right arms as they face you and see you raise your left, then have all the children face one direction. You stand in front of them and also face in that direction.

I MAKE MY TURTLE GO

Why?

☐ To practice identifying their left and right with armbands as a guide

🏃 To practice commands used to move the turtle

🏃 To practice following verbal directions

What Is Needed?

A pair of armbands for each child—a red one marked "R" and a blue one marked "L"
A tagboard turtle for each child

How?

Have the children listen to the song and help their turtle to follow the commands in the song.

(To the tune of "Looby Lou")

Chorus:
The turtle turns to the right.
The turtle turns to the left.
The turtle turns to the right.
Oh what a beautiful sight.

Verse:
I turn my turtle right.

I turn my turtle right.
I give my turtle an "F" command,
Then forward it will go.

Repeat chorus.

Verse:
I turn my turtle left.
I turn my turtle left.
I give my turtle a "B" command,
Then backward it will go.

Making It Your Own:

To simplify, color the turtle's right legs red and left legs blue. Mark an "L" on the left legs and an "R" on the right ones.
Have the children stand up and be the turtle. The verse could be adapted a bit to go like this: "The turtle turns to the right. The turtle gets an 'F' command . . ."

Going Beyond:

If children are getting ready to use **Logo** with the screen turtle, give each child a triangular turtle (a cardboard triangle) and a "screen" (a piece of white paper). Have the children move the "turtle" on the screen as they sing the song.

TURTLE TASKS

Why?

☐ To provide practice using the turtle commands

人 To encourage children to work cooperatively

What Is Needed?

A turtle-robot and the appropriate software
Rubber insects
A blue paper pond taped to the ground around the edge
Boxes or large hollow blocks decorated with paper reeds, rocks, or cattails.
A set of right and left armbands for each participant
Some previous unstructured experience using the turtle

How?

Have the rocks, reeds, and cattails around the periphery of the "swamp" (the floor area the turtle will use). Scatter the insects around the swamp. The children use the keyboard to command the turtle around the swamp. The turtle can have specific tasks like: find an insect for dinner, go for a swim, or sit in the shade of some reeds.

One or two children can use the keyboard. One child can be a "tail watcher" (to be sure the tail does not get tangled when the turtle turns). Other children can help determine which commands are needed by standing near the turtle to help figure out its orientation. Children can also rearrange the props after each task is completed. If another role is needed, one child can choose the turtle's task. Children can take turns with each of the roles.

It is important that the children remain sitting unless they have a particular task. The importance of moving carefully around the turtle should be stressed so that no one falls on it or bumps into it.

Making It Your Own:

Add other props for the turtle to roam among—other turtles, city scenes, or other props that fit the needs of your classroom.

Dress the turtle up as something else—a dinosaur (as in **Stanley Stegosaurus**, p. 246), a fire engine, a flying saucer, or anything that fits the interests or current theme of your classroom.

Provide picture task cards that indicate where the turtle should move.

PEN DOWN

Why?

- ☐ To become comfortable with the turtle-robot commands
- 🚶 To practice giving clear verbal directions
- 🚶 To practice following verbal directions
- 🚶 To encourage social interaction and cooperation

What Is Needed?

A roll of newsprint or brown butcher's paper

A 3-foot-long pole with a marker taped securely to the end so that the tip extends beyond the end of the stick

Experience using the turtle-robot

Blue paper armbands marked with an "L" and red armbands marked with an "R" (1 set for each participant)

How?

Cut two lengths of paper, each 4 yards long. Tape the pieces together along the long edge to make a piece 4 yards x 2 yards. One child is the "turtle." This child, who wears a set of armbands, stands on the paper and holds the stick vertically. Another child, or group of children, are the command givers. They use turtle commands to tell the child where to move—"right," "left," "forward," "backward," "up" (to lift penpoint up off paper), and "down" (to put penpoint down onto paper.) The children can either draw randomly or try to draw a specific shape.

Making It Your Own:

Read **Harold and the Purple Crayon** by Crockett Johnson (1959), in which Harold draws scenes that he then inhabits, as a good follow-up or lead-in to this activity. The child-drawer could be Harold, and the command-givers can help him to get through an adventure.

A Comment on Turtle-Robot Activities. If a turtle-robot is not available, many other types of robots, or computerized toys such as cars, also use left, right, forward, and backward commands. It is important to remember that these activities are intended to provide an example of how to design activities to support an individual piece of software. Even if you do not have a robot, the activities illustrate this process of designing activities to meet needs created by certain software. Many of the activities can be adapted for noncomputer goals if the teacher does not have access to a robot or similar toys.

Activities Generated by the Use of Bumble Games

Bumble Games was one of the earlier pieces of software developed for children. Its graphics are less sophisticated than many of the newer pieces. It also resembles much of the earlier software in the way that it includes a range of games from extremely simple to very complex. The first two games are appropriate for nonreaders, whereas the later games are not.[1] Because the number of games that are usable for nonreaders is small, I would not recommend purchasing this software specifically for this age group. But elementary schools or after-school programs with a wide age range may purchase this with the intent of using different parts for different age groups. Although all teachers would like ideally to have unlimited purchasing power to select the software that best fits their needs, in reality many teachers find they must make do with the software currently available. This often necessitates adapting the software to make it fit the class, and providing activities to help develop skills to make independent use of the software possible.

Some software introduces teachers and children to skills and concepts they might not otherwise have explored. For example, **Bumble Games** addresses the ability to locate coordinates on a graph. This is not a skill that young children are likely to develop on their own. However, it is a skill they can easily develop and one they are excited to possess and eager to use once it has been mastered. Although **Bumble Games** is not on my recommended purchase list, it did generate some interesting learning and some excellent support activities. Some of the support activities are more appropriate for young children than the original software. Software-stimulated activities can occasionally add more to the curriculum than the software itself. The activities to teach graphing skills are an example of this.

The second game on the **Bumble Games** disk, "Find the Bumble," asks the children to find Bumble, a round space creature. In the game, Bumble is hiding behind one of the boxes in a 4 × 4 grid. The vertical columns are marked with letters, and the horizontal rows are marked with numbers. The child enters a letter, which lights up all the boxes in that column, and a number, which lights up all the boxes in the row. The box in which the lines cross is outlined. If this is where Bumble is hiding, Bumble appears and a song is played. If it is the wrong place, arrows will show whether Bumble is higher or lower, and to the right or left. The child then keeps guessing until Bumble is found. It would appear that in order to play with this software that children must have the following skills and concepts:

1. Understanding that the numbers and letters stand for rows and columns on the grid.
2. Being able to decipher the meaning of the arrows—that Bumble can be found in the direction in which the arrow is pointing.
3. Understanding that combining the information from two guesses significantly increases what is known about Bumble's location. (For example, if a number is higher than 2 and lower than 4, it must be 3.)

Understanding That Numbers and Letters Stand for Rows and Columns. Few children already know that the numbers and letters at the side and bottom of the grid represent the rows and

---

[1]When only some of the options are appropriate for the children, the teacher should only highlight the appropriate options on the rebus directions. In **Bumble Games,** the first two games—"Find Your Number" and "Find the Bumble"—are the only two appropriate for nonreaders. The rebus directions for **Bumble Games** should have a "1" and a picture of the 5-point number line used in "Find Your Number" and a "2" illustrated with a Bumble peeking out of a grid for "Find the Bumble."

columns they mark. This is a concept that is well illustrated in the software itself. Whenever children select a letter, the whole column is highlighted, illustrating that the letter represents the column. It does, however, require practice to become fluent at using the numbers and letters to designate a specific coordinate. Off-computer activities can offer opportunities to practice this skill. (Children should have the ability to recognize or at least discriminate letters and numerals before teachers consider teaching grid reading skills.)

Children are constantly sorting and labeling things in the classroom, both spontaneously and in response to teacher-designed activities. Children sort blocks by size when they put them away, matching the size and shape of the block to the block pictures labeling each shelf. When placing pegs in a pegboard, children may decide to make one row red, the next one blue, and so on. Teachers may put out a muffin tin and a bowl of buttons for children to sort. These are all forms of classification. The grid labeling is another form of classification: all the points in each single row are labeled with a letter (e.g., top row is "4"). Reading coordinates is a more complex form of classifying because it deals with two intersecting sets of characteristics: "A,4" is a point contained both in the set of all "A" points and in the set of all "4" points. Some 5- and most 6-year-olds can consider two characteristics simultaneously when classifying. Those children who cannot do this can still "read" a grid. They do it by considering the row position and the column position sequentially rather than concurrently. Grids help children build classification skills, which are important to mathematics and general problem solving.

Deciphering the Meaning of the Arrows. Some children already understand that the arrow is a clue to where Bumble is hiding. They know to make their next guess in the direction in which the arrow is pointing. In contrast, other children do not yet know that the pointed part of the arrow signifies the direction in which to go. Arrow activities such as **Arrow Hunt** (p. 222) and **Where's Bumble?** (p. 224) provide practice in understanding and using arrows. Arrow-reading skills can also be reinforced through

use of software such as **Magic Crayon** or the **Explore-a-Story** series, which use the arrow keys on the keyboard to direct the cursor.

Children often see arrows used in their environment: one-way street signs, the arrows marking turn lanes on roads, arrows marking how to line up at the bank to wait for a teller, arrows on traffic lights telling when to turn. Being able to read such environmental symbols gives the child a sense of competence and is the precursor to the more complex skill of reading words made with letter symbols.

Combining Information Received from Two Guesses. This is the most difficult of the three skills. Not all young children master this. On the other hand, they need not all master it to use the software. Children can eventually arrive at the answer by making random guesses. It is interesting that each child approaches this task in an idiosyncratic way. Some guess until they hit the correct spot by chance. Other children systematically pick each numeral in order until they find the spot. Still other children are able to deduce the spot by recalling information gained from previous guesses. Although each of these methods can arrive at the answer, the last is the most efficient.

With practice, children are more likely to develop a detection system that is effective for them. Off-computer activities, such as **Where's Bumble?** (p. 224), that ask for similar types of higher/lower clues can provide this practice. It is important to realize that it is easier to use previous clues for guessing when only one coordinate is involved. The first game on **Bumble Games**, "Find Your Number," provides practice in guessing whether a number is higher or lower. The second game asks children to remember clues for column and row locations (although previous guesses are highlighted to act as a reminder.) Teachers can help children to realize that they can consider each coordinate separately. First, they can think about a letter that is after "B" but before "E." Then they can try to find a number that is lower than "2" but higher than "0." Off-computer practice, such as **Where's Bumble**? (p. 224), encourages development of the skill and offers additional opportunity for teachers to help children find effective ways to consider the problem.

ACTIVITIES TO TEACH GRAPHING SKILLS FOR BUMBLE GAMES

ARROW HUNT

Why?

⋔☐ To practice "reading" arrows

⋔ To encourage social problem solving

What Is Needed?

20 index cards (4"x 6") with an arrow drawn
   lengthwise on each
Masking tape
A large hall area
At least 2 teachers (or other adults) in the classroom

How?

Tape the arrows along the hallway of the school to
   make a path that eventually leads back to the
   classroom. Have groups of 4-6 children go on an
   "arrow hunt" with a teacher. They follow the arrows
   in the hallway to see where they lead.
This is a particularly good activity for rainy days, as it
   reduces the number of children in the room at any
   one time, provides a substitute for the missing
outside exercise, and adds a novelty that relieves
   the tedium of rainy days.

Making It Your Own:

If no hallway area is available, set up arrows around
   the yard. Because the space is so open, it is easy to
   accidentally jump from one part of the trail to
   another, missing many arrows on the way.
   Therefore, outside, the arrows must be positioned
   with less space between them.
If the class only has one teacher, either a parent
   volunteer or a child from an older class could
   accompany the arrow hunters on their search.

Going Beyond:

Have the first group of children tape up the arrows for
   the next group to follow. The second group can take
   down the arrows as they go, then make a new trail
   for the third group.
Have one class make an arrow hunt for children in
   another class to follow.

DOT TO DOT

Why?

🧍☐ To practice locating coordinates on a grid

🧍 To exercise small-muscle control

What Is Needed?

Dittos with the following grids and directions: Each grid should be 5 squares by 5 squares, with the intersections darkened and the lines lightly drawn. The grid should be marked from 0 to 4 going up the left side, and from A to E going along the bottom. With each grid should be a set of directions. (See the drawing below for an example.)

A pencil or magic marker

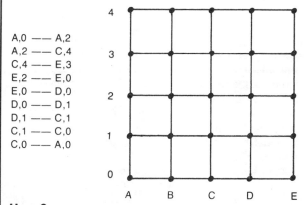

A,0 —— A,2
A,2 —— C,4
C,4 —— E,3
E,2 —— E,0
E,0 —— D,0
D,0 —— D,1
D,1 —— C,1
C,1 —— C,0
C,0 —— A,0

How?

The child places a pencil or marker on the first grid-point listed in the directions, and moves it in a straight line to the next grid-point. The child continues following the directions from point to point until the picture is completed. For example, if the children are using the grid and directions in the drawing, they will place their pencil on A,0 and move it to A,2, and so on.

Making It Your Own:

Instead of dittos, make the grid and directions on tagboard. Laminate the tagboard. The children write directly on the tagboard with marker. They wipe it off with a damp sponge when finished.

The directions can describe steps for making simple objects, shapes, or letters.

Going Beyond:

For older children, offer blank grids. In pairs, they can make a design and write down the coordinates for each point in the sequence. One student can make the designs, the other writes the coordinates. These directions can then be used by other children.

Make a larger grid to allow for more complex designs.

Instead of a paper grid, label a rubber band board with coordinates. Have the children stretch the rubber bands between the two designated nail coordinates.

A similar activity could be done with a pegboard. The tactile pegboards that hold 25 of the large knobbed pegs would work well. The left side of the pegboard can be labeled with numerals going up from 0 to 4. The bottom could be labeled with letters from A to E. The coordinates could be written in different colors. Red pegs go in the coordinates written in red, and so on.

WHERE'S BUMBLE?

Why?

☐ To develop the graphing skills used in **Bumble Games**

🏃 ☐ To develop problem-solving skills

🏃 ☐ To provide practice in understanding and using arrows

Where's Bumble?

What Is Needed?

A game board made of an 18- × 24-inch rectangular piece of tagboard (The game board should contain a rectangle 15 inches tall and 20 inches long drawn so that the top and right edges of the rectangle are the edges of the tagboard, leaving extra tagboard to the left and below the rectangle.) 12 stiff-paper pockets (like those found in library books) should be mounted in the rectangle. They should be spaced in 4 rows across and 4 columns down. Each pocket should be marked with a distinctive shape and color, such as hearts in the top row, circles in the middle row, and triangles in the bottom row; orange shapes in the right column, blue shapes in the next column, red shapes in the next, and yellow shapes in the left-most column. Along the left margin of the rectangle are plain-colored shape silhouettes or outlines—a heart by the first row, a circle by the middle row, and a triangle by the bottom row.

Below each column is a crayon matching the color of the shapes in that column. Strips of velcro the length of the rectangle run along the far left and the bottom of the game board.

2 large cardboard arrows with velcro attached lengthwise to the back at the center of the shaft

A cardboard replica of Bumble that will fit inside the pockets

A bulletin board or wall on which to mount the game board

WHERE'S BUMBLE?
(Continued)

How?

The children close their eyes. The teacher hides
Bumble in one of the pockets. The children guess a
color. If Bumble is in that column, the teacher places
the arrow on the velcro below that column pointing
upward. If Bumble is not in that column, the teacher
points the arrow to the left or right indicating the
direction of Bumble's column. The children guess a
shape, and the teacher uses the arrow to indicate
the correctness of their guess in the same way. The
children keep guessing columns and rows until they
find Bumble. The teacher should encourage them to
explain why they made each choice.

Once the children have completed the game, ask one
child, or a group of children, to hide Bumble and use
the arrows to give clues. They may need help from
the teacher at first to give accurate clues.

Making It Your Own:

Use other objects instead of shapes to mark the rows.
Pick objects that fit the topics of interest in the class.

Use letters and numerals to mark the columns and
rows. To make it simpler, put the coordinates on
each pocket. To make it harder, mark only the sides
of the grid and leave the pockets blank.

Going Beyond:

For an older group, include more coordinates in the
grid.

DELIVER THE MAIL

Why?

♟☐ To practice using grid coordinates

♟ To stimulate real and/or pretend writing in the classroom

What Is Needed?

A box with dividers that create a compartment for each child and teacher in the class (boxes that wine or liquor come in have such dividers)

Letter labels for the columns to go at the bottom of the box, with the left-most column marked "A" and the others progressing through the alphabet in sequence

Numeral labels for the rows to go at the left side of the box, with "1" in the bottom row and each higher row labeled with the sequentially higher number

A reference chart listing the children alphabetically by first name with a different coordinate after each name; also include teachers' names

Pencils

Paper

Envelopes

Stamps (the kind that come in magazine orders)

How?

Use the boxes as mailboxes. Children can write or draw messages for each other. To mail the letters, children can find the recipient's name on the list to determine the correct mailbox coordinates, then mail the letter by finding the needed coordinates. If children are frustrated when they do not have a letter, encourage them to write someone because that is the best way to get mail. The teacher should respond to any letters she or he gets to model the importance of writing back to people who write to you.

Making It Your Own:

For a younger class, with children who cannot read each others' names, place a small snapshot next to each name on the list.

If children have trouble locating coordinates, label each compartment with its coordinate as well as the labeling the bottom and side of the rows and columns.

Going Beyond:

If your classroom has daily jobs, the mailboxes could be used to notify people of their job.

Set up a post office dramatic play. Children can write a coordinate on the letter and let the "letter carrier" deliver it.

Label notices to parents with coordinates, and let a couple of children read the coordinates and deliver the papers to the mailboxes. (The teacher may wish to check after delivery to be sure that no box was overlooked.)

A Comment on *Bumble Game* Activities. Like the activities to support the use of the turtle-robot, it is important to remember that the activities to support **Bumble Games** are intended as an illustration of how you can develop activities to fit specific pieces of software that you have in your school. As shown here with **Bumble Game** activities, you may start by devising activities to support particular software and find that the value of the activities exceeds the value of the software. These activities take on a life and value of their own even when the software is not used.

Activities Generated by the Use of Auxiliary Drawing Devices

Some software employs peripheral devices such as the joystick, touch pad, or mouse, rather than the keyboard, to move the cursor. In using **Color Me** with a mouse, the child pushes the mouse toward the back of the table to move the cursor up on the monitor screen. Moving the mouse toward the forward edge of the table creates a downward movement of the cursor. (It is recommended that the mouse be used on a mouse pad, a thin piece of foam-backed rubber that sits on the tabletop. The pad increases the precision of the mouse.) Moving the mouse to the right or left on the horizontal plane of the table results in a corresponding movement to the right or left on the vertical plane of the screen. With the Koala pad, a similar relation exists between the movement of the stylus (or drawing stick) on the pad, and the movement of the cursor on the screen. The joystick involves a further level of abstraction. The cursor will go up when the child's hand pushes forward on the joystick and down when the child's hand pulls back. Unlike the mouse and the touch pad, the joystick itself does not move; motion on the screen is set by the direction in which the top of the joystick is leaning.

The idea of using a secondary device (the peripheral) to create motion in a different location (on the screen) is new to most children. Children can learn to operate these devices and often, with practice, they are easier than using the keyboard.

Some children find it confusing at first to use these secondary devices to create movement on a different plane. It appears that in order to use these peripherals independently, children must develop the following skills and concepts. They must

1. Realize that motion of the secondary device can create movement on the monitor
2. Have enough fine-motor control to move the device smoothly and precisely
3. Be able to translate directional movements on the horizontal surface into directional movements on the monitor
4. Be able to gauge the amount of movement required of the peripheral device to produce the desired amount of movement on the screen.

Realizing That Movement of a Secondary Device Can Cause Movement on the Monitor. Most children will have had some experience in which the movement of one object will create the movement of another. When riding a tricycle, they must turn the handlebars to get the tricycle to turn, and keep the handlebars straight in order to go straight. When children first ride tricycles, they are surprised that when they turn to look to the side that the tricycle turns along with their head and arms. Through trial and error, they begin subconsciously to realize that the position of the handlebars determines the direction in which the tricycle moves. In the same way, through use of the mouse (or other peripheral) children will realize that its movement will cause the cursor on the monitor to move. Still, sometimes children forget and point to a spot on the screen where they want the cursor to move, temporarily forgetting how to move it there. An Etch-a-Sketch offers a similar experience. This toy allows children to create a picture on a screen by turning a dial (another secondary device). Using an Etch-a-Sketch also reinforces the idea that movement of a secondary device can cause movement on the screen.

Developing the Fine-Motor Precision to Control the Peripheral. Dan is using the mouse to draw a picture with **Color Me**. He is trying to cover all of the screen with green. He is having trouble filling in the last few spots. He cannot seem to manipulate the mouse with enough precision to catch those last few spots. Finally he calls a teacher to help him cover the spots he cannot get. All classroom activities that aim at developing fine-motor control will improve Dan's skill at manipulating the mouse. Activities like **Marble Painting** (p. 229) can promote this development. It is important to note that Dan's task, filling in the whole screen, was one that he imposed on himself, not one that was set by the software. Teachers must observe as children use the computer. If certain software or hardware easily frustrates the children, this particular task may be too difficult for this age child. When possible, field test programs with children of the appropriate age before introducing them to the whole class to ensure that overly difficult software is avoided.

Translating Movement from a Horizontal to a Vertical Plane. Often when children first use a stylus on a touch pad or a mouse, they try to move the drawing device vertically, to match the required movement on the screen, rather than horizontally across the touch pad or mouse pad. As they use the peripheral, they become more accustomed to moving it away to make the cursor go up or toward them to make the cursor go down. This is a skill that seems to improve with practice. Activities such as **Copy the Pattern** (p. 230), which ask a child to transfer information from a horizontal to a vertical plane, strengthen their ability to understand the relation between motion on the two planes.

Gauging the Amount of Movement Needed to Move the Cursor. When children first begin using the mouse, they often make large sweeping movements, causing the cursor to go right off the screen and disappear. Suggesting smaller movements and allowing opportunities to practice using the mouse will help children to develop a sense of how much to move the mouse (or other device). Providing two or three pieces of software that require the same auxiliary device enables children to become familiar with how it works in the context of different programs.

Both following the mazes that fit over the Etch-a-Sketch, and using the mazes with marbles inside that are tipped to move the marble through the maze, help children to realize the importance of small, precise movements. **Marble Painting** (p. 229) may also help children to tie the amount of movement of one thing (the box) to the amount of movement of another (the marble) in the same way that the amount of movement of the mouse is tied to the amount the cursor moves.

ACTIVITIES TO SUPPORT THE USE OF AUXILIARY DRAWING DEVICES

MARBLE PAINTING

Why?

🏃☐ To increase precision of hand movements

🏃☐ To help children realize that the speed of their motion affects the speed of the marble (or the mouse)

🏃 To provide an opportunity for creativity

What Is Needed?

6 boxes that are 9 × 12 inches and at least 3 inches high

3 damp sponges each on a plate or bowl

9- × 12-inch black construction paper

9 shallow bowls of paint—3 white, 3 red, and 3 powder blue, arranged so that each color can be reached by each child

18 marbles, 2 in each bowl of paint

Smocks

A place for drying pictures

How?

The children place a piece of paper at the bottom of the box. Then they put a paint-covered marble in the box, and tip the box so that the marble leaves a path on the paper. Children repeat the procedure with marbles from other colors of paint. Children should be free to experiment freely with the materials. Teachers can comment on the various speeds at which marbles are going. Encourage the children to see how fast they can make the marble go and how slowly they can make it go, to try to get a marble to follow a trail left by an earlier marble, to go to a certain spot on the paper, etc. Discuss how different results are obtained. The discussion of marble movement should come from the children's actions and build on their ideas and comments; the first priority should be to have an open-ended creative activity. If discussion and exploration of the effects of various ways of tipping the box can be achieved, this is an added bonus. Children can use the sponges to wipe off paint-covered fingers.

Making It Your Own:

Use a variety of small spheres—marbles of different sizes, golf balls, wiffle balls, rubber balls—and compare the different paths each leaves.

Pick any combination of paper and paint colors that result in a pleasing effect.

Adjust the box size, but for convenience it is best to have all the boxes the same size so that the paper will fit them consistently.

Going Beyond:

After children have had a chance to experiment, mark the sides of the box "R right," "L left," "F forward," "B backward." Have another child or teacher give directions telling which way to tip the box. This will help children with the commands for using **Logo**. (Armbands can be used as well.)

COPY THE PATTERN

Why?

🚶☐ To help children move between vertical and horizontal planes

🚶 To exercise small-muscle skills

What Is Needed?

A container of 1″ colored cubes (red, blue, green, and yellow)

A 3- × 3-inch piece of white tagboard divided evenly into 9 1-inch squares (3 rows of 3 squares each)

5 pieces of 3- × 5-inch tagboard with the bottom 3 inches divided into 9 1-inch squares, each square colored red, blue, green, or yellow

A 7- to 10-inch-tall box

A clothes pin

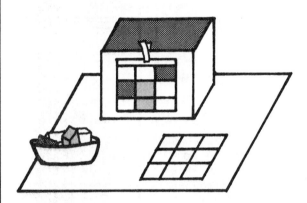

How?

Put the box on the table with the open end up. Attach one of the colored grids to the box with a clothes pin so that the grid part hangs down the side of the box. Place the plain grid on the table in front of the box. The child looks at the colored pattern on the box grid and tries to recreate the pattern with the colored cubes on the plain grid.

Making It Your Own:

Use other types of materials for making patterns, such as jumbo pegs on a 25-hole pegboard, Beginning Mosaics—a clear plastic holder 1″ deep divided into a 10 x 10 grid of small boxes that can hold cylindrical or squared colored wooden pegs,[2] or other materials that you have. It is important that the patterns are relatively small and simple at first.

Going Beyond:

Let the children color plain grids and then use these as patterns to follow.

[2]This is made by Teaching Resources. A wide variety of other kinds of pegboards could be used for this activity as well.

PROVIDING WAYS TO CIRCUMVENT SKILLS THAT ARE TOO DIFFICULT FOR THE CHILDREN

Some software or hardware—which otherwise seems appropriate for young children—has one feature that appears too difficult to allow for independent use—although the rest of the program is fine. Some features that are difficult are

1. A menu that requires reading
2. A loading process that is too lengthy and complex
3. A program that requires children to locate many different keys or has many steps
4. A program that varies in level from part to part

In many cases, teachers can find ways to circumvent the difficult features of the program, making it possible to use the software without the skills that seem to be required.

Programs That Include Some Text That Must Be Read

Software that relies heavily on written directions is usually inappropriate for young children. However, if only a small amount of reading is needed, teachers can often provide pictorial aids that allow children to negotiate the program without having to read. Many programs that are otherwise appropriate for young children, such as **Kindercomp, Kidwriter, Facemaker,** and **Letter-Go-Round**, have written rather than pictorial menus. In **Letter-Go-Round** and **Kindercomp**, the initial menu (from which the child selects the desired program option) is written. Once children have selected the option, no more reading is required. In this case, teachers can make pictorial menus on the disk cover to show children each of the games next to the numeral that will select the game. The pictorial menu for **Kindercomp** could have a linear design next to the "1" to depict "draw" (which allows children to draw designs using a group of letter keys). Three rows of the same letter repeated next to the "2" would show that the

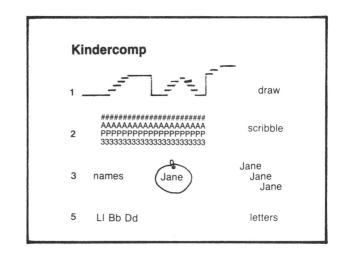

second game is "scribble" (which makes a whole row of any letter, numeral, or symbol that is typed). Similar picture clues can be made for each item on the menu.

Programs such as **Kidwriter** have a series of written menus to follow. Picture clues can also be made for these, but they are more complicated to construct and to follow. The directions must indicate which choices are possible at each level. (See the drawing of the **Kidwriter** rebus directions.) The more pictures that must be included on the directions, the harder it is to for children to find the clues they need. Directions such as those for **Kidwriter** may require more initial teacher time to help children understand how to decipher the clues. Programs that require lengthy pictorial clues are better used with older groups and with children who have already had experience reading picture directions and using computers.

There is a limit to the length of instructions that can be clearly depicted pictorially. Programs such as **Garfield** have so many sets of written directions that picture directions for each step would be too complicated for young children to follow easily. Although some children can learn to use these programs at home with parental help and sufficient practice to memorize enough of the steps to use them independently, they are not appropriate for a school pro-

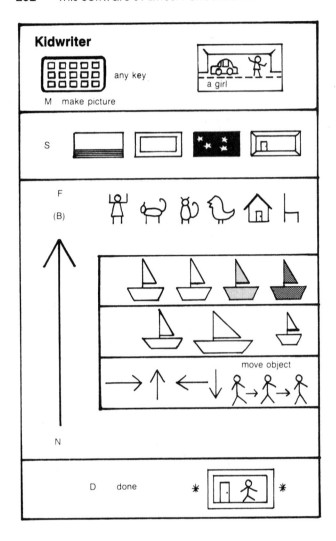

and the disk must be in the disk drive when the computer is turned on. After the computer is turned on, the user must type a series of commands to enter the desired program. For **Astro-Grover**, the user must type "L"-"O"-"A"-"D" [Space Bar] "C"-"B"-"S" "8," press the [Return] key, then type "R"-"U"-"N." Entering the Commodore program can be extremely difficult, if not impossible, for (1) children just beginning to learn the keyboard, (2) those who have trouble correctly hitting the needed key, or (3) those who have trouble following a line of directions to "read" each step in order.

The teacher can deal with this problem in two ways. For the younger and less proficient children, the teacher could preload the software. A big **STOP** signs could be placed on the disk drive and the power switch, to indicate that the disk should be left in and the computer left on.

For older children, who are able to hit the intended key accurately and follow the directions sequentially, the teacher could add labels to expedite location of the needed keys. Peel-off labels, such as those used for file folders, can be cut and placed on each key needed for the loading process. The letter or symbol for that key should then be printed on the label. This type of labeling will make the needed keys stand out from the other keys and make finding their location easier because the children need only to look at the labeled keys, rather than the whole keyboard, when searching for a specific key.

Color-coding the keys makes it still easier to find the needed keys. The letters for LOAD can be in green, the ["] key and the [Shift] key can be in blue (the [Shift] key must be held down while the ["] key is struck). And other colors can be used for the other sections of the loading procedure. The rebus loading directions can then be color-coded to match the keys. When children are looking for an "L," they need only scan the four green keys. The blue " and **Shift** on the directions will indicate that blue labels should be sought next.

Some software also requires a series of commands to get the child to the desired part of the program. **Talking Screen Textwriter** and **Turtle Tot Logo** are both complex programs with many parts. Each has a part that is appropriate for use with

gram, in which large amounts of teacher time should not be spent on helping children to learn a single program.

Machines That Require Complex Loading Procedures

The procedure for loading programs for the Commodore is neither easy nor automatic. It is necessary to turn the disk drive on before the computer, young children. Because the majority of the program is designed for older children and because the software contains so many options, a long series of commands is required to get to each part of the program. Programs on the Macintosh also require following a number of steps through a series of written menus in order to locate specific activities. For programs such as these, teachers need to consider carefully the steps involved in the loading process. Are these steps that picture directions can describe for younger users? Are they steps that young children could complete successfully given the appropriate directions? If the answer to these two questions is "yes," then the teacher can provide a combination of labeling and pictorial guides for children to use. If the answer to these questions is "no," the teacher should plan to either preload the software or look for software that requires less complex loading procedures.

Programs That Require Location of Many Keys

Some children find it difficult to locate specific keys on the keyboard. To search 26 letter keys for one desired letter can be a time-consuming process. This is especially difficult for the child who still does not have a clear mental picture of each letter. For these children, it is best to use programs that do not require the child to locate many specific keys. If the program seems to meet the class's needs in all other ways except for the number of keys that need to be located, teachers can label the needed keys to make location easier. If the children using **Facemaker** become frustrated looking for the 6 keys that make the face move—"T," "S," "C," "W," "F," and "E"—then labels can be added to highlight these keys, making them easier to find. Such labeling should be used judiciously. The more labels that are added, the less the child needs to learn key location. Labeling should be used if finding the keys frustrates the children so that the software cannot be used effectively without it. Once the children have become accustomed to the software, the labels should be removed to encourage them to begin locating the keys independently. It is important that

such labeling be used selectively and for a brief time only; otherwise, the keyboard becomes so crowded with labels that they become ineffective.

There are times when labels should be added and left on the keyboard. **Magic Crayon** and the "draw" option of **Kindercomp** both use letter keys to move the cursor in different directions. There is no logical relationship between the keys used and the direction in which the cursor moves. Adding arrow labels to the keys, pointing in the appropriate direction, will make these drawing programs more usable for both children and adults. Placing the arrows on the front (or vertical plane) of the keys rather than on the top surface will keep the letters visible for use with other kinds of software.

Programs with Many Different Levels

Chris, who is 4 years old, likes making dotted paths and diamonds on **Color Me**. He likes to use the "fill" option to make the screen blue, then green, then black, then white. He likes to fill in every inch of the screen. Lily, who is 7 years old, also uses **Color Me**. She draws a picture of a person with a variety of line widths and colors. After outlining the shirt, she uses the "fill" option to make the whole shirt yellow. She adds a sentence to the picture: "Lily is going to a party." Then she saves her picture onto another disk; later, she retrieves the picture, adding sky, sun, and grass. When the picture is completed to her satisfaction, she prints it.

Both these children are using **Color Me**, but at different levels of complexity. Many programs have different levels at which they can be used. This enables the software to be challenging and exciting to the wide range of skills and interests that exists in every class. At the complex level that Lily is using it, **Color Me** appears too difficult for younger children, but the manner in which Chris is using the same program obviously *is* appropriate. For programs such as **Color Me**, it is important to introduce the options gradually to the class so that the children are not overwhelmed with too many choices.

In introducing **Color Me** to the class, let the children begin by experimenting with drawing and perhaps with changing the colors. Some child is likely to stumble into the fill option by mistake. The menu in **Color Me** is across the top of the screen, and children new at using the mouse, joystick, or touch pad often unknowingly move the cursor through the fill part of the menu and select it accidentally. When it is discovered, the teacher can explain what the fill option is. After children have explored the software and become familiar with basic drawing, changing colors, and filling, then teachers can gradually introduce other parts of the program. For example, when a child is telling you about the picture, you could ask whether he would like to add those words to the screen to tell about the picture. If the child is interested, the typing option can be explained.

Some children explore all the options on their own, whereas other children are satisfied to use the familiar parts of the program without venturing into new areas. In many cases, children learn about a part of the program from other children who have already mastered it. This type of peer teaching should be encouraged. When children want to know how to try something new, ask a child who has used that option to help explain to the novice what to do.

When making rebus directions for programs, it is important to consider which options to introduce to the children first, and include only these on the initial rebus directions. **Magic Crayon** allows children to draw, change color, erase the screen, save the picture, and recall previously drawn pictures. The first two options—drawing and changing color—are relatively simple; the later ones are more complicated. If this is one of the first programs introduced to the class, it is wise to limit the rebus directions on the disk only to those telling how to select colors. The rebus card could show

1. A "C" key next to a spectrum of colors (to indicate that pressing "C" will bring the menu of colors)
2. A small arrow pointing each way under the spectrum (to indicate that the arrows move the cursor along the spectrum)
3. A [Return] key at the end (to indicate that pressing [Return] will bring back the picture with the new colored cursor).

Directions for the other options can either be added to the card later, when they are introduced to the children, or be placed on the back of the cover, where they will not distract children who have not yet learned to use them.

In some programs, like **Bumble Games**, only some of the games are appropriate for young children. The first two games on **Bumble** can be used with nonreaders. The others all require at least some beginning reading. In making a rebus card to illustrate the options on the **Bumble** program, depict only those games that you feel the children will be able to use successfully. If the children accidentally stumble onto the more complex program, they are likely to get frustrated and will spontaneously move back to the more appropriate programs that you have shown on the directions. If the child finds that he or she can use the program successfully, then this option can be added to the menu. (If it is an option that is too difficult for most of the class, but appropriate for that child, you can give that child a card that shows how to locate the game again later.)

SOFTWARE-GENERATED ACTIVITIES TO FACILITATE DEVELOPMENTAL GOALS

At CAPP, we found that software often sparked ideas for enjoyable activities that did not necessarily promote any specific computer skills. These activities, however, *would* promote general developmental goals. Some of these activities mimicked or complemented activities done on the computer. For example, **Bowling Bop** (p. 235) involves bowling with the pins dressed up to look like the objects in **Stickybear Bop**. The off-computer activity offers the children another way to be involved with the software, and may defuse some of the tension developed in waiting for a turn. **Snoopy's Table Maze** (p. 236) was modeled after **Peanuts Maze Marathon**. These off-computer activities also provide children experience with concrete objects. Good teachers seek ideas everywhere, so they can use software as another source to spark creative classroom activities and materials.

DEVELOPMENTAL ACTIVITIES GENERATED BY SOFTWARE

BOWLING BOP

Why?

- ♀ To develop hand-eye coordination
- ♀ To provide an outlet for energy
- ♀ To provide a meaningful context for rational counting

What Is Needed?

9 pictures from **Stickybear Bop**—an apple, a hat, a duck, a ball, a star, a heart, and a bag, and the word BOP—drawn on cardboard and laminated (see picture)

9 of the double unit blocks (2-3/4 inches x 11 inches) with one of the preceding pictures taped to the top of each

A 6-8 inch rubber ball

*Bowling Bop is similar to **Stickybear Bop**.*

How?

Arrange the blocks in a staggered line. Have the child roll the ball and knock down the pins. See how many pictures can be knocked down before the player is "bopped" by knocking over the BOP pin. After each roll, the children, as a group, can count how many pins are down and how many are left to go. (Obviously, the counting part of the activity is only appropriate for children who can count rationally.)

Note: this game should not be done in a competitive way. If children tend to make it competitive, move the BOP pin way to the side to make it easy to avoid hitting it until the end.

Let each child pick her or his own spot from which to roll the ball. Children who find it difficult tend to move closer and closer until success is assured.

Making It Your Own:

Add some pictures that fit with the theme being discussed—farm animals, birds, vehicles, etc.

Going Beyond:

Have a laminated "menu" of the picture pins with a box next to each pin. Have another child check off the pins as they are toppled.

Let children arrange the pins in whatever way they please, in an effort to knock down more at the same time. Stacking pins on top of each other should not be discouraged.

SNOOPY'S TABLE MAZE

Why?

- 🧍 To facilitate small-muscle development
- 🧍 To build visual-tracking skills
- 🧍 To help children understand that lines in mazes represent walls
- 🧍 To build problem-solving skills

What Is Needed?

A maze drawn on posterboard with posterboard walls attached vertically
A small rubber Snoopy (or other figure)
A paper bone at the end of the maze

Snoopy's Table Maze.

How?

The child will move the Snoopy figure through the maze until it gets to the bone at the end. Encourage children to add other objects to the maze and invent their own destinations or tasks for Snoopy.

Making It Your Own:

Change the character that moves through the maze, or use a fire truck or other vehicle instead of a character.

Make a maze that does not have an endpoint but has a variety of things to visit: a pond, a playground, a store, and so on. The children can then move the characters around to create their own stories.

Going Beyond:

Use paper mazes as a follow-up to this activity. One of the mazes could match the one with stand-up walls.

SUMMARY

Ideally, each piece of computer equipment would be perfect as it is, but realistically, they often need to be adapted or have supportive aids supplied to make the independent use of the software or hardware possible. If children cannot use the materials independently, the computer cannot be another of the autonomous, child-directed activities that are the essence of the good early childhood program. In looking at individual software and hardware, consider the skills required. Are these skills in the child's current repertoire? If not, are they within reach, or can that skill be circumvented? Teachers can then design activities to develop the necessary skills or methods for circumventing these skills. Pieces of software that need no skill development, or even pieces that are inappropriate for young children, can often serve as a stimulus for developing exciting noncomputer activities for the classroom.

11

Integrating the Computer into the Early Childhood Curriculum

The most exciting aspect of having computers in classrooms for young children is using them to support the other learning and development that occur. The computer should be seen as a tool to promote a wide variety of learning, not merely as an entity to be learned about. One of the strongest arguments for having the computer in the classroom, rather than in a lab, is that it must be present in the classroom to be truly integrated into the learning that is occurring.[1]

Good early childhood programs do not segregate learning into separate "curriculum areas," as is so often done in later grades. For example, children learn science as they paint with water on the blackboard and watch it evaporate, as they watch the garden they have planted growing, as they observe how cars move down the ramps they have built in the block area, as they see the ingredients combine and change form in the pretzel dough they mix, and in many other classroom experiences. In the same way, the classroom provides an environment with opportunities to build skills in mathematics, social science, and language, as well as the other curriculum areas that are studied in more isolated units in the later grades.

These cognitive areas are only a small part of the learning that occurs in the early childhood classroom. Programs are designed to facilitate the development of the whole child—physically, socially, emotional, and linguistically, as well as cognitively. As with the science learning described, each developmental area is strengthened by a myriad of experiences throughout the day. For example, children develop physical skills as they pour juice for snack, carefully place blocks to make them balance, dance to music, paint a picture, ride a tricycle, work to turn their jacket sleeves right side out, or participate in many other ways.

[1]In " 'I'm the Thinkist, You're the Typist': The Interaction of Technology and the Social Life of Classrooms," Sheingold, Hawkins, and Char (1984) suggest the computer's importance as a tool to support the elementary school curriculum in much the same way that I am recommending it support the early childhood curriculum.

The computer is only one part of a rich early childhood classroom.

In many classrooms, teachers organize activities and materials around a theme or unit of study. Each content unit, which lasts for a week or two, provides a focus for the classroom; the unit theme then becomes a vehicle for providing opportunities to encourage development in all areas. As children play and work in this kind of classroom, observant teachers may recognize new, emerging skills in individual children; the teacher can then encourage the further development of these skills by offering appropriate activities. For example, if children have become interested in cutting, then many opportunities to cut are made available to build on this interest. Other activities that strengthen the muscles needed for cutting will also be provided, such as paper punches, tongs, or clothes pins.

Computers are another medium teachers can use when designing an environment in which children can learn and develop. Computers, and computer-related activities, can be used to support units, promote the development of specific skills, and encourage the development of the whole child.

USING COMPUTERS TO SUPPORT A UNIT

Unit themes are often used as a focus for the learning and development that occurs in the classroom. Materials and activities in many areas of the classroom, as well as group-time stories and songs, may center around the chosen theme. If the unit is dinosaurs, children may build caves for rubber dinosaurs in the block area; excavate for dinosaur bones and fossils in the sand table; ride tricycles in a life-sized chalk outline of a dinosaur on the playground; use stencils to outline and then color a variety of different types of dinosaurs; sort dinosaur pictures by what they like to eat; write stories about dinosaurs; make dinosaur-shaped cookies; listen to dinosaur stories; make a graph of favorite dinosaurs; see how many people are needed to stretch the whole length of a brontosaurus; move like dinosaurs to a story narrated by the teacher; or role-play a paleontologist working in a lab where fossils are

---

INPUT FOR TEACHERS:

"TEACHING" SKILLS TO CHILDREN

When "developing skills" is discussed, it is important to remember that the teacher should not expect to "teach" each child a set list of skills. Many skills depend on biological maturation as well as the development of new thinking processes necessary to learn and use the skill. Instead, the teacher can provide materials and activities that spark children's interest in trying a new skill, or that provide additional opportunities to practice a skill that the child has been developing.

In the process of growing and developing, children practice and strengthen a variety of skills. The child may begin making random crayon marks on paper as young as at 1 year of age. But with increasing age and opportunities for using crayons, the child's ability to control the crayon increases. The child's grip becomes more sophisticated, moving from a clutching with the whole hand to the more sophisticated grip that is used in writing. Drawing is not a skill that can be taught to a child. It is an ability that develops with age and practice. Teachers cannot "teach" children to draw, but they can provide activities that encourage children to draw.

---

studied and dinosaur bones are put together. The activities provide opportunities to encourage all areas of development, as well as learning in the more traditional school areas—language arts, science, social science, etc.

During the "dinosaur unit," children use blocks, sand, outside play, movement experiences, mathematics, dramatic play, books, language arts, cooking, and many other types of activities to explore dinosaurs. Teachers can also use computers to enhance units. There are three levels on which computers can support a unit:

1. Specific software can provide unit-related information
2. Tool software—such as graphics or writing programs—can be used for creating unit-related products
3. Computer-related activities—those designed to support specific computer skills or concepts—can be designed to support the unit theme as well.

Rather than an abstract discussion regarding the use of computers to support unit themes, this chapter describes some ways that each of these three levels of computer support can enhance a specific unit—dinosaurs.

Using Unit-Related Software

The easiest way to support a unit with the computer is to supply unit-related software. This is not always possible because there is still a relatively limited supply of software appropriate for nonreaders, and because teachers often do not have the budgetary resources to obtain the software that might be appropriate. In the case of a dinosaur unit, there are at least two pieces of software that teachers could use. **Dinosaurs** is more closed-ended software. It allows children to discover through trial and error which dinosaurs are meat eaters or plant eaters; to learn which dinosaurs live in water, on land, or in the air; to match dinosaur pairs; to match sets of dinosaurs; and to match dinosaurs to their names. The program is designed as drill and practice with which children learn, through repeated use of the software, which dinosaurs belong in which categories.

In this program, the "habitat" option has children place the dinosaurs in the water, on the land, or in the air. The child uses the cursor to point to where the dinosaur belongs. If the child selects the wrong habitat, nothing happens. If the right habitat is chosen, the dinosaur is moved there. When all the dinosaurs have been correctly placed, they parade across the screen. Some children are fascinated by the different habitats, the eating habits, and the

length of the dinosaur names. They select this software often until they can easily sort and label the dinosaurs. Other children are not interested. Children should be free to use or not use the software as their personal interests and skills dictate. As mentioned earlier, drill-and-practice software, such as this, should only be a small part of the software available. It *must* be offered on a self-selecting basis.

For those children who enjoy mastering this information, teachers can provide additional off-computer sorting. Plastic dinosaurs or pictures of dinosaurs can be sorted by type, habitat, or eating habits. Children could be encouraged to use **Dinosaur** as a resource for checking the accuracy of their off-computer sorting.

What Makes a Dinosaur Sore?, part of the **Explore-a-Story** series, is more open-ended software that can enhance a dinosaur unit. This software is designed to mimic a book. It has a "cover page," and five other "pages" or scenes. Some of the pages show realistic dinosaur scenes, others show imaginary scenes of dinosaurs visiting the present world. Children can use the cursor to pick up and move, and thereby animate, any character or object on the screen. Children can select additional objects, characters, or words to add to each scene. This program can be used in a number of ways.

A child using **What Makes a Dinosaur Sore.**

Children can create stories, narrating them as they move the various characters and objects around, and even off, the screen. They can create more formal stories by arranging a scene and then typing or narrating text to complement their picture. Older children may choose to create a continuing story, by illustrating and writing text on each "page," or screen of the software. The pictures can be printed and compiled into a dinosaur book.

Using Software as a Tool To Support Unit Activities

Children often spontaneously incorporate topics they find interesting into their activities and creations. If the class is discussing dinosaurs, dinosaurs are likely to appear in children's paintings, playdough creations, dramatic play, and drawings. Graphics programs on the computer offer another medium for creation of unit-related pictures. Children can draw dinosaurs, dinosaur habitats, dinosaur paths (which can be used for rubber dinosaurs to follow), or jumbles of dinosaur bones.

During a dinosaur unit, dinosaurs may be found in children's word processing as well. They may copy dinosaur names by typing them into the computer. Children may narrate dinosaur stories for teachers or parent volunteers to type. The creation of stories can be child-initiated, or the teacher can suggest dinosaur-related story themes such as "the day a dinosaur came to school," or more realistic stories describing "when the dinosaurs lived." The class can construct a "fact sheet on dinosaurs" with the word processor. The list can be sent home to parents or distributed to other classes.

Other nondinosaur software can also be incorporated into the dinosaur unit. For older children who are more adept typists, it is fun to type out the lengthy names of the dinosaurs. **Kindercomp** has a game called "Name," which allows the user to type in a name. The software then recreates the name many times in a variety of colors, sizes, and designs. Children who like typing the dinosaurs' names may enjoy seeing these names repeated in many styles by **Kindercomp**.

Stanley Stegosaurus going for a walk.

If a turtle-robot is available, children can "dress it up" as a dinosaur by adding a construction paper dinosaur tail and head. Large armored plates taped along the back can turn the robot into a stegosaurus. The children can then direct the "dinosaur-robot." **Stanley Stegosaurus Goes Walking** (p. 246) describes an activity built around a dressed-up turtle-robot.

Computerized toys, such as Simon, can also be used to supplement units. Simon is a memory game with four illuminated colored buttons, each with its own special sound. When the child starts the game, one of the lights blinks, making its accompanying noise. The child watches and listens, and then tries to echo the machine by pressing the button that blinks. If the child is right, **Simon** will repeat the first light-sound button and add a second one. The child must repeat the button sequence in the correct order. This process continues, adding an additional light-sound button with each correct response. This game could be incorporated into a dinosaur unit by attaching a different dinosaur sticker to each button. The child can then remember the sequence of dinosaur names instead of the color sequence. **Simon** could also be used in this same manner with different pictures to support other unit themes.

Using Computer-Related Activities To Support Units

With slight modification, many typical preschool activities can be readjusted to support a specific unit. For example, sewing cards can be made to look like (1) various forms of transportation for a transportation unit, (2) doctors' tools for a doctors unit, or (3) dinosaurs for a unit on dinosaurs. In the same way, many of the computer activities presented in this book can be redesigned to incorporate a particular unit. **Name Jumping** (p. 84) develops keyboard skills as children jump out the letters of their names on a floor keyboard. Instead of, or in addition to, typing out their own names, children can use labeled picture cards of dinosaurs to jump out dinosaur names. Children could receive a dinosaur sticker of each dinosaur whose name they jump out. **Meet Timothy Turtle** (p. 146), which introduces the turtle-robot, could be changed to **Meet Stanley Stegosaurus**. The robot could be decorated with paper dinosaur plates on its back and a dinosaur head, tail, and legs.

Old McDonald Had a Farm (p. 121) could be modified to teach about dinosaurs as well as providing an opportunity to read picture directions. The title could be changed to ''Old McDonald Had Some Dinosaurs,'' with the lyrics changed as follows.

Old McDonald had some dinosaurs, E I E I O.
With a tyrannosaurus here and a tyrannosaurus there

Here a tyrannosaurus, there a tyrannosaurus,
Everywhere a tyrannosaurus,
Old McDonald had some dinosaurs, E I E I O.

As in the original activity, pictures should be available for each animal—dinosaur in this case—are added to the song. At the end of the verse, repeat the names of all the preceding dinosaurs, in order. These are just a few ideas on ways to adapt previous activities to complement a unit on dinosaurs. Teachers can find their own way to adjust the activities to meet their needs.

New activities can also be designed to encourage the development of specific computer skills or concepts as well as adding to the current classroom unit. **Digging for Bones** (p. 244), in which children use a graph to locate the correct quadrant of the sand table in which to excavate for bones, promotes both computer- and dinosaur-related goals. In this activity, the children are practicing moving between horizontal and vertical planes, they are practicing graphing skills needed for **Bumble Games**, and they are using picture clues—all computer-related skills. They are also learning about dinosaurs (e.g., scientists discover dinosaur remains buried in the sand), and they are learning to match dinosaur models to the appropriate picture by noticing the different characteristics of each of the dinosaurs from the ''Making It Your Own'' and ''Going Beyond'' suggestions that use rubber dinosaurs and pictures.

ACTIVITIES TO SUPPORT LEARNING ABOUT BOTH COMPUTERS AND DINOSAURS

DIGGING FOR BONES

Why?

♱ ☐ To practice reading the coordinates on a graph

♱ ☐ To practice using picture clues

♱ ☐ To practice moving between horizontal and vertical planes

♱ To encourage thought and discussion about how dinosaur bones were discovered

What Is Needed?

A sand table
Yarn
Tape
8 cards, each with one letter from A to H
3 numeral cards, each with one numeral from 1 to 3
A pocket chart (made out of tagboard equal in size to the sand table, with 24 pockets attached to the tagboard in 3 horizontal rows and 8 vertical columns). Mark each row to the left with a numeral; the top row is 3, the middle row is 2, and the bottom row is 1. Beneath each column is a letter. The left-most column is A. The other columns are labeled in alphabetic sequence, with the right-most column being H.)
Three pieces of cardboard cut into the shape of bones
Three chicken-leg bones
A wall

Digging for bones.

DIGGING FOR BONES
(Continued)

How?

Tape the yarn across the sand table to make a grid of 24 squares, with 3 horizontal rows and 8 vertical columns. Tape the letter labels below the columns from A to H, going from left to right. Tape the numeral cards to the left of the rows, going down from 3 to 1.

Mount the pocket chart on the wall behind the sand table. Bury the three bones in different quadrants of the sand table. Place the cardboard bones so that they stick out of the corresponding pockets on the pocket chart.

The children try to find the buried bones by using the pocket chart as a reference. Once the bones have all been found, the children can bury them in new quadrants, leaving the cardboard bones as clues in the appropriate pockets.

Making It Your Own:

Instead of digging for bones, dig for treasure. Hide various objects in the sand table. Make pictures to represent each for the pocket chart.

Change the number of squares in the sandbox and pocket chart grid to fit your sandbox so that you can make relatively square quadrants in your sand table.

Search for rubber dinosaurs instead of their bones

Instead of using the sand table, glue 16 small gift boxes onto a sheet of cardboard in four rows of 4 each. Make the lids of each row a different color. On the wall behind the boxes, hang a piece of tagboard with 16 squares of felt in colors and arrangement to match the box lids. Hide rubber dinosaurs in the boxes. Pictures of the dinosaurs, attached to felt or velcro backing, can be hung on the felt square grid as clues.

Although grids do have the numbers running down from highest to lowest, some teachers may prefer to have the numbers run from lowest to highest to reinforce the top-to-bottom sequence used in reading.

Going Beyond:

Instead of using the pocket chart for clues, provide a dittoed grid that corresponds to the sand table. The children may role-play paleontologists digging for bones. When they find bones, they mark the coordinate where the bones were found on their "record sheet." Children can rebury the bones, if they wish, for other children to find.

STANLEY STEGOSAURUS GOES WALKING

Why?

- ☐ To encourage children to give more precise commands to the turtle-robot

- ☐ To practice using left and right (with the armbands as clues) to command the turtle

- ☀ To encourage social interaction and cooperation

- ☀ To encourage thought and discussion about dinosaurs and their habitat

What Is Needed?

A turtle-robot and the appropriate software
Paper to dress the robot like a dinosaur
Paper towel rolls decorated with paper palm leaves to represent trees
Hollow blocks or boxes with pictures of dinosaurs taped on

How?

Arrange the dinosaurs and trees around the area where Stanley can go walking. The children can give commands to make the robot say hello to, or run away from, each of the dinosaurs. Stanley can bump into the trees and topple them over.

Making It Your Own:

Attach dinosaur pictures to the paper towel tubes so that they can be toppled over as well.

Going Beyond:

Have the children help determine and then construct the props that belong in a dinosaur environment. They may not be as ''beautiful,'' and they may take longer to make, but the thinking process is worth it.

Stanley Stegosaurus knocking over trees.

DINOSAUR PRINTING

Why?

☐ To build keyboarding skills

🯅 To encourage fine-motor skills

🯅 To encourage thought and discussion about dinosaurs

What Is Needed?

Letter stamps
A model of the computer keyboard, sized to be in scale with the letter stamps (laminate the keyboard)
A cloth for wiping off keyboard if it gets inky
A stamp pad
Dinosaur word cards, each with a word and a picture
Paper

How?

Place the letter stamps on the appropriate letter on the model keyboard. The children use the letter stamps to make their own names and various dinosaur words. After each stamp is used, it should be returned to the proper place on the keyboard.

Making It Your Own:

For a younger class, use the stamps for random stamping.
Use other word cards to fit other units.

Rubber stamp pad keyboard.

USING COMPUTERS TO HELP DEVELOP SKILLS

The children in the kindergarten class have been creating patterns.[2] When they sing their "Good Morning" song, they use a pattern to clap out the rhythm. They tap their knees then clap, tap their knees then clap, and repeat this pattern over and over as they keep time to the song. Each day, they try different rhythm patterns for accompanying their songs. The children had a pattern party. They made the refreshments by stacking patterns of black raisins, yellow raisins, and carrot circles on toothpicks. They designed placemats with patterned borders. They choreographed and performed dances made out of a series of simple patterned motions. They might step-jump, turn-step, or jump-turn, repeating the pattern until the music ends. Pattern creation is a skill that the teacher introduced, but it sparked the interest of many children. They often create patterns spontaneously. When placing pegs in the pegboard, they may make a row of red, then blue, then red, and so on. When threading beads, they may invent a pattern like two green, two blue, then one yellow, and repeat this pattern to string a whole necklace.

The children delight in new media for creating patterns. The computer is an excellent material for pattern making. Using **Facemaker**, children can program a repeated pattern of movements for the face to make it wink-cry, wink-cry, wink-cry, wink-cry, and so on. When using a word processing program, a child may type alternating letters—"B"-"D"-"B"-"D"-"B"-"D"-"B"-"D"-"B"-"D"—to create a pattern. There is also software designed to support the development of patterning skills. **The Pond** asks children to help a frog hop through the lily pads to reach the end of the pond. The pads are arranged in a pattern such as 2 down, 3 across, 2 down, 3 across. The child can move the frog more quickly to its friend after discovering the pattern.

Computer-related activities can be adapted, either intentionally by the teacher or spontaneously by

the child, to facilitate the development of various noncomputer skills. Many of the activities described in this book could be adapted to support the patterning skills discussed earlier. For example, programming activities such as **Program a Face** (p. 164), **Programming the Piano** (p. 170), or **Program an Obstacle Course** (p. 166), could be used to program a repetitive pattern. For older children, who are using **Logo**, patterns could be represented in **Logo** language like this—**Repeat (red dot, blue dot) 6**— indicating that the necklace should have 6 repetitions of the red–blue bead pattern.

As can be seen by the description of patterning activities, the computer can be used to facilitate the development of specific skills in a number of ways.

1. Teachers can provide software that is designed to foster the skill.
2. Children can spontaneously use the software to practice a skill—as when they type letters in a pattern.
3. Computer-related activities can be adapted either spontaneously by the child, or in response to teachers' suggestions, in order to support a specific emerging skill.

In thinking of computers as a means for skill development, it is also important to remember that most of the computer-related skills discussed in Chapters 4 through 6 have corresponding noncomputer skills. This chapter takes a brief look at a few of these skills. Children who learn to turn computer switches on and off are expanding their skill with all switches. The majority of switches they will use in their lives will not be connected to a computer. They are also learning to see themselves as competent individuals who can have an effect on their surroundings. Loading the computer requires children to remember and follow a sequence of steps in order—again another skill that has wide applicability beyond the computer. Chapter 4 explores the noncomputer use of each of these skills in greater detail.

[2]The pattern activities described here are ones used by Nancy Edwards in the University of Delaware Laboratory Preschool kindergarten class as part of the mathematics curriculum. Many of the activities Nancy uses are based on Baratta-Lorton's **Mathematics Their Own Way** (1976).

USING COMPUTERS TO SUPPORT DEVELOPMENT OF THE WHOLE CHILD

The goal of early childhood programs is to further the development of the whole child. Computers are one of the many media that teachers can use to facilitate development. Specific pieces of software claim to promote certain types of learning. For example, according to its documentation, **Letter-Go-Round** allows children to "practice reading skills." The specific skills listed are "letter recognition and matching, uppercase/lowercase matching, word recognition and matching, and simple spelling." Software companies often promise more than the software can actually deliver. The **Letter-Go-Round** software states that the children will practice the skill of word recognition and spelling. In Level 3, "one little word"—a three-letter word is on the screen. The child must pick letters off the Ferris wheel to spell the word again. The children *do* need to match letters to construct the word, but they do not need to match *words*, nor do they have to recognize the word. The program provides no pictorial clue as to what the word is. With a reader nearby reading the word out loud, the child may learn to recognize it. But when the software is used independently, the child must be able to read the word already in order to recognize it.

Many pieces of software, especially drill-and-practice software, purport to facilitate some aspect of cognitive development. Often, as is the case in **Letter-Go-Round**, adult help is required if the software is to accomplish some of its stated goals. This is not to say that software never fulfills the claims it makes, but rather that the claims must be carefully evaluated rather than blindly accepted.

Some of the goals in software documentation pertain to the acquisition of specific skills. Others are more general. For example, **Stickybear ABC's** documentation suggests that the software will encourage children to "be little scientists." The documentation for **Big Bird's Fun House** states that "CTW [Children's Television Workshop] games allow children to experiment and explore, to think and solve problems." Mr. Rogers's introductory letter to the **Many Ways to Say I Love You** says that this software will provide a means to "express feelings that adults and children have for each other." The documentation for the **Bald-Headed Chicken** suggests that using the software will help children to discover "their own imaginations." These more general goals are often not software-specific. They tend to be applicable to a variety of open-ended software.

Examining only the use of specific software and its effects provides a limited view of how computers can support children's growth and development. To see the wider view, teachers must look at computer use more generally. When children interact freely with appropriate software in a child-centered environment, the development of the whole child can be enhanced. A look at the different developmental areas highlights some of the many ways in which computers can support development.

Computers Facilitate Language Development

Children learn language by using language. Children, like adults, use language more and use richer language when they are communicating about something that they find meaningful. The computer provides many meaningful contexts for language use. Some software, like the **Explore-a-Story** series, lends itself easily to dramatic play, a particularly meaningful context for language. In the **Bald-Headed Chicken**, a series of scenes are available for the children to select. The children can "pick up" any of the objects and move them around the screen. Children often create stories and dramatic play around this software. Four-year-old Sarah was particularly fond of this software. She used it to create the following story by moving objects around the screen and narrating the events of the story as she worked.[3]

First, Sarah uses the cursor to remove the cracked egg shells from around the chicks. Then she moves each of the chicks to the mother. The mother walks around checking on them. The chicks are thirsty, but the pond look too deep for

---

[3]The incident described is from the University of Delaware Laboratory Preschool's 4-year-old class.

*Children using **What Makes a Dinosaur Sore?***

the little chicks. Sarah picks up a piece of water and moves it to a new spot to make a smaller drinking area. The Momma and chicks all walk over for a drink. Sarah decides that the family needs a Daddy chicken. She goes up into the menu to get another chicken. The Mom, Dad, and chicks play by the pond, fly up into the trees, go to visit the sun, then come back to the flowers at bedtime to go to sleep. Sarah narrates the events of the story as she works. Jesse wanders by and sits down. She listens to Sarah and watches. Occasionally she adds a suggestion to the unfolding story.

Children create stories around less open-ended software as well. When using **Facemaker**, children often discuss what is happening to the face. "Now his friend is leaving, so he is crying. But another friend is coming, so he is smiling again." Dramatic play tends to elicit language. Some children, like Sarah, will narrate the story to themselves as they work. Children who are working together will use language to decide on, and develop, the plot together. Providing software with dramatic play potential, and encouraging children to add stories to programs such as **Facemaker**, offers many opportunities for language use and development.

If social use of the computer is encouraged, language is sure to result. Two children working together on **Facemaker** will debate which feature to add next and which particular set of eyes are best. These children will use language to describe the choices they want and to explain why these are the best. In many situations, the children decide on a special type of face they want to create—"Let's make a scary face." Then they discuss which eyes or ears are scariest and why. Not only do these children need to use language to explain their ideas, but they must do it in a way that convinces the other child that the idea is right. When children use **Peanut's Maze Marathon** together, they often try to guess which reward will result when the maze is completed. They may tell each other which path to take and have to explain why the path they suggest is the correct one.

Teachers who encourage children to share their knowledge of a program with other children are providing another wonderful avenue for language. In order to explain how to do something, children must use clear, precise language. It is important to realize that children have a tendency to show others, rather than tell them, how to do it, but they can use words when they try. Teachers can encourage verbal assistance by modeling good helping language themselves and by asking children to "use their words" to explain what to do.

Word processing programs also elicit language. Some children may narrate a story as they type random strings of letters. Other children may have a clearer notion of the connection between the letters used and the words read back. These children might type out their stories or labels using "invented spelling."[4]

Children can also dictate stories to a teacher, who does the typing. The stories can be printed and compiled into a class book to be read and reread. Word processing programs can also be used to record stories composed by groups of children, to compile lists, to print thank-you notes or other messages, or for as many uses as there are reasons for writing.

---

[4]Schickedanz (1986), Teale and Sulzby (1986), and Sampson (1986) discuss the emergence of early literacy. They stress that early "writing" is often a random series of marks that children use to represent their words. This later moves to a closer interconnection between letters and words as children develop a clearer understanding of how the writing system works and as they develop the phoneme-letter relation.

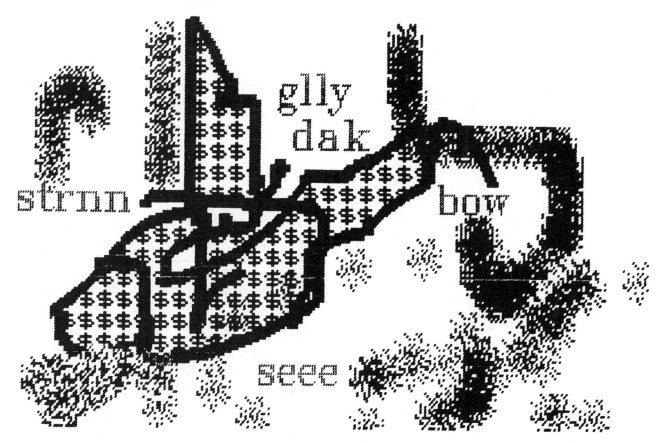

During a boat unit, a child made and labeled a boat with the computer.

Computers Facilitate Social and Emotional Development

In my classroom, children rarely use the computer alone. When new software is introduced, a group of children always gathers around the computer to watch one another experiment with it. Older software is used in groups as well. Sometimes, two children come over to use the software together. At other times, one child is on the computer when another child becomes interested and sits down too. Many times, children urge others to come over to "see what I have done!" or to watch a new discovery they have made.

Because the computer is a social activity, it requires children to use a variety of social interaction techniques. The children have to negotiate who does what on the computer. They need to find ways to convince others, or if that does not work to develop compromise solutions.

Christin had decided to type everyone's names using **Bank Street Writer**. Christopher wandered by and wanted to use the computer too. He sat down and started randomly hitting keys, then giggling. Christin looked a bit annoyed, then giggled when he giggled. She continued trying to type names. He continued distracting her by typing other letters. They would laugh together at the silly words that resulted. Christopher began typing faster. Christin was no longer laughing. She said softly, "Don't." Christopher continued. Christin looked upset and said, "Stop that!" Christopher continued typing and giggling, trying to draw Christin back into his game. A teacher came over and said, "Christopher, I think Christin is trying to tell you something." Christin repeated her request to "stop that."

Christopher tried silliness as a way to initiate a social interaction with Christin. It did work as an entrance, but he was unable to successfully maintain the interaction because he did not recognize Christin's desire to type the names correctly. The teacher who stepped in helped him to realize that Christin's intent was different than his. Christin was willing to have Christopher join her. She was even willing to adjust her game to include his silliness. She was unsure how to stop the silliness when it got out of hand, so she needed to rely on the teacher's help. All social interaction requires some understanding of the other person's intent and some ability to adapt and compromise to keep the interaction going in a way that satisfies the people involved.

Dramatic play, which is often seen when children use the computer, provides a vehicle for both social and emotional development. In creating and enacting stories, children are designing their own world. In this world, they can try out different roles, and social interactions. Children can also use dramatic play to come to terms with emotional issues in their lives. A child who is worried about being left with babysitters, can create a story on **Bald-Headed Chicken** in which the chicks are left with a sitter. Through a story, children can try on powerful roles that they do not get to enact often in real life.

In watching children use the computer in my classroom, I have observed pairs of children who rarely, or never, played with each other brought together by joint interest in a piece of software. Sometimes, the interactions begin as peer teaching, with an "expert" at the program guiding a "novice" classmate. At other times, a child sees something intriguing on the computer, sits down to watch what is happening, and becomes involved with the child using the computer. Thus, the computer can expand the child's social network by prompting interaction with a wider range of peers.

The peer teaching, which computer use can foster, also increases the child's social development. Helping others requires a new set of skills. The child has to learn how to explain what is happening so that others can understand, to recognize what the other child does not know, and to explain what to do slowly enough so that the other child can follow. Being an "expert" and able to "teach" others may provide the child with a new social status. In my own classroom, I have seen three children (in 4 years of using computers) who did not have many friends each sought out to be a companion at the computer. In two cases, the children were quiet members of the class, who watched others but had no effective strategies for initiating interactions with peers. Their skill at the computer made other children seek them out. The third case was a younger child who had not attempted much social interaction. Her desire to use the computer encouraged her to participate with peers when it was their turn. She then began to offer help to others who spent less time on the computer. Using the computer provided a stimulus for increasing her level of social interaction.

When using computers independently, and especially when they are able to show others what they have learned on the computer, children feel competent. They are learning to see themselves as someone who can manage the world in which they live. Children often discover something the computer does that is even new to the teacher, which makes them feel like the important, successful learners that they are.

I do not mean to imply by these examples that the computer is the prescription for increasing all children's social interactions. All good early childhood teachers can cite examples of activities or materials that have served to increase individual children's level of social interaction. A child who has a rich imagination may be sought when children are playing pretend; the child who is creative at the art table may spark classmates' ideas; and a child who is uncomfortable in dramatic play may find that a non-speaking role, such as "dog" or "baby," provides a nonthreatening means of entry. There are many things that can stimulate a child's interest in, and skill at, social interaction. The computer can add an additional stimulus for social interaction to the class-room.

Computers Facilitate Physical Development

Children are constantly stretching their physical abilities as they use their bodies to explore the world. Using the keyboard, mouse, joystick, or touch pad all require the children to use their hands in a controlled, precise way. The children's enjoyment of the computer and their desire to control what is happening on the screen encourage them to exercise and extend their small-muscle abilities. While playing with **Peanut's Maze**, children learn to move their hands more quickly in order to stop the cursor at the opening to the desired maze path. Children using **Color Me** may work to position the cursor accurately in a small hole they wish to fill. The children are not consciously stretching their physical development; this growth comes as a by-product of their using the computer. Many of the off-computer activities described in this book also facilitate small-muscle development.

On-computer activities rarely facilitate large-muscle development, although some children find ways of being physically active while using the software. For example, the "reward" for successfully completing a section of **Astro-Grover** is to watch Grover dance to some lively music. The 5-year-olds at the University of Delaware Laboratory Preschool invented their own **Astro-Grover** dance to do along with the computer. In another class, children would dance along with **Creature Creator** after they had programmed it to move. Children using the turtle-robot move both in response to its movements and to map out the moves they are planning for the turtle. Many off-computer activities also encourage children to use their bodies actively. **Hokey Pokey** (p. 216), **Bowling Bop** (p. 235), **Jane Commands** (p. 152), and **Program an Obstacle Course** (p. 166) are just a few of the activities that promote large-muscle development along with computer-related goals.

Program an Obstacle Course *promotes large-muscle development.*

Computer use facilitates visual and auditory development as well. Children carefully track the cursor as they move it around the screen in graphics programs, through a maze in **Peanut's Maze** or through a menu of options. They must watch to see that the cursor is positioned correctly to accurately indicate their choices. Many programs have music or other sounds to accompany various parts of the software. Children who do not read will often use the sound effects as an additional way to know where they are in a program. When using **Color Me** the children may recognize the "whoosh" sound of the fill option even before they notice the expanding fill diamond on the screen.

Computers Facilitate Cognitive Development

Children learn by constructing their own knowledge. As they explore and experience the world, they learn through "a complex process that results from the interaction of [their] own thinking and their experiences in the external world" (NAEYC [Bredekamp, Ed.], 1986, p. 47). When a child drops something in water and sees it sink, that child might conclude that all things sink in water. With more experience, the child will realize that some things sink and some do not. As the child explores and experiments with objects and water, a personal theory will evolve to explain why things sink and why they do not. If, by chance, the floating things have all been brown the child may conclude that brown things float and things of other colors sink. When the child finds that a blue plastic cup floats in water, the earlier conclusion is challenged. The child will need to revise the theory to accommodate this new event. Children constantly go through this process of constructing concepts, some accurate and others not, which are often later revised or expanded to account for conflicting evidence or ideas.

Some children who are busy learning in a preschool program illustrate this process. As Sharon mixes paint on paper, she is learning about how colors combine to make new colors and how the paper reacts to the wetness of the paint. When Charlotte tries to get the doll Mark is cuddling, she may discover that Mark's needs and hers do not coincide. Depending on the action she decides to take, and on Mark's reaction, she may learn that she can affect Mark's actions, or that she cannot. Christopher has discovered that by turning the contrast and darkness dials on the side of the monitor, he can make the picture fade away and come back. Outside, Andrew and Sean play with icy blocks of snow, discovering that all but the thickest blocks will shatter when dropped. Even these can be shattered by stomping on them. As children play, they learn about the world. It is this process of exploring and explaining the world, not the learning of set facts, that is the essence of cognitive development.

Teachers carefully design the classroom environment to create a place rich with materials to explore and time in which children can ponder and create conclusions about what they discover. As can be seen from the previous example, the computer is one of the materials in the classroom that children can explore and with which children can experiment in the process of constructing their own knowledge. It is this use of the computer—the computer as thought-provoker—that most powerfully facilitates the child's cognitive development.

The computer also poses many opportunities to solve meaningful, self-defined problems. When children begin to use new programs, they experiment with commands used in old programs to see whether the commands will have similar effects on this new software. As they experiment with programs, they learn the constraints imposed by each piece of software. The cursor in **Magic Crayon** will not go beyond the end of the screen, but it will in **What Makes a Dinosaur Sore**. In the latter software, the pictures can be picked up and dropped off the screen. But once they are dropped, they cannot be retrieved. Although characters and objects can be dropped off the screen, letters must remain on the screen once they are typed. This poses a problem to be solved. What can be done to dispose of unwanted letters? Sarah discovered she could cover letters by dropping other objects on top of them. Sarah has learned that, like all materials in the world, computer programs have constraints. Other materials that children use impose some kinds of constraints: blocks can only be stacked so high before they topple; if two colors of wet paint are touching each other, the colors are likely to blend a little; playdough can only be stretched so thin before breaking into two pieces, and so on. And as children explore software, they discover the software's constraints and experiment with ways to reach their goals within those constraints.

Although the Computer Can Foster Development, It Does Not Do So Automatically

How the computer is used in the classroom directly affects its ability to support development. If, contrary to the recommendations of this book, the computer is viewed as a solitary activity and children are discouraged from watching each other or from working together, then the computer will not encourage social development or language development. On the other hand, if children are encouraged to involve each other in their computer work, discuss what they are doing, and seek peer assistance from children who have become more experienced, then the computer is a medium that facilitates social interaction and provides many opportunities for children to use, expand, and develop a variety of social skills. It also offers an excellent stimulus for language development. But if computers are perceived as drill-and-practice machines, they will only promote a limited range of cognitive skills. On the other hand, if the computer is viewed as a **thought-provoker**, children will be allowed to explore and experiment in the process of constructing knowledge for themselves.

CONCLUSION

It is clear why there has been so much debate about the appropriateness of computers in early childhood classrooms. Because the computer is a chameleon whose essence depends on the way it is perceived and used, it has the potential for being misused. However, it also has the potential for enriching and supporting a child-oriented, developmental classroom by providing another open-ended material that can facilitate the development of the whole child. The computer is a relatively new material. It is up to us as early childhood teachers to define and refine computer use with children. If we do this, we can help the computer to live up to its potential. With our help the computer can become a tool that children can use to learn, a material that can be used to stretch and extend children's thoughts, promote social development, encourage physical development, spark rich meaningful language, and thus become a vital component of the developmental early childhood classroom.

Appendix I: List of Software

Many different pieces of software are mentioned throughout the book. They are used in discussions of how children use computers. The following software list is intended to describe software so that readers can understand references in the text dealing with the software. **This list is not meant as an endorsement.** To see criteria for selecting appropriate software, read Chapter 3.

Note: The addresses of the manufacturers appear at the end of the list of software.

ASTRO-GROVER

Description: Five games that provide practice in counting, adding and subtracting. The graphics and animation have an outer space motif.

Company: CBS software

Computer: Commodore 64, Apple (the animation is better on Commodore)

Print capacity: No

Keys needed: Number keys, and on the Commodore a 17-key sequence needed for loading. The program uses a keyboard overlay once it is loaded.

Aides needed: A pictorial menu depicting the levels to supplement the written one. The program must either be preloaded or have colored labels on keys and a color coded guide to ease loading.

Skills needed: Must be able to count rationally

BALD-HEADED CHICKEN

Description: This program is formatted like a book. It has a title page and four picture pages. Children can pick up and move any of the characters or objects in the picture. Additional characters can be added as well as words. The story can be saved, and/or printed.

Company: Collarmore Educational Publishing, D. C. Heath & Company

Computer: Apple with 128K memory

Peripherals: Can use the keyboard or any of these: mouse, joystick, or koala pad. The keyboard makes the program much slower; use with peripheral is recommended.

Print Capacity: Color or black and white

Keys needed: Arrow keys (to move the cursor if peripheral not being used)

BANK STREET WRITER

Description: A children's word-processing program. The editing functions are accessed with the **[Esc]** key. The program can be used for free typing or taking dictation.

Company: Broderbund Software

Computer: Apple

Print Capacity: Black and white (many command steps needed to print)

Keys Needed: No specific keys for free typing

BIG BIRD'S FUN HOUSE

Description: A memory game with five levels. Children try to guess which Muppet characters are hiding.

Company: CBS Software

Computer: Commodore 64

Print Capacity: No

Keys Needed: There is a 16-key sequence for loading. Once the computer is loaded a keyboard overlay is used.

Aids needed: Preload or have colored labels on keys and a colored guide to ease loading. Picture menu for levels needed to supplement written one on program.

BUMBLE GAMES

Description: Grid plotting activities from simple to complex. The first two levels do not require reading.

Company: The Learning Company

Computer: Apple

Print Capacity: No

Keys Needed: For Levels 1 and 2, the keys needed are the numerals 1-7 to choose a game, and ''A,'' ''B,'' ''C,'' ''D.''

Aides needed: Picture guide to supplement written menu for levels.

CHARLIE BROWN'S ABC'S

Description: This is an animated alphabet book. When the children presses a letter, they get the letter and a word and a picture of something starting with that letter on the screen. Pressing the letter again animates the picture. Only half of the alphabet is on each side of the disk.

Company: Random House Software

Computer: Apple, Commodore 64, IBM jr.

Print Capacity: No

Keys needed: Any letter keys on that side of the disk will work.

Aids needed: Perhaps a sheet to show which letters are on which side of the disk.

COLOR ME

Description: Children use a mouse, joy stick, or Koala Pad to draw pictures. Text can be added. Children can change colors, size of crayon, use spray paint, or use a fill option. The program can be used at a variety of skill levels.

Company: Mindscape

Computer: Apple, Commodore 64 (128K memory required), IBM

Peripherals: One of these is required—mouse, joystick, or koala pad

Print Capacity: Color or black and white (color preferable)

Keys Needed: ''J,'' ''K,'' or ''M'' to indicate type of peripheral

CREATURE CREATOR

Description: Children can make a creature by selecting arms, legs, heads, and bodies. They can make the creature dance with single keystrokes, or program a dance. There is also a game to recreate the creature's dance. Making and moving are simple. Programming the dance requires understanding the meaning of a grid.

Company: Design Ware

Computer: Apple, IBM

Peripheral: Joystick is optional.

Print Capacity: No

Keys needed: Spacebar, **[Return]**, ''R,'' ''T,'' ''W,'' ''G,'' ''H,'' ''S,'' and arrows

Aids needed: Rebus pictures for moving commands

Skills: For programming dance and playing game, child must understand grid.

DELTA DRAWING

Description: A drawing program that allows children to move the cursor in straight line segments, ''wrap'' the line so it goes off the end of the screen and comes up on the other side, fill parts of the picture, and use five colors. Single letters are used for commands for example—D (draw), L (left), M (move without drawing) E (erase). As the picture is drawn, commands are stored for later editing. Pictures can be printed. Similar to LOGO. This can be used at a more complex level as well.

Company: Spinnaker Software Corp.

Computer: Apple, IBM jr., Commodore 64

Print capacity: Yes

Keys Needed: ''D,'' ''R,'' ''L,'' ''M,'' ''E,'' ''C,'' 1-5, and additional keys for more advanced commands

Aides needed: Rebus picture menu depicting command letters and their uses

DINOSAURS

Description: This program offers five dinosaur games: matching dinosaurs, classifying by food type, classifying by habitat, counting dinosaurs, and matching dinosaurs to their written names. The program requires no reading. Excellent self-explanatory picture menus and clues. Animation is used to reinforce correct responses. Incorrect answers receive no response.

Company: Advanced Ideas

Computer: Apple, Commodore 64, IBM (128K memory required)

Keys Needed: **[Return]** key and arrow keys

EXPLORE-A-STORY SERIES

A software series that is presented like books. Each has a number of pages. Children can pick up and animate characters and objects. Words can be added. Pictures can be printed. Some of the titles in the series are **Bald-Headed Chicken, Lima Bean Dream, What Makes a Dinosaur Sore?** (See **Bald-Headed Chicken** and **What Makes a Dinosaur Sore?** for individual descriptions.)

Company: Collarmore Educational Publishing, D. C. Heath & Company

Computer: Apple (128K memory required)

Print Capacity: Yes

FACEMAKER

Description: Children use the spacebar and **[Return]** key to select features and construct a face. The children can then use six letters to move the features of the face. They can ''write a program'' for a series of movements. A memory game is available that is too fast for many young children.

Company: Spinnaker Software Corp.

Note: The **[Caps Lock]** key must be down for the moving part of the program to run. This version has been discontinued a description of the newer version (Golden edition) appears below

Computer: Apple, IBM PC & jr., Commodore 64, Atari

Print Capacity: No

Keys Needed: Spacebar, **[Return]**, "1," "2," "W," "C," "E," "T," "S," "F"

Note: The **[Caps Lock]** key must be down to use the moving part of the program.

Aids needed: Rebus menu to show which number to press for making and moving parts of the program, and to illustrate letters for moving the face

Note: The introductory questions can be bypassed by pressing "1" when they appear.

FACEMAKER GOLDEN EDITION

Description: This is an updated version of **Facemaker**. It begins with a demo that can be ended by pressing the **[Return]** key, but the demo is slow to end. Compared to the original version, the menu for features is clearer, bodies, and accessories are available. Two new movements—crossed eyes and dancing—are added, as well as a printing option.

Company: Spinnaker Software Company

Computer: Apple, Amiga

Print Capacity: Yes

FREDDIE FROG

Description: A program available on PLATO that runs on a main frame computer. This uses a touch screen. The children touch a spot on the screen and Freddie Frog will jump where they touch. Later they must touch where he has jumped.

JUGGLE'S RAINBOW

Description: Three games that explore right/left, and up/down by adding a design to the screen to the side that corresponds to the side of the keyboard that is touched. At the beginning, the designs respond to where the child touches, then the child is expected to touch where the clues on the screen indicate. If the child completes the drill, then touching the screen creates a butterfly, rainbow, or windmill. Touching the spacebar allows children to advance to picture and bypass the drill. Children are sometimes confused with the menu and believe that "4" will let them make a question mark; it really gets them into instructions.

Company: The Learning Company

Computer: Apple, IBM, Commodore 64

Print Capacity: No

Keys needed: 1-3 to pick game, "4" for instructions and to cancel instructions that are accidentally entered

Note: The **[Caps Lock]** key must be down for this program to work.

KINDERCOMP

Description: This program includes six games: a drawing program using the arrows with a variety of colors; an option that repeats symbols typed; one that presents a name typed in many formats; and three drill and practice pieces involving uppercase/lowercase matching, shape matching, and finishing a sequence of numbers.

Company: Spinnaker Software Corp.

Computer: Apple, IBM PC & jr., Commodore 64, Atari

Keys Needed: 1-6 to pick options, for drawing—"F," "S," "B," "W," spacebar, and **[Return]** key

Aids needed: Picture menu to supplement written menu on program

Peripherals: Can use joystick

KIDWRITER

Description: Children can select from a variety of backgrounds and 100 objects to make a picture. Children can alter the size, color, and location of each object before moving to the next one. Children can invent stories as they move the character. Text can be added. Once the text is saved, it can not be edited.

Company: Spinnaker Software Corp.

Computer: Apple, Commodore 64, IBM PC & jr.

Print capacity: Black and white, and color

Keys Needed: "S," "C," "B," "F," "P," "S," "N," "M," "D," and arrow keys. The **[Caps Lock]** must be down for this program to work.

Aids needed: Picture menu to supplement written one on program

Skills needed: Ability to use a multistepped menu

LETTER-GO-ROUND

Description: Children use the spacebar to stop the ferris wheel and match upper- and lowercase letters, and to make three-letter words. Sesame Street characters used in the animation.

Company: CBS Software

Computer: Commodore 64, Atari

Print capacity: No

Keys needed: Commodore has a 16-key sequence for loading. Keyboard overlay used once the program is loaded.

Aids needed: Either preload the Commodore version or color-code the loading keys and provide a rebus guide for loading.

MAGIC CRAYON

Description: The children use the arrow keys to move the cursor horizontally, vertically, and diagonally. A variety of colors may be used. Pictures may be saved.

Company: C & C Software

Computer: Apple

Print Capacity: Color or black and white

Keys needed: Must type name to enter, arrow keys, **[Return]** key, "R" (remember), "P" (picture)

Aids needed: Stickers on the sides of keys for diagonal arrows, these come with the software, and a rebus menu for how to find colors. Later may want to add "how to save" and "retrieve" pictures to the rebus menu.

MANY WAYS TO SAY I LOVE YOU

Description: Children design their own "greeting card." They use the spacebar and **[Return]** key to select backgrounds, characters, borders, and music to go with the message. The card can be saved. When it is recalled, it is rolled up. It unrolls, and the characters are animated as the music plays.

Company: CBS Software

Computer: Apple, Commodore 64 (the animation is significantly better on the Commodore version)

Print Capacity: No

Keys Needed: **[Space]** bar, arrows, and **[Return]** key

Skills needed: Ability to move between a variety of menus

MASK PARADE

Description: Children can create masks and other costume accessories by selecting the designs they wish to combine. Once a choice has gone by, the child must go through all the other options to see it again.

Company: Springboard

Computer: Apple, IBM PC & jr., Commodore 64

Print capacity: Color or black and white

Peripheral: A joystick is optional.

Keys Needed: Spacebar, **[Return]** key, ''I,'' ''J,'' ''K,'' and ''M.'' The spacebar and **[Return]** key are used in the opposite way from many other programs. The **[Return]** moves the cursor through the menu and the spacebar registers the choice.

Aids needed: Arrows added to front edge of ''I,'' ''J,'' ''K,'' and ''M,'' to indicate direction, or a rebus card to use with the keys

NEWSROOM

Description: A program that allows you to create a newspaper. This can not be used independently by children.

Company: Springboard

Computer: Apple, IBM PC, Commodore 64/128

PEANUTS MAZE MARATHON

Description: Children move through a maze on the screen. When the maze is completed, the Snoopy characters will be animated. Simple mazes are on one side of the disk; more complex ones are on the other side.

Company: Random House Software

Computer: Apple, Commodore 64, IBM jr.

Print capacity: No

Peripherals: Joystick optional, but it makes the movement of the cursor smoother.

Keys Needed: **[Return]**, and arrows if using keyboard

Aids needed: indication on disk label to show which side of the disk has easy, and which side has hard mazes

PRINT SHOP

Description: A program that allows user to create a banner, sign, or greeting card. This can not be used independently without first having many repetitions with adult help.

Company: Broderbund

Computer: Apple, IBM PC & jr., Macintosh, Atari

Print capacity: Yes

PRIMARY EDITOR

Description: A word-processing program for children. The print is large. Stories can be saved and edited.

Company: IBM Educational Systems

Computer: IBM PC & jr. (requires 128K memory)

Print capacity: Yes

Keys Needed: Must type name and number to enter

Aids needed: A rebus guide listing the steps to enter would be helpful.

STICKYBEAR ABC

Description: When using this program, the child presses a letter, and an animated picture of something starting with that letter appears. There are two different pictures for each letter.

Company: Weekly Reader Software

Computer: Apple, Atari, Commodore 64

Print capacity: No

Keys Needed: Any key pressed will get a response.

STICKYBEAR BOP

Description: This is like a video arcade game. Children use a seesaw-like lever to launch balls into the air to shoot down objects.

Company: Weekly Reader Software

Computer: Apple, Atari XL, Commodore 64

Print capacity: No

Peripheral: Joystick required

TALKING SCREEN TEXT WRITER

Description: This program allows user to type in text and have the computer's word synthesizer ''read'' the text. Can be used at a much more complex level as well.

Company: Computing Adventures Ltd.

Computer: Apple

Print Capacity: Yes

Peripherals: Voice synthesizer

Aids needed: Teacher will need to load the program and provide a rebus menu for getting it to talk.

TASMIN TURTLE CONTROL SOFTWARE

Description: **Logo** software for controlling the Terrapin Turtle robot

Company: Flexible Systems

TURTLE TOT CONTROL SOFTWARE

Description: **Logo** software for controlling the Turtle Tot robot

Company: Harvard Associates

TOYBOX

Description: Children can create a picture. Each key will place a different shape, color, or special effect on the screen, the placement of the objects is random.

Company: Data Integration Services, Corp.

Computer: Commodore 64, Apple (128K required)

Print capacity: No

Keys Needed: Any key will get results.

WHAT MAKES A DINOSAUR SORE?

Description: This is formatted like a book. There is a title page and seven picture pages. Children can pick up and animate the characters and objects on the screen. Additional characters can be added as well as words. Stories can be saved and/or printed.

Company: Collarmore Educational Publishing, D.C. Heath & Company

Computer: Apple with 128K memory

Peripherals: Can use the keyboard or any of these: mouse, joystick, or koala pad. The keyboard makes the program much slower; use with other peripheral is recommended.

Print Capacity: Color or black and white

Keys needed: Arrow keys (to move the cursor if peripheral not being used)

ADDRESSES OF SOFTWARE MANUFACTURERS

Advanced Ideas, Inc.
2550 Ninth Street
Berkeley, CA 94710
    (415) 526-9100

Broderbund Software
P.O. Box 1294
San Rafael, CA 94913-2947
    (415) 479-1185

C&C Software
5713 Kentford Circle
Wichita, KS 67220
    (316) 683-6056

CBS Software
CBS INC
One Fawcett Place
Greenwich, CT 06836
    (203) 622-2500

Collarmore Educational Publishing
D. C. Heath & Company
125 Spring Street
Lexington, MA 02173
    (800) 225-1149

Computing Adventures Ltd.
P.O. Box 15565
Phoenix, AZ 85060
    (602) 954-0293

Data Integration Services Corp.
1728 K Street, NW, Suite 614
Washington, DC 20006
    (202) 785-8585

Design Ware, Inc.
185 Berry Street
San Francisco, CA 94107
    (415) 546-1866

Flexible Systems
219 Liverpool Street
Hobart, Tasmania
Australia 7000

Harvard Associates
1260 Beacon Street
Sommerville, MA 02143
    (617) 492-0660

IBM Educational Systems
P.O. Box 2150
4111 Northside Parkway, NW
Atlanta, GA 30055
    (800) 426-2468

The Learning Company
545 Middlefield Road, Suite 170
Menlo Park, CA 94025
    (800) 852-2255

Mindscape, Inc.
3444 Dundee Road
Northbrook, IL 60062
    (312) 480-7667

Random House Software
400 Hahn Road
Westminster, MD 21157
    (800) 638-6460

Spinnaker Software Corp.
1 Kendall Square
Cambridge, MA 02139
    (800) 826-0706

Springboard
7808 Creekridge Circle
Minneapolis, MN 55435
    (612) 944-3915

Weekly Reader Software
245 Long Hill Road
Middletown, CT 06457
    (800) 852-5000

Appendix II: List of Activities

CHAPTER 5: ACTIVITIES TO DEVELOP SKILLS

Activities to build skills in turning the computer on and off	70
First, second, third	70
Obstacle course by the number	71
1, 2, 3, 4 . . . Orange juice	72
You turn me on	73
Activities to support development of skills for selecting and loading software	77
Pick a movement	77
Activities to develop keyboarding skills	82
Make your name	82
Name jumping	84
Keyboard Bingo	85
Office	86
Move a face	87
Keyboard puzzle	88
Bag a letter	89

CHAPTER 6: ACTIVITIES TO DEVELOP MORE SKILLS

Activities to Build Menu-Reading Skills	98
Soda machine	98
Create a creature	100
Taco by the menu	102
Treasure hunt	105
Activities to develop skills in following and generating procedures	109
Pizza parlour procedure	109
Necklace factory	111
Book bindery	113

Plan the planting procedure 114
Peanut butter planning 115

Activities to develop picture-reading skills 119
Pets on parade 119
Use your body and make some music 120
Old McDonald had a farm 121
Picture treasure hunt 122

CHAPTER 8: ACTIVITIES TO TEACH ABOUT THE COMPUTER

Activities to teach about computer parts 141
Computer easel 141
Build a computer 143
This is a song about computers 144
Meet Timothy Turtle 146
Joy Stick and the computer 148

Activities to teach about commands 152
Jane commands 152
Robot cleaners 154
Find what I command 155
If you're a Facemaker monitor 156
Simple dance to do 157
I'm gonna clap 158
I command you to draw 159
Good-bye commands 161

Activities to teach about programming 164
Program your face 164
Program an obstacle course 166
Robot orchestra 168
Programming the piano 170
Purple cloud 171
Fruit salad programming 172

CHAPTER 9: MORE ACTIVITIES TO TEACH ABOUT THE COMPUTER

Activities to teach about computer uses 184
I want some money, please 184
A trip to the bank 187
Children's bank and trust 188
The wishing stone 189

Activities for teaching about the computer's strengths and limitations 194
The art show 194
Recitation time 195

Activities to teach about input/CPU/output 198

Many kinds of processors	198
People input and output	200
They're playing our song	201
Popcorn processing	202
Shake a color	203
Microwaved cheese melt	204

CHAPTER 10: ACTIVITIES TO SUPPORT SPECIFIC SOFTWARE

Activities to teach turtle-robot skills	212
Feed the turtle	212
Fire! Fire!	214
Hokey pokey	216
I make my turtle go	217
Turtle tasks	218
Pen down	219
Activities to teach graphing skills for Bumble Games	222
Arrow hunt	222
Dot to dot	223
Where's bumble?	224
Deliver the mail	226
Activities to support the use of auxiliary drawing devices	229
Marble painting	229
Copy the pattern	230
Developmental activities generated by software	235
Bowling bop	235
Snoopy's table maze	236

CHAPTER 11: COMPUTER ACTIVITIES TO SUPPORT THE CURRICULUM

Activities to support learning about both computers and dinosaurs	244
Digging for bones	244
Stanley Stegosaurus goes walking	246
Dinosaur printing	247

Bibliography

Almy, Millie. (1969). Spontaneous Play: An Avenue for Intellectual Development. *Young Children.* 22(5), 265-277.

Ball, Stanley. (1985). "Valuable Alternatives to Keyboarding in Grades K-3." Paper presented at Young Child and the Computer conference in Austin Texas. *ERIC* Ed 264 957.

Bamberger, J. (1983). "The Computer as Sandcastle. In *Chameleon in the Classroom: Developing Roles for the Computer.* (Tech. Rep. No.22) pp34-39. New York: Bank Street College of Education, Center for Children and Technology.

Baratta-Lorton, Mary. (1976). *Mathematics Their Own Way: An Activity Centered Mathematics Program for Early Childhood Education.* CA: Addison Wesley.

Barnes, B. J., & S. Hill. (1983). "Should Young Children Work with Microcomputers—Logo before Lego? *The Computing Teacher.* 10(9), 11-14.

Baskin, Linda, & Mima Spencer. (1986). "Computer Resources for Early Childhood Teachers." In James L. Hoot (Ed.), *Computers in Early Childhood Education: Issues and Practices.* Englewood Cliffs, NJ: Prentice-Hall.

Beaty, Janice J., & W. Hugh Tucker. (1987). *The Computer as a Paintbrush: Creative Uses for the Personal Computer in the Classroom.* Columbus, Ohio: Merrill Publishing Company.

Beeson, B. S. & R. A. Williams. (1985). "The Effects of gender and Age on Preschool Children's Choice of the Computer as a Child-selected Activity. *Journal of the American Society for Information Science. 36,* 339-341.

Bert and Ernie's Sing-Along (1975). Children's Televison Workshop. New York: Children's Records of America. (CTW22068)

Borgh, Karen, & W. Dickson. (1986). "Two Preschoolers Sharing One Microcomputer: Creating Prosocial Behavior with Hardware and Software." In Patrica Campbell & Greta G. Fein (Eds.), *Young Children and Microcomputers.* Englewood Cliffs, NJ: Prentice-Hall.

Bredekamp, Sue (Ed.). (1986). *Developmentally Appropriate Practice.* Washington, DC: NAEYC.

Buckleitner, Warren. (1987). *1987 Survey of Early Childhood Software.* Ypsilanti, Michigan: High/Scope Foundation.

Burg, K. (1984). "The Microcomputer in the Kindergarten." *Young Children.* 39(3), 28-33.

Campbell, Patricia, & Greta Fein (Eds). (1986). *Young Children and Microcomputers.* Englewood Cliffs, NJ: Prentice-Hall.

Campbell, Patricia, & S. Schwartz. (1986). "Microcomputers in the Preschool: Children Parents and Teachers." In Patrica Campbell & Greta Fein (Eds.), *Young Children and Microcomputers.* Englewood Cliffs, NJ: Prentice-Hall.

Center for Children and Technology. (1983). *Chameleon in the Classroom.* (Technical Report #22). New York: Bank Street College of Education.

Church, Marilyn, & June Wright. (1986). "Creative Thinking with the Microcomputer." In Patricia Campbell & Greta Fein (Eds.), *Young Children and Microcomputers.* Englewood Cliffs, NJ: Prentice-Hall.

Clements, Douglas H. (1985a) *Computers in Early and Primary Education.* Englewood Cliffs, NJ: Prentice-Hall.

Clements, Douglas H. (1985b). "Young Children and Computers: What Have We Learned from Research?" Paper presented at NAEYC conference.

Clements, Douglas H. (1987). "Computers and Young Children: A Review of Research." *Young Children.* 43(1), 34-44.

Clements, Douglas H., & Gullo, D. F. (1984). "Effects of Computer Programming on Young Children's Cognition." *Journal of Educational Psychology.* 76(6), 1051-1058.

Copple, Carol, Irving Sigel, & Ruth Saunders. (1979). *Educating The Young Thinker: Classroom Strategies for Cognitive Growth.* New York: D. Van Nostrand.

Cuffaro, Harriet. (1984). "Microcomputers in Education: Why is Earlier Better?" *Teacher's College Record.* 85(4), 559-568.

Donohue, W. Anthony, Karin Bough, & W. Dickson. (1987). "Computers in Early Childhood Education." *Journal of Research in Childhood Education.* 2(1), 6-16.

Davis, Alice (1940). *Timothy Turtle.* New York: Harcourt, Brace and Company.

Dramatic Play—An Integrative Process for Learning. (1973). a film distributed by Campus Films Distributers.

Elkind, David. (1981). *The Hurried Child: Growing Up Too Fast, Too Soon.* Reading, Ma: Addison-Wesley.

EPIE Institute. (1986-87). *T.E.S.S. Educational Software Selector.* New York: Teacher's College Press.

Favaro, Peter. (1983). "My Five Year Old Knows Basic." *Creative Computing.* 9(4), 158-166.

Fein, Greta. (1986). "Microcomputers and Young Children an Interactive View." in Patricia Campbell & Greta Fein (Eds.), *Young Children and Microcomputers.* Englewood Cliffs, NJ: Prentice-Hall.

Forman, George , & David Kuschner (1983). *The Child's Construction of Knowledge: Piaget for Teaching Young Children.* Washington, DC: NAEYC.

Freeman, Don (1959). *Norman the Doorman.* New York: Viking Press, Inc.

Galland, Frank. (1983). *Dictionary of Computing.* New York: John Wiley and Sons.

Goodwin, Laura, William Goodwin, & Mary Beth Garel. (1986). "Use of Microcomputers with Preschoolers: A Review of the Literature." *Early Childhood Research Quarterly. 1*(3), 269-286.

Hadlock, James, & Sandra Morris (1984). *Computers and Classrooms: Physical Considerations.* Paper presented at Tennessee State University.

Hainstock, Elizabeth. (1968). *Teaching Montessori in the Home.* New York: Random House.

Hap Palmer (1969). *Learning Basic Skills Through Music: Volume 1. New York: Educational Activities Inc. (AR514)*

Haugland, Susan, & Daniel Shade. (1988). "Developmentally Appropriate Software for Young Children." Young Children. 43(4), 37-43.

Hawkins, J., K. Sheingold, M. Gearhart, & C. Berger. (1982). "Microcomputers in Schools: Impact on the Social Life of Elementary Classrooms." *Journal of Applied Developmental Psychology. 3,* 361-373.

Hendrick, Joanne. (1985). *The Whole Child.* Merill.

Hendrick, Joanne. (1986). *Total Learning.* Merill Publishing.

Hess, Robert, & L. McGarvey. (1987). "School-relevant Effects of Educational Uses of Microputers in Kindergarten Classrooms and Homes." *Journal of Educational Computer Research. 3*(3), 269-286.

Hirsch, Elizabeth S. (Ed.). (1984). *The Block Book.* Washington, DC: NAEYC.

Hoot, James (Ed.). (1986). *Computers in Early Childhood Education: Issues and Practices.* Englewood Cliffs, NJ: Prentice-Hall.

Hoover, Jeanne, & Ann Austin. (1986). "A Comparison of Traditional Preschool and Computer Play from a Social/Cognitive Perspective." Paper presented at the American Educational Research Association in San Francisco. *ERIC* Ed 270 220.

Hyson, Marion, & Sandra Morris (1985). "Computers? I Love Them!": Young Children's Concepts and Attitudes about Computers. *Early Childhood Development and Care. 23,* 17-29.

Johnson, Crockett (1959). *Harold and the Purple Crayon.* New York: MacMillian Books.

Kamii, Constance. (1985). "Leading Primary Education towards Excellence: Beyond Worksheets and Drill." *Young Children.* 40(6), 3-9.

Kamii, Constance, & DeVries, R. (1978). *Physical Knowledge in Preschool Education.* NJ: Prentice-Hall.

Klinzing, D. & A. Hall. (1985). *A Study of the Behaviour of Children in a Preschool Equipped with Computers.* Paper presented at the Annual Meeting of the American Educational Research Association, Chicago April 1985.

Kull, Judith A. (1986). "Learning and Logo." In Patricia Campbell & Greta Fein (Eds.), *Young Children and Microcomputers.* Englewood Cliffs, NJ: Prentice-Hall.

Kurland, P. Midian. (1983). "Software for the Classroom: Issues in Design of Effective Software Tools." *In Chameleon in the Classroom: Developing Roles for Computers.* (Tech. Rep. No. 22). New York: Bank Street College of Education, Center for Children and Technology.

Lee, Marjorie. (1984). "An Electric Preschool: Pros And Cons" paper presented at the 1984 NAEYC conference in Los Angeles. *ERIC* ED 257 551.

Levine, Milton. (1966). "Early Sex Education." *Young Children.* 22(1), 11-15.

Lipinski, Judith, Robert Nida, Daniel Shade, & Allen Watson. (1986). "The Effects of Microcomputers on Young Children: An Examination of Free-play Choices, Sex Differences, and Social Interactions." *Journal of Educational Computing Research. 2,* 147- 168.

Martin, John H. (1981). "On Reading, Writing, and Computers." *Educational Leadership. 41,* 60-64.

Mathews, Walter (Ed.). (1980). *Monster or Messiah?: The Computer's Impact on Society.* Jackson: University Press of Mississippi.

Muller, A.A., & Perlmutter. (1985). "Preschool Children's Problem-solving Interactions at Computers and Jigsaw Puzzles." *Journal of Applied Developmental Psychology. 6,* 173-186.

Ormerod, Jan. (1982). *Moonlight.* New York: Puffin Books.

Piaget, Jean (1964). *The Child's Conception of the World.* Translated by J.A.Tomilson. New York: Harcourt Brace Jovanovich.

Papert, S. (1980). *Mindstorms: Children and Computers, and Powerful Ideas.* New York: Basic Books.

Papert, S. (1986). "Are Computers Bad for Children?" In Patricia Campbell & Greta Fein (Eds.), *Young Children and Microcomputer.* Englewood Cliffs, NJ: Prentice-Hall.

Paris, Cynthia. (1985). "Skills and Concepts of Successful Computer Use." *ERIC* ED 259 837.

Paris, Cynthia, & Sandra Morris. (1985). "The Computer in the Early Childhood Classroom: Peer Helping and Peer Teaching. Paper presented a the Microworld for Young Children Conference College Park MD. *ERIC* ED 257 555.

Parish, Peggy (1963). *Amelia Bedelia.* New York: Harper and Row.

Pea, R. D. (1983). "Logo Programming and Problem Solving." *In Chameleon in the Classroom: Developing Roles for the Computer.* (Tech. Rep. No. 22) pp.25-33. New York: Bank Street College of Education, Center for Children and Technology.

The Random House Book of Poetry for Children. (1983). selected by Jack Prelutsky. New York: Random House

Sampson, Michael (Ed.). (1986). *The Pursuit of Literacy: Early Reading and Writing.* Dubuque, Iowa: Kendall/Hall Publishing.

Sardello, Robert, J. (1984). "The Technological Threat to Education." *Teacher's College Record.* Summer 1984.

Schickedanz, Judith. (1986). *More Than The ABC's: The Early Stages of Reading and Writing.* Washington, DC: NAEYC.

Shade, Daniel, Robert Nida, Judith Lipinski, & Allen Watson. (1986). "Microcomputers and Preschoolers: Working Together in a Classroom Setting." *Computers in the Schools.* 3(2),53-61.

Sheingold, Karen, Jim Hawkins, & Cynthia Char. (1984). "I'm the Thinkist, You're the Typist: The Social Interaction of Technology and the Social Life of the Classroom." (Tech. Rep. No. 27). New York: Bank Street College of Education, Center for Children and Technology. *ERIC* ED 249-924.

Sheingold, Karen. (1986). "The Microcomputer as a Symbolic Medium." In Patricia Campbell & Greta G. Fein (Eds.). *Young Children and Microcomputers.* Englewood Cliffs, NJ: Prentice-Hall.

Sherman, J., K. P. Divine & B. Johnson (1985). "An Analysis of Computer Software Preferences of Preschool Children. *Educational Technology.* May, 39-41.

Software Reports: The Guide to Evaluated Educational Software. (1986) Winter 1986-67. Trade Service, 10996

Spencer, Mima, & Linda Baskin. (1986). "Guidelines for Selecting Software for Children." In James L. Hoot (Ed.), *Computers in Early Childhood Education: Issues and Practices.* Englewood Cliffs, NJ: Prentice-Hall.

Sponseller, Doris (Ed.). (1974). *Play as a Medium for Learning.* Washington, DC: NAEYC.

Sponseller, Doris. (1982). "Play and Early Education." In B. Spodek (Ed.) *Handbook of Research in Early Childhood Education.* New York: Free Press.

Sprigle, J. E. & L. Schaefer. (1984). "Age, Gender, and Spacial Knowledge Influences on Preschoolers' Computer Programming Ability." *Early Child Development and Care. 14,* 243-250.

Stangl, Jean. (1976). *The No-Cook Cookery Cook Book.* Camarillo, CA: Jean Stangl.

Swigger, Kathleen M., J. Campbell, & B. K. Swigger. (1983). "Preschool Children's Preferences of Different Types of CAI Programs." *Educational Computer Magazine.* January/February, 38- 40.

Swigger, Kathleen M., & B. K. Swigger. (1984). "Social Patterns and Computer Use Amoung Preschool Children." *AEDS Journal, 17*(3), 33-41.

Taylor, Robert (Ed.). *The Computer in the School: Tutor, Tool, Tutee.* (1980). New York: Teachers College Press.

Teale, William, & Elizabeth Sulzby. (Eds.). (1986). *Emergent Literacy: Writing and Reading.* Norwood, NJ: Ablex Publishers.

Veitch, Beverly, & T. Harmes. (1981). *Cook and Learn.* California: Addison-Wesley.

Watson, J. Allen, Robert Nida, & Daniel D. Shade. (1986). "Educational Issues Concerning Young Children and Microcomputers: Lego and Logo? *Early Child Development and Care. 23,* 299-316.

Webster's Seventh New Collegiate Dictionary (1967). Springfield, MA: G & C Merriam Company.

Weiner, I. B. & Elkind, David. (1972). *Child Development: A Core Approach.* New York: John Wiley.

Wright, June L., & Anastasia S. Samaras. (1986). "Play Worlds and Microworlds." In Patricia Campbell & Greta Fein (Eds.), *Young Children and Microcomputers.* Englewood Cliffs, NJ: Prentice-Hall.

Ziajka, A. (1983). "Microcomputers in Early Childhood Education? A First Look." *Young Children. 38*(5), 61-67.

Index

Abacus, computer as, 14
Age, software appropriate for, 47
Aggressiveness, 7, 35, 47
Alphabet book, computer as, 14
Alphabet keys, 79
Alphabet programs, 11, 177–178
Apple IIe, 26, 36, 66, 137
    disk drive, 25
    keyboard, 23, 67, 68
    turn-on sequence, 37–38
    video interface, 178
Appropriateness of software content, 47–48
Arrow keys, 5, 9, 10, 45, 50, 78–79, 133, 221
Arrows, deciphering meaning of, 221
Art media, 11–12
    use of computers in, 179
Astro Grover, 59, 129, 232, 252
Atari, 66
Attitude toward computers, 7

Backup copy, 48, **49**
Bald-Headed Chicken, 13, 33, 94, 96, 190, 191,
    249, 252
Banking, computers in, 179, 182
    activities to teach about, 184–189
Bank money machine, 175, 182
    keyboard, 23
Bank Street Writer, 4, 5, 27, 78, 162, 251
BASIC, 28
Behavior, teaching, and computer, 32–33
Big Bird's Fun House, 249
Block Book, The, 1
Boot, 139
Booting, **128**
Building block, computer as, 14, 15
Bumble Games, 56, 234, 243
    activities generated by, 220–221, 227
    activities to teach graphing skills for, 222–226

Cable, **21**, 31, 131, 139
    labeling, 29

CAI. *See* Computer-assisted instruction
Card, 139
Cash registers, computerized, 133, 175, 176, 180
Central processing unit (CPU), 22, 27, 29, 36, 66,
    134, 139, 175, 186–197
    activities to teach about, 198–204
Charley Brown's ABC's, 76
Charts
    pictorial, 118
    for sequencing steps in using computer, 37–38,
        67–68
    see also Labeling
Child-directed activities, 3–4, 10–11, 18, 33, 46,
    50
    see also Independent use of computer
Chip, **179**
Circumventing difficult skills, 231–234
Classroom computer
    computer lab for, 33–34
    introducing to children, 38–41
    learning computer parts for, 22–29
    number needed, 34–35
    placement, 35–38
    purchasing, 29–31
    teaching behavior and, 32–33
    uses of, 117–178
Classroom environment, 17–19
Cognitive development, 4–5, 15–16, 35, 57, 253–
    254, 255
Collection, building software, 50–51
Color coding, directionality and, 210
Color Me, 13, 24, 25, 27, 48, 52, 94, 95, 117,
    133, 138, 233–234, 252
Command(s), **15**, 139
    activity to teach about, 152–161
    people needed to give, 150–151
    series, 162–163
    two-step, 210–211
Commodore, 59, 66, 78, 133
Communication, computer in, 178
Community, computers in, 178–179
    field trips to, 180–182
Computer(s)
    acquiring knowledge through using, 128–130
    classroom, 21–41

guidelines for using, 17–19
learning, *see* Learning about computers
metaphors for, 12–17
parts, 22–29
potential problems with, 8–12
skills, *see* Computer skills
strengths and weaknesses, 190–193
    activities for teaching about, 194–195
system, purchasing, 29–31
uses of, 175–183
    activities to teach, 184–189
values of, 2–8
Computer-assisted instruction (CAI), **10**, 14
Computer drawings, 12
Computer labs, 33–34
    borrowing from, 177
Computer language, **17**
Computer skills, developing children's
    auxiliary drawing devices, 227–228
        activities for, 229–230
    basic, 55–56
    command, 150–151
        activities about, 152–161
    community computers, 178–183
        activities about, 184–189
    computer parts, 137–140
        activities about, 141–149
    following picture directions, 117–118
        activities about, 119–122
    graphing, 220–222
        activities about, 223–227
    keyboarding, 78–81
        activities about, 82–89
    information processing, 196–197
        activities about, 198–204
    keystroke, using single, 90–91
    loading, 37–40, 74–76
        activity about, 77
    menu reading, 93–97
        activities about, 98–106
    multistepped procedures, 107–108
        activities about, 109–116
    objections to, 56–57
    picture reading, 117–118
        activities about, 119–122

programming, 162–163
   activities about, 164–172
selecting software, 74–76
   activity about, 77
support for, 57–59
teacher help with, *see* Teacher assistance in
   developing skills
time spent on, 61–62
turning computer on and off, 66–69
   activities about, 70–73
turtle-robot, 207, 208–211
   activities about, 212–219
Computers as Partners Project (CAPP), 32, 38,
   107, 208
Concept building
   input/CPU/output, 196–197
      activities about, 198–204
   people in computer control, 205–206
   strengths and weaknesses, computer, 190–193
      activities about, 194–195
   uses of computer, 176–183
      activities about, 184–189
Concepts, children's, construction and revision
   of, 5–6, 15, 47, 138, 140
Conferences, computer, 53
Content, software, 47–48
Cook and Learn, 108
Cooking, 10, 108
   activities about following recipes, 109–110
Cooperative computer use, 3, 18, 37, 80, 252–
   253
CPU. *See* Central processing unit
Crayon, computer as, 14
Creature Creator, 162, 253
Curriculum, integrating computers into
   cognitive development, 253–254
   language development, 249–251
   physical development, 253
   skill development, 248–249
   social development, 251–253
   unit themes, 240–243
      activities for, 244–247
Cursor, 9, **10**, 22–23, 45, 49, 50, 133, 139, 150,
   227
   moving secondary device and, 228

Damage to computer, environmental, 36–37
Data Disk, **28**
Delete key, 78
Delta Draw, 11, 129, 162
Developmental classroom, 18, 255
   facilitating goals in, 234–236
Developmentally Appropriate Practice, 17
Digitizers, **27**
Dinosaurs, 240–241
   activities to learn about, 244–247
Directionality, 208, 209–210
Disk, **26**, 39, 130, 139
   loading, 74–76, 77
Disk drive, 25–26, 27, 31, 36, 59, 66, 68, 130,
   137–138, 139, 182
   loading disks into, 74–76, 77
Disk sleeve, **38**
Dramatic play, 183, 249–250, 252
*Dramatic Play—An Integrative Process for Learn-
   ing*, 6
Drawing devices, auxiliary, 227–228
Dust sensitivity of computers, 36

Electrical power, 36
Emergent literacy, 191
Emotional development, 251–253
Enter key, **5**
Environment
   classroom, 18
   computer damage caused by, 36–37
   interacting with, 10, 15
Esc key, 45, 108, 127
Etch-a-Sketch, 227, 228
Evaluation, software, 51–53
Expandability, 30–31, 48, 50
Experience, children's
   computer software and, 46
   functional knowledge and, 129
   as prerequisite for computer learning, 130
   weaknesses of computer vary by, 190–191
Explore-a-Story, 6, 49, 50, 51, 177, 190, 221,
   241, 249

Facemaker, 26, 35, 38, 45, 59, 60, 75, 78, 94,
   96, 117, 131, 133, 150, 151, 162, 193,
   231, 233, 250
Field trips, planning good, 180
Finger Print, 26
Freddie Frog, 192
Functional knowledge, 126–128
   computer experience and, 129
   developmental level and, 129–130
   in situational context, 130
Function keys, **22**, 50
Furniture, for use with computers, 36

Garfield, 232
Gender, computer use by, 7–8, 35
Graphics, **6**, 11–12, 14, 16, 23, 27, 30, 31, 46,
   50, 179
   to support unit activities, 241
Graphing skills, 220–221, 227
   activities for, 222–226
Group activity, computer as, 3, 8, 18, 251–253
Guessing, clues for, 221
Guidelines
   for classroom computer placement, 35–38
   for computer use, 17–19
   for software collection, 53

Hands-on approach in software evaluation, 51–
   53
Hard copy, 26
Hardware, 31n, **33**, 133
   activities for using specific, 207–237
   auxiliary, 178
   people-controlled, 205–206
Heat sensitivity of computers, 36
Hurried Child, The, 56

IBM, 66
Imaginative play, 6–7, 252–253
Inanimate object, computer as, 191–192
Independent use of computer, 3, 8, 18, 37, 44,
   46, 177, 181, 207, 252
   with specific software and hardware, 208–211,
      220–221, 227–228

Information processing, 134, 196–197
   activities to teach, 198–204
Input, **25**, 134, 139, 175, 196
Input/CPU/output, 196–197
   activities to teach about, 198–204
Input devices, 22–26, 29, 36
   comments on, 25
Instruction, formal and informal, 131, 132, 182
Interface card, **25**, 31

Joystick, **9**, 23–24, 25, 31, 49, 50, 56, 61, 134,
   139, 227
Juggle's Rainbow, 35, 51, 94, 95, 132

K (kilobytes), **28**
Key(s), **5**, 9, 10, 45, 55, 134, 139, 182
   labeling to locate, 233
Keyboard, 22–23, 29, 36, 49, 51, 57, 61–62, 66,
   130, 131, 137–138, 139
Keyboarding, 65, **66**
   developing skills in, 78–81, 82–89
   typewriter as aid to, 80
Keystroke, using single, 90–91
Kidwriter, 49, 162, 231
Kindercomp, 94, 231–232, 233, 242
Knowledge
   functional, 126–128
   operational, 126
Koala Pad, 24, 95, 133, 139, 227

Lab, computer, 33–34
   borrowing from other, 177
Labeling
   cables, 29
   complex loading procedure, 232–233
   grid, 221
   to locate keys, 232
   sequence in turning computer on and off, 37–
      38
Language development, 8–9, 249–251
Learning about computer, children's
   activities for, 141–149
   formal instruction, 132
   helping with, 137–140
   informal instruction, 131
   need for, 126–128
   using computer for, 128–130
   what can be learned, 130–132
   when to learn, 130–132
Left arrow key, 5, 78
Lego, 57, 192–193
Letter Go Round, 14, 231, 249
Levels, programs with different, 233–234
Library software collections, 54
Lighting, 36
Literacy, emergent, 191
Loading a program, 37–40, **48**, 50, 55, 56, 62,
   67, 74–76, 139, 248
   activity for, 77
   complex procedures for, 232–233
Logico-mathematical knowledge, 5
Logo, 4–5, 11, 14, 15, 56, 107, 162, 207, 248

McDonald's
cash register, 133, 175
keyboard, 23
MacVision, 178
Machines
 computers as parts of, 179–180
 learning to operate, 62, 68
Magic Crayon, 9, 11, 12, 27, 45, 47, 51, 60 75,
 78, 80, 96, 108, 127, 129, 133, 150, 162,
 178, 192, 221, 233, 254
Magnetic fields, 37
Mainframe, **192**
Maintenance, computer, 31, 205
Many Way to Say I Love You, 133, 162
Mask Parade, 45, 177
Memory, 27–29, 36, 49, 177
 expandibility, 30–31
Menu, 10, **23**, 46, 55, 56, 62, 139
 developing skills in reading, 93–97, 98–106
 picture, 94
Metaphors for computers, 13–17
Micro, **181**
Microcomputer, **18**, 182
Microprocessor, **179**
Monitor, **3**, 26, 29, 66, 68, 130, 131, 137–138,
 139
 moving secondary device and, 227
Moral values, software content and, 47
Motherboard, **138**, 139
Motor skills, 18, 55, 228
Mouse, 24, 25, 31, 49, 50, 56, 133, 139, 227–228
 pad, 25
Multistepped procedures, 55, 56, 62, 107–108
 activities for, 109–116
Muppet Keys, 79
Music Programs, 8, 16, 248

National Association for the Education of Young
 Children (NAEYC), 5, 17
Newsroom, 177n
No-Cook Cookery Cook Book, The, 108
Number of computers, optimal, 34–35
Numeral sequences, 37–38, 69, 70–72

Offices, computers in, 179
Open–ended activities, 5, 10–11, 18, 43, 47, 51,
 241, 255
Operational knowledge, 126
Output, 139, 175, 196–197
 activities to teach about, 198–204
Output devices, 26–27, 29, 36, 134

Pace, program, 46
Paintbrush, computer as, 14
Parents
 borrowing software from, 53, 177
 workplace computers, 178
Parts, computer
 activities for learning about, 141–149
 connecting, 29, 133
 helping children learn about, 137–140
 input devices, 22–26
 output devices, 26–29

recognition by children, 181
Peanuts Maze Marathon, 76, 234, 250, 253
Peer teaching, 3, 18
People, computers and, 133–134, 150–151, 152,
 175, 176, 205–206
Peripherals, 29, 30, 31, 36, 49, 228
Personal computer (PC), **22**, 175
Physical development, 8, 18, 55, 57, 58, 62, 253
 activities to promote, 234–236
Piaget, Jean, on constructing concepts, 5
Picture directions, 94, 117–118
 activities for, 119–122
 see also Rebus pictures
Placement guidelines for classroom computer,
 35–38
PLATO terminal, 192
Play, stimulating, 6–7
Playmate, computer as, 15
Port, **25**
Positive attitude toward computers, 7
Power strips, 36
Practice, acquiring computer knowledge through,
 128–130
Primary Editor, 27, 90, 162
Primary storage, 28
Print buffer, 26
Printer, 26–27, 29, 31, 36, 56, 68, 134
Print It, 26, 107
Print Shop, 94, 162, 177
Problem–solving skills, 4–5
Problems with computer use, 8–12
Procedure, 55, **56**
 multistepped, 55, 56, 62, 107–108, 109–116
Program, 3, **4**, 22, 46, 62, 139
 concept of, 162
 different levels for, 233–234
 run a, 139
Programmer, 133, **134**
Programming, 162–163
 activities for, 164–172
Programming language, **17**
Purchasing computer system, 29–31
 teacher involvement in, 33

Random access memory (RAM), 28
Reading, 16, 45
 programs that include, 231–232
Rebus pictures, **38**, 39, 45, 62, 94, 96, 107
 activities for, 119–122
 directions for following, 117–118, 231
Retailing, computers in, 178–179
Return key, **5**, 45, 60, 78, 79, 80, 108, 117, 127
 139, 162, 232
Right arrow key, 9, 10
Roles of computers, 14–17
Run a program, 139

Sales record, computerized, 176
Save, 139, 162
Schools, software collections in, 54, 177
Science, computers in, 179

Secondary storage, 28–29
Self–concept, child's, 3–4, 18, 47, 150
Sequence
 pictorial, 118
 of steps for using computer, 37–38, 67–68
Services, public, computers in, 179
Sex–role stereotyping, 7–8
Sharing arrangements, 35
Shift bar, 78, 232
Simon, 242
Simulation, **12**, 179
Skills. *See* Computer skills
"Skills and Concepts of Successful Young
 Computer Users," 55n
Small-muscle development, 62
Social development, 2–3, 8, 9, 18, 35, 251–253
Software, **2**, 30, 31, 33, 39
 activities for specific, 96, 207–237
 characteristics to consider, 44–50
 collections, 50–51
 developing skills in selecting, 74–77
 drill-and-practice, 11, 12, 13, 16
 guides, 53
 hands-on approach in evaluating, 51–54
 "ideal," 43–44
 introducing new, 40–41
 menus, characteristics of, 93–97
 people and, 133–134, 205–206
 unit-related, 240–241
Software Reports: The Guide to Evaluated Educa-
 tional Software, 52, 53
Space bar, 45, 96, 133, 150, 232
Speech recognition, 25
Speech synthesizer. *See* Voice synthesizer
Sprites, 28
Static electricity, 37
Stereotypes, 7–8, 47
Stickybear ABC, 47, 51, 80, 177, 249
Stickybear BOP, 234
Storage, 27–29
 components, 22
Stores, computer, 54
Strengths, computer, 190
 activities to teach about, 184–195
 what children can learn about, 192–193
Student teachers, 32
Stylus, **24**, 56, 227, 228
Subject, computer as, 17
Supermarkets, computers in, 180, 181
Surge suppressors, 36
Survey of Early Childhood Software, 53
Switches, locating and operating, 66–69, 248
 activity for, 73
Symbolic development, 9, 117–118
System, computer, **30**, 31

Talking Screen Text Writer, 78, 232
Tapes, 28–29
Tasks
 dissecting, 57–58, 62, 95
 modifying, 59–60, 96
Teacher(s)

assistance in developing skills, 37–38, 5. –61, 75–76, 78–81, 90–91, 95–97, 107–108, 117–118, 137–140, 162–163, 196–197, 208–211, 220–221, 227–228, 231–234
evaluating community computers, 182
evaluating software, 51–53
explaining role of people with computers, 205–206
introducing computer to children, 38–41
involvement in computer purchase, 33
questions to ask about computer, 180
teaching behavior with computer, 32–33
time spent on computer use, 11, 61–62
and varied uses of computer, 182–183
Teaching Montessori in the Home, 57
Technical quality, software, 48
Terminology, correct computer, 138–140
Terminal, **192**
Terrapin Logo, 78, 95
T.E.S.S. Educational Software Selector, 53
Thought–provoker, computer as, 15–16, 17, 46, 50, 51, 255
Time, teacher, spent using computer, 11, 61–62

Toggle switches, 66
Tool, computer as, 13, **14**, 16, 17, 50
Touch pad, 24, 25, 31, 56, 134, 227–228
Towerifics, 57
Toy Box, 47
Training guides for computer use, 61
Transportation, computer in, 179
Trial-and-error exploration, 47, 51
Turning computer on and off, 37–40, 55, 56, 62, 66–69
    activities to teach about, 70–73
Turtle-robot, 207, 220, 242
    activities generated by using, 208–211
    activities to teach skill with, 212–219
Turtle Tot Logo, 232
Tutee, computer as, 13, **14**, 15, 16, 17, 50
Tutor, computer as, 13, **14**, 16, 17, 50
Typewriter, and developing keyboarding skills, 80

Unit, using computer to support, 240–243
    activities for, 244–247
Uses of computers, 175–183
    activities to teach, 184–189

Values of computer use, 2–8, 43
VCR. *See* Videocassette recorder
Video arcade games, 175, 176
Video interface, 178
Videocassette recorder (VCR), 175, 179
Violence–based software, 47
Vocabulary, computer, 138–140, 162
Voice box, **138**, 178
Voice synthesizer, **16**, 27

Watercolor painting, 12–13
Weaknesses, computer, 190–191
    activities to teach about, 194–195
What Makes a Dinosaur Sore, 6, 46, 241, 254
Word processing, 4, **5**, 13, 16, 30, 78, 241, 250–251
Workbooks, computers as, 10–11
Workshop, computer, 53
Writing, 16